THE AUSTRALIAN
Women's Weekly

Everyday
CAKES &
COOKIES

Project editor Stephanie Kistner
Editor Deidre Livolsi
Designer Corey Butler
Food director Pamela Clark
Food editor Cathie Lonnie

ACP Books
Editorial director Susan Tomnay
Creative director Hieu Chi Nguyen
Director of sales Brian Cearnes
Marketing director Matt Dominello
Brand manager Renée Crea
Production manager Cedric Taylor

Chief executive officer John Alexander
Group publisher Pat Ingram
Publisher Sue Wannan
General manager Christine Whiston
Editorial director (AWW) Deborah Thomas

Produced by ACP Books, Sydney.

Printed by Everbest Printing Co. Ltd., China.

Published by ACP Magazines Ltd,
54 Park St, Sydney, NSW 2000 Australia;
GPO Box 4088, Sydney, NSW 2001.
Ph: +61 2 9282 8618 Fax: +61 2 9267 9438
www.acpbooks.com.au
acpbooks@acpmagazines.com.au
To order books phone 136 116.
Send recipe enquiries to
reccipeenquiries@acpmagazines.com.au

RIGHTS ENQUIRIES
Laura Bamford, Director ACP Books.
lbamford@acpmedia.com

UNITED KINGDOM: Distributed by
Australian Consolidated Press (UK),
Moulton Park Business Centre, Red House Rd,
Moulton Park, Northampton, NN3 6AQ
Ph: (01604) 497 531 Fax: (01604) 497 533
books@acpmedia.com

AUSTRALIA: Distributed by Network
Services,GPO Box 4088, Sydney, NSW 2001.
Ph: +61 2 9282 8777 Fax: +61 2 9264 3278
networkweb@networkservicescompany.com.au

CANADA: Distributed by Whitecap Books Ltd,
351 Lynn Ave, North Vancouver, BC, V7J 2C4
Ph: (604) 980 9852 Fax: (604) 980 8197
customerservice@whitecap.ca www.whitecap.ca

NEW ZEALAND: Southern Publishers Group,
44 New North Rd, Eden Terrace, Auckland.
Ph: (64 9) 309 6930 Fax: (64 9) 309 6170
hub@spg.co.nz

SOUTH AFRICA: Distributed by PSD
Promotions (Pty) Ltd, PO Box 1175, Isando,
1600, Gauteng, Johannesburg, SA.
Ph: (011) 392 6065 Fax (011) 392 6079
orders@psdprom.co.za

Clark, Pamela.
The Australian women's weekly
everyday cakes & cookies.

Includes index.
ISBN 1 86396 536 X.
1. Cakes. 2. Cookies. 3. Biscuits.
4. Quick and easy cookery.
I. Title. II Title: Australian women's weekly
641.865

Cover
Photographer: Alan Benson
Stylist: Marie-Helene Clauzon

Back cover
Photographer: Andre Martin
Stylist: Sarah O'Brien

CONTENTS

IF I KNEW YOU WERE COMING…

There's something about a home-baked cake or batch of cookies that makes everyone smile. Wherever they're on offer, whether in a gathering of friends or family or, if you're lucky, at the office, you know you'd better be quick. Cakes and cookies can speak of home, of something lovingly crafted to be shared with others, as well as of celebration. We can live without them, unlike lots of other foods – but who would want to? Sweet, gooey, crunchy, creamy, fragrant, spicy, spongy… they're a delight to the senses.

More than anything, cakes and cookies are made to be passed around. You *could* make a sacher torte for yourself and eat it all alone, but it wouldn't be quite the same.

Everyday Cakes & Cookies is full of recipes for sweet sensations you can make to have on hand whenever you need them – for after school, morning or afternoon tea, to celebrate family events or just the fact that it's the weekend. And everyone can try their hand at making them.

Baking lets you get creative, especially when it comes to the finishing touches. What a delight it is to make something beautiful to look at as well as heavenly to eat. This is show-off territory, even when you're using the simplest of recipes. The oohs and aahs you'll get make the small effort worth it.

This book offers something for everyone: elegant biscotti, comforting muffins and luscious brownies, plus glamorous gateaux that make for a spectacular finish to a dinner party. You'll find rich mudcakes, and cakes that revel in the freshness of fruit; superb special occasion cakes rich with liqueurs, rum and brandy; christmas puddings big and small – and, of course, fruit mince tarts. There are plenty of old favourites like cupcakes – great for school lunchboxes – and butterfly cakes. Fabulous dessert cakes are included, as are exquisitely flavoured, moist syrup cakes, and delicious cakes for those who can't normally tolerate certain ingredients. There are quick and easy one-bowl cake recipes, and some using packet cake mixes – often where we first discovered the joys of cake-making – as a base. That light-as-air queen of cakes, the sponge, gets a chapter, and there are ideas for birthday cakes that are more fun than fuss, as well as scrumptious and easy-to-make muffins and scones. Our collection of icings, frostings and glazes tops it all off.

Biscuit and cookie baking is one of the most satisfying things you can do, and as most will keep well, you know you'll always have something on hand to go with that pot of tea or freshly brewed coffee when someone drops in. They'll be so much more special because you made them yourself. Here you'll find recipes for gingernuts, florentines, macaroons, shortbread, choc-chip cookies, classics such as honey jumbles and monte carlos, and lots more.

Many of these cakes and cookies can be made ahead of time and stored, often frozen.

Whether you're new to baking or not, you can be confident following these recipes. To help you perfect your baking, we've included information on oven types, preparing cake pans and testing to see whether your creation is cooked. There are useful cake-making tips, advice on cooling and storing, and some troubleshooting suggestions if your result was less than perfect. At the back of the book you'll find a comprehensive glossary, and an index to help you locate your favourite recipes again quickly. There is also a conversion chart you can refer to for accurate measuring and oven temperatures.

Enjoy *Everyday Cakes & Cookies* – every day. Happy baking.

Pamela Clark

Food Director

ABOUT CAKES AND COOKIES

CAKES

HOW TO PREPARE A CAKE PAN

We prefer to use aluminium pans for baking wherever possible. Pans made from tin and stainless steel do not conduct heat as evenly as does aluminium. If using these pans, reduce the oven temperature by 10°C.

Cake pans made from materials that have various coatings, such as non-stick, work well provided the surface is unscratched.

To grease a cake pan, use either a light, even coating of cooking-oil spray, or a pastry brush to brush melted butter evenly over the base and side(s). Cakes that are high in sugar, or have golden syrup, treacle or honey as an ingredient, have a tendency to stick. We recommend lining the base and/or side(s) of the pans for these. The recipes will indicate when this is necessary. Use greaseproof or baking paper, and use a pencil to trace around the base of the pan onto the paper; cut out the shape, slightly inside the pencil mark, so that the paper fits snugly inside the greased pan. In most cases it's not necessary to grease the baking paper once it's in position.

If the recipe indicates that the sides of a pan need to be lined, make a baking paper "collar", extending about 5cm above the edge of the pan, to protect the top of the cake.

Fruit cakes need more than a single layer of paper to prevent the cake drying out during the longer baking times specified in these recipes. The following method of lining round or square cake pans, using greaseproof or baking paper, allows for this:

– For side(s), cut three paper strips long enough to fit around the inside of the pan and 8cm wider than the depth of the pan. Fold strips lengthways about 2cm from the edge and make short diagonal cuts about 2cm apart, up to the fold. This helps ease the paper around the curves or corners of the pan, with the cut section fitting around the base.

– Using the base of the pan as a guide, cut three paper circles (or squares) as instructed previously; position these in the base of the pan after you've lined the sides.

CAKE-MAKING TIPS

Use an electric beater for mixing cakes, and always have the ingredients at room temperature, particularly the butter. Melted or extremely soft butter will alter the texture of the baked cake.
– Start mixing ingredients on a low speed; once they are combined, increase the speed to about medium and beat for the required time.
– Creamed mixtures for cakes can be mixed with a wooden spoon, but this will take more time (and elbow grease!).
– When measuring liquids, always stand the marked measuring jug on a flat surface and check at eye level for accuracy.
– When measuring dry ingredients, spoon and cup measurements should be levelled off with a knife or spatula.

OVEN TYPES AND RACK POSITION

There are many different types of ovens and energy sources, so it's important you get to know your own oven – particularly when it comes to baking cakes. The recipes in this book were tested in domestic-size electric fan-forced ovens. If you have a fan-forced oven, make sure you're familiar with the operating instructions for best results.
As a rule, you need to reduce the baking temperature by 10°C to 20°C when using the fan during baking (we indicate this in each recipe); cakes might also take slightly less time to bake than specified. Some ovens give better results if the fan is used for part of the baking time; it's usually best to introduce the fan about halfway through the baking time.
We positioned the oven racks and cake pan(s) so that the top of the baked cake would be roughly in the centre of the oven.
Best results are obtained by baking cakes in an oven preheated to the desired temperature; this takes at least 10 minutes. See the Conversion Chart on page 400 for a guide to oven temperatures for conventional ovens.

TO TEST IF A CAKE IS COOKED

All cake baking times in this book are approximate. We recommend you check your cake just before the suggested cooking time is due; it should be browned and starting to shrink from the side(s) of the pan.
Feel the top of the cake with your fingertips; it should feel firm.
You may want to insert a thin skewer in the deepest part of the cake from top to base (we prefer to use a metal skewer rather than a wooden one because any mixture that adheres to it is easier to see). Gently remove the skewer; it shouldn't have any uncooked mixture clinging to it.

COOLING A CAKE

We have suggested standing cakes for up to 15 minutes before turning onto wire racks to cool further. The best way to do this, after standing time has elapsed, is to hold the cake pan firmly and shake it gently, loosening the cake from its pan.

Turn the cake upside down onto a wire rack, then turn the cake top-side up immediately, using a second rack (unless directed otherwise).

Some wire racks mark the cakes, particularly soft cakes such as sponges. To prevent this, cover the rack with baking paper.

We have indicated when it is best to cool a cake in the pan; this applies mostly to fruit cakes, which are usually covered with foil before cooling.

HOW TO KEEP A CAKE

Most cakes will keep well for two or three days, depending on the climate and the type of cake. As a rule, remember that the higher the fat content, the longer the cake will keep.

– Make sure your cake is at room temperature before storing it in an airtight container as close in size to the cake as possible; this will minimise the amount of air around the cake.

– For those cakes that are suitable for freezing, we recommend icing and filling the cake after thawing. Icing will often crack during the thawing process. Wrap or seal un-iced and unfilled cakes in freezer wrap or freezer bags, expelling as much air as possible. To thaw, it's best to leave the cake overnight in the refrigerator.

– We prefer to store rich fruit cakes in the refrigerator simply because they'll cut better; once sliced, they quickly return to room temperature.

WHAT WENT WRONG?

MY BUTTER CAKE WASN'T PERFECT...

Sinks in the centre after removal from oven:
   This generally means that the cake is undercooked.

Sinks in the centre while still baking:
   The mixture has been forced to rise too quickly because the oven is too hot.

Sugary crust:
   Butter and sugar have probably not been creamed sufficiently.
   Excess sugar was used.

White specks on top:
Sugar has not been dissolved enough; in a light butter cake, it is better to use caster sugar, which dissolves easily during baking.
Mixture has not been creamed sufficiently

Excessive shrinking:
Cake has over-cooked due to the oven being too hot.

Crumbles when cut:
Mixture may have been creamed too much, particularly in fruit cakes.

Sticks to pan:
Too much sugar or other sweetening ingredient in the recipe.
If a recipe contains honey or golden syrup, or if you're using a new pan, it's best to line the evenly greased pan with baking paper, greased if you wish, to prevent sticking.

Rises and cracks in centre:
Caused by using a cake pan that is too small; most cakes baked in loaf, bar or ring pans will crack slightly due to the confined space of the pan.
Oven may have been too hot.

Collar around top outside edge:
Cake was probably baked at too high a temperature.

Pale on top, brown underneath and sides:
This is caused by using a pan that is too large or extending lining paper too high around the side(s) of pan.

Coloured streaks on top:
Ingredients have not been mixed together enough.
Bowl scrapings have not been mixed thoroughly into the cake mixture.

Uneven rising:
This might be because the oven shelf has not been set straight or the oven is not level on the floor.
Mixture not spread evenly in pan (use a wet spatula to level the top of the cake mixture).

Holes in baked cake:
This can occur if the mixture has not been creamed sufficiently.
Oven may have been too hot.

Crusty, over-browned, uncooked in centre:
Cake has been baked too long or at too high a temperature.
Cake pan is too small, causing the top of the cake to overcook while the rest is not cooked through.

MY FRUIT CAKE WASN'T PERFECT...

Fruit sinks to the bottom:
Fruit not dried thoroughly after washing.
Cake mixture is too soft to support weight of the fruit (caused by over-creaming).
Fruit should be finely chopped to about the size of a sultana so mixture can support it more easily.
Self-raising flour may have been used in the recipe instead of plain flour.

Doughy in centre:
Cake has been baked in too cool an oven, or not long enough.

Burnt bottom:
Cake has been wrongly positioned in oven.
Cake has been baked at too high a temperature.
Pans have not been lined correctly.
Rich fruit cakes require protection during long, slow baking times. Cakes that are 22cm or smaller require three thicknesses of baking-paper lining; larger cakes need one or two sheets of brown paper and three sheets of baking paper.

Cracks on top:
Cake has been baked at too high a temperature.

Uneven on top:
Oven shelf or oven not level.
Mixture spread unevenly in pan (use a wet spatula to level the top of cake mixture).

Creamed mixture curdles:
Eggs and butter not at room temperature to begin with.
Eggs not added quickly enough to creamed butter and sugar mixture.
Eggs used are too large for mixture to absorb the excess liquid. If eggs used are larger than 60g in weight, omit one of the number shown in ingredients list, or add only the yolk of one of the eggs. Curdled creamed mixture could cause the finished cake to crumble when cut.

Sinks in the middle:
Self-raising flour used, or too much bicarbonate of soda. (Usually only plain flour is used in rich fruit cake, but sometimes a small portion of self-raising flour is added.)
Cake may not have been baked properly. To test, push a sharp-pointed knife rather than a skewer through centre to base of pan; the blade surface helps distinguish between uncooked mixture and fruit combined with cooked mixture. Test only after the minimum specified baking time.

MY SPONGE CAKE WASN'T PERFECT...

Small white specks on top:
Caused by undissolved sugar; sugar should be added gradually to beaten eggs and beaten until completely dissolved between additions.

Shrinks in oven:
Cake has been baked at too high a temperature or for too long.

Shrinks and wrinkles during cooling:
Insufficient baking time
Cake has been cooled in a draughty area.

Flat and tough:
Incorrect folding in of flour and liquid. Triple-sifted flour should be folded into the mixture in a gentle, circular motion.

Pale and sticky on top:
Cake has been baked at too low a temperature, or in wrong oven position.

Crusty:
Cake has been baked at too high a temperature, in wrong oven position or too small a pan. Using high-sided cake pans protects the cake mixture.

Sinks in centre:
Pan is too small, causing the cake to rise quickly, then fall in the centre.

Streaks on top:
Scrapings from the mixing bowl have not been mixed into the sponge mixture; scrapings are always slightly darker than the rest of the cake mixture. It's best to put them towards the side of the pan – not in the centre of the mixture.

Sponge rises too quickly:
Oven temperature may be too high.

Sponge is undercooked:
Oven door may have been opened during the first half of baking.

COOKIES
OVEN TRAYS

We used aluminium oven trays with no or very shallow sides, which allows heat to circulate freely around the biscuits. The recipes will indicate whether to grease or line trays. It is important that you don't over-grease trays. Over-greasing not only makes washing up more difficult but it can cause the biscuits to burn on the bottom.

OVEN POSITION

Two or more trays of biscuits can be baked in an oven at the same time provided none of the trays touch the oven sides or door when it is closed. There must be at least a 2cm space around each tray or pan to allow for proper heat circulation and browning.

For even baking, alternate the position of the trays or pans on the oven's shelves halfway through the cooking time. Some ovens have hot spots, so trays or pans need to be rotated to ensure even browning.

As a general rule, the top half of a gas oven will produce the best baking results, but in an electric oven the lower half is best.

Fan-forced ovens can bake and brown about four trays of biscuits at a time without the need to alternate shelf positions.

It's a good idea to check the manufacturer's manual for any instructions peculiar to your oven.

MIXING

For best results, have all the ingredients for a recipe at room temperature. Do not over-beat the butter and sugar mixture as this will result in a soft mixture that will cause biscuits to spread too much during baking.

It's usually best to stir in dry ingredients in two batches, and often a recipe will instruct you to change to a larger bowl.

Individual recipes will tell you when it is necessary to cool biscuits on trays or if they should be transferred to racks to cool.

PIPING BAG

In some recipes, we used a piping bag to force out the mixture; however, only smooth biscuit and cookie mixtures without any chunky ingredients like nuts or raisins can be piped.

COOKIE CUTTERS

There are myriad cutter shapes available, from cats to Christmas stars to the classic gingerbread man (and don't forget the original simple round cutter). Use whatever shape appeals to you as long as it's of a similar dimension to what's called for in the recipe. We do recommend using metal cutters.

TESTING BISCUITS

Baking times in this book are a guide only. Biscuits generally feel soft in the oven and become firmer when cold. To test if a biscuit is cooked, push it gently with your finger; if it can move on the oven tray without breaking, it's cooked.

STORING AND FREEZING BISCUITS

To prevent biscuits from softening, completely cool them before storing. Keep them in an airtight container just large enough to hold them.

To freeze un-iced or unfilled biscuits, place cooled biscuits in an airtight container, using sheets of baking paper between the layers.

To avoid softening, biscuits that have cream or jam fillings are best assembled just before serving.

Biscuits should be stored in a separate container from cakes, bread or scones as they will absorb moisture and go soft.

If plain biscuits or slices (unfilled and/or un-iced) do soften, you can place them on oven trays in a single layer and reheat, uncovered, in a moderate oven for 5 to 10 minutes to re-crisp; lift onto wire racks to cool.

WHAT WENT WRONG?

MY COOKIES WEREN'T PERFECT...

Spread on the tray:

The mixture is too soft due to overbeating.

Ingredients have been measured incorrectly.

The wrong flour has been used (such as self-raising flour instead of plain).

Oven was not hot enough to set the mixture quickly.

Too hard:

The ingredients have been measured incorrectly.

Biscuits have been baked for too long or at too high a temperature.

Too soft:

Ingredients have been measured incorrectly.

Biscuits have not been baked enough or have been softened by steam when stacked on top of each other to cool.

Too brown underneath:

Trays have been over-greased, causing the oven heat to be attracted to the biscuits' bases. Use a pastry brush dipped in a small amount of melted butter to grease trays lightly and evenly.

Incorrect oven position and/or temperature could also cause over-browning, as could over-generous measuring, particularly with sweet ingredients such as sugar, honey or golden syrup.

BIG CAKES

Cut and keep butter cake

preparation time **15 minutes** cooking time **1 hour 15 minutes** serves **10**

125g butter, softened
1 teaspoon vanilla extract
1¼ cups (275g) caster sugar
3 eggs
1 cup (150g) plain flour
½ cup (75g) self-raising flour
¼ teaspoon bicarbonate of soda
½ cup (125ml) milk

1 Preheat oven to moderately slow (170°C/150°C fan-forced). Grease a deep 20cm round cake pan; line base with baking paper.
2 Beat ingredients in medium bowl on low speed with electric mixer until just combined. Increase speed to medium; beat until mixture is smooth and lighter in colour. Pour mixture into prepared pan.
3 Bake cake for about 1¼ hours. Stand cake in pan 5 minutes before turning onto wire rack; turn cake top-side up to cool. Dust cake with sifted icing sugar, if desired.

tips To give this cake a slight caramel flavour, substitute 1⅓ cups (295g) firmly packed brown sugar for the caster sugar. The cake will keep in an airtight container for up to three days. It can be frozen for up to three months.

Buttery orange cake

preparation time **20 minutes** cooking time **1 hour** serves **12**

250g butter, softened
2 tablespoons finely grated orange rind
1½ cups (330g) caster sugar
4 eggs
1½ cups (225g) self-raising flour
½ cup (75g) plain flour
¾ cup (180ml) orange juice

Glacé icing
1½ cups (240g) icing sugar
1 teaspoon soft butter
2 tablespoons orange juice

1 Preheat oven to moderately slow (170°C/150°C fan-forced). Grease a deep 22cm round cake pan; line base and side with baking paper, extending paper 5cm above the edge.
2 Beat butter, rind and sugar in a large bowl with electric mixer until light and fluffy. Add eggs one at a time, beating until just combined after each addition. Fold in combined sifted flours and juice in two batches. Spread cake mixture into prepared pan.
3 Bake cake for about 1 hour. Stand cake in pan 5 minutes before turning onto a wire rack to cool.

Glacé icing Sift icing sugar into a small heatproof bowl. Stir in butter and juice to form a firm paste. Place bowl over a small saucepan of simmering water and stir until icing is a spreadable consistency; do not overheat. Top cake with glacé icing.

tips This recipe can be made four days ahead; store in an airtight container at room temperature. The un-iced cake is suitable for freezing for up to three months. The icing can be microwaved.

Apple pecan cake with maple frosting

preparation time **30 minutes** baking time **50 minutes** serves **12**

You will need 1 large apple (200g) for this cake; we used a granny smith.

90g butter, softened
½ cup (80g) wholemeal self-raising flour
1 cup (150g) white self-raising flour
1 teaspoon ground cinnamon
¾ cup (150g) firmly packed brown sugar
¼ cup (60ml) maple-flavoured syrup
3 eggs
1 cup (125g) coarsely chopped pecans
½ cup (85g) coarsely chopped raisins
1 cup (170g) coarsely grated apple
½ cup (60g) pecans, toasted, extra

Maple frosting
90g butter, softened
1 cup (160g) icing sugar
1 teaspoon maple-flavoured syrup

1 Preheat oven to moderate (180°C/160°C fan-forced). Grease a 20cm ring pan; line base and sides with baking paper.
2 Beat butter, flours, cinnamon, sugar, syrup and eggs in a medium bowl on low speed with electric mixer until ingredients are combined. Beat on medium speed until the mixture is smooth and changed in colour.
3 Using a wooden spoon, stir in nuts, raisins and apple. Spoon the mixture into prepared pan; spread evenly with plastic spatula.
4 Bake cake for about 50 minutes. Stand cake in pan for 5 minutes then turn onto a wire rack; turn cake top-side up to cool.
5 Beat ingredients for maple frosting in a small bowl with electric mixer until light and fluffy. Spread frosting over cooled cake; top with extra nuts.

tips Sultanas or finely chopped seeded dates or prunes can be substituted for the raisins, and walnuts for the pecans. Cake will keep for up to three days in an airtight container in the refrigerator. It can be frozen for up to three months.

Upside-down cashew and maple syrup loaf

preparation time **25 minutes** cooking time **1 hour** serves **8**

90g butter, softened
½ cup (100g) firmly packed brown sugar
2 tablespoons maple-flavoured syrup
1 cup (150g) unsalted roasted cashews, chopped coarsely
125g butter, extra
¾ cup (150g) firmly packed brown sugar, extra
2 eggs
1 cup (150g) self-raising flour
½ cup (75g) plain flour
½ teaspoon mixed spice
½ cup (125ml) sour cream
2 tablespoons maple-flavoured syrup

1 Preheat oven to moderate (180°C/160°C fan-forced). Grease 15cm x 25cm loaf pan; line base and two long sides with baking paper, extending paper 2cm above edge.
2 Beat butter, sugar and syrup in small bowl with wooden spoon until smooth; spread over base of prepared pan. Sprinkle with cashews.
3 Beat remaining ingredients in medium bowl with electric mixer on low speed until combined; beat on medium speed until mixture is smooth and changed to a lighter colour. Spread cake mixture over cashews.
4 Bake loaf for about 1 hour. Stand loaf in pan 10 minutes before turning onto a wire rack to cool.

Coffee and walnut cake

preparation time **20 minutes** cooking time **45 minutes** serves **8**

30g butter
1 tablespoon brown sugar
2 teaspoons ground cinnamon
200g walnuts, toasted
½ cup (125ml) milk
1 tablespoon dry instant coffee
185g butter, extra
1 ⅓ cups (300g) caster sugar
3 eggs
1 cup (150g) self-raising flour
¾ cup (110g) plain flour

Toffee
½ cup (110g) caster sugar
2 tablespoons water
3 teaspoons cream

1 Preheat oven to moderately slow (170°C/150°C fan-forced). Thoroughly grease and lightly flour a 22cm baba cake pan; shake out excess flour.
2 Melt butter in small saucepan and add brown sugar, cinnamon and walnuts. Stir well; cool.
3 Combine milk and coffee in small bowl; stir until coffee has dissolved.
4 Beat extra butter and caster sugar in small bowl with electric mixer until light and fluffy. Add eggs one at a time, beating well after each addition. Fold in sifted flours, then milk mixture.
5 Spread one-third of the cake mixture in base of prepared pan, sprinkle with half walnut mixture and top with remaining cake mixture. Bake about 45 minutes or until cooked when tested. Stand cake 5 minutes in pan before turning onto wire rack to cool.
6 Make toffee.
7 Place cake on wire rack over oven tray. Drizzle some of the toffee on top of cake, press on remaining walnut mixture; drizzle with remaining toffee.

Toffee Combine sugar and water in small saucepan. Stir over low heat until sugar dissolves. Bring to a boil, then reduce heat and simmer, uncovered, until sugar browns slightly. Add cream and stir 1 minute or until thickened slightly.

Caramel mud cake

preparation time **30 minutes** (plus cooling time)
cooking time **2 hours 10 minutes** serves **12**

250g butter, chopped
200g white eating chocolate, chopped coarsely
2¼ cups (450g) firmly packed brown sugar
1½ cups (375ml) water
2 cups (300g) plain flour
⅔ cup (100g) self-raising flour
1 teaspoon vanilla extract
3 eggs, beaten lightly

Caramel frosting
125g butter, chopped
1 cup (200g) firmly packed brown sugar
⅓ cup (80ml) milk
1½ cups (240g) icing sugar

1 Preheat oven to slow (150°C/130°C fan-forced). Grease deep 22cm round cake pan; line base and side with baking paper, extending paper 5cm above edge.
2 Combine butter, chocolate, sugar and the water in medium saucepan; stir over low heat until mixture is smooth. Transfer mixture to large bowl; cool 15 minutes. Whisk in flours, then extract and eggs.
3 Pour mixture into prepared pan; bake in slow oven about 2 hours. Stand cake in pan 10 minutes; turn onto wire rack to cool. Place cooled cake, top-side up, on serving plate until completely cold.
4 Make caramel frosting; spread over cold cake.

Caramel frosting Melt butter in small saucepan. Stir in brown sugar and milk. Bring to a boil, then reduce heat and simmer, uncovered, for 3 minutes; cool. Gradually stir in icing sugar until frosting is of spreadable consistency.

Almond butter cake

preparation time **20 minutes** cooking time **1 hour** serves **10**

250g butter
1 teaspoon almond essence
1 cup (220g) caster sugar
4 eggs
1 cup (150g) self-raising flour
½ cup (75g) plain flour
¾ cup (90g) almond meal

1 Preheat oven to moderate (180°C/160°C fan-forced). Grease a deep 19cm square cake pan; line base with baking paper.
2 Beat butter, essence and sugar in medium bowl with electric mixer until light and fluffy. Add eggs one at a time, beating until just combined after each addition (mixture may curdle). Fold in sifted flours and almond meal in two batches (mixture will be stiff).
3 Spread mixture into prepared pan; bake for 30 minutes. Reduce oven temperature to moderately slow (170°C/150°C fan-forced); bake for another 30 minutes. Stand cake in pan for 5 minutes; turn onto wire rack to cool.

Melt'n'mix coffee cake

preparation time **20 minutes** cooking time **50 minutes** serves **10**

125g butter, chopped
⅔ cup (130g) firmly packed brown sugar
⅓ cup (75g) caster sugar
½ cup (125ml) milk
2 teaspoons instant coffee granules
2 eggs
1½ cups (225g) self-raising flour

1 Preheat oven to moderate (180°C/160°C fan-forced). Grease 14cm x 21cm loaf pan; line base with baking paper.
2 Place butter, sugars, milk and coffee in medium saucepan; stir over low heat, without boiling, until butter is melted. Stand 10 minutes.
3 Stir in eggs and flour. Pour into prepared pan. Bake for about 40 minutes. Turn onto wire rack to cool. Serve dusted with icing sugar, if desired.

Carrot cake with lemon cream cheese frosting

preparation time **35 minutes** cooking time **1 hour 15 minutes** serves **12**

You will need approximately 3 large carrots (540g) for this recipe.

1 cup (250ml) vegetable oil
1 ⅓ cups (250g) firmly packed brown sugar
3 eggs
3 cups firmly packed, coarsely grated carrot
1 cup (120g) coarsely chopped walnuts
2½ cups (375g) self-raising flour
½ teaspoon bicarbonate of soda
2 teaspoons mixed spice

Lemon cream cheese frosting
30g butter, softened
80g cream cheese, softened
1 teaspoon finely grated lemon rind
1½ cups (240g) icing sugar

1 Preheat oven to moderate (180°C/160°C fan-forced). Grease deep 22cm round cake pan; line base with baking paper.
2 Beat oil, sugar and eggs in a small bowl with electric mixer until thick and creamy.
3 Transfer mixture to large bowl; using wooden spoon, stir in carrot and nuts then sifted dry ingredients. Pour mixture into prepared pan.
4 Bake cake for about 1 hour and 15 minutes. Stand cake in pan for 5 minutes then turn onto wire rack; turn cake top-side up to cool.
5 Make lemon cream cheese frosting; spread over cold cake.

Lemon cream cheese frosting Beat butter, cream cheese and rind in a small bowl with electric mixer until light and fluffy. Gradually beat in the icing sugar.

tip This cake will keep for up to three days if refrigerated in an airtight container. Frosted or unfrosted, it can be frozen for up to three months.

Honey yogurt cake

preparation time **15 minutes** cooking time **45 minutes** serves **10**

200g butter, chopped
¾ cup (180ml) plain yogurt
½ teaspoon ground cinnamon
½ cup (125ml) honey
2 eggs
¼ cup (55g) caster sugar
1 ¾ cups (260g) self-raising flour
½ teaspoon baking powder
1 tablespoon icing sugar
½ teaspoon ground cinnamon, extra

1 Preheat oven to moderate (180°C/160°C fan-forced). Grease a 15cm x 25cm loaf pan; line base with baking paper.
2 Beat butter, yogurt, cinnamon and honey in small bowl with electric mixer until just combined and smooth. Transfer mixture to large bowl.
3 Beat eggs and sugar in a small bowl with electric mixer until thick and creamy. Stir egg mixture into yogurt mixture. Fold in sifted flour and baking powder. Spread into prepared pan.
4 Bake cake for about 45 minutes. Stand cake in pan for 10 minutes before turning onto wire rack to cool. Serve dusted with combined sifted icing sugar and extra cinnamon.

Pumpkin date cake

preparation time **15 minutes** cooking time **1 hour 15 minutes** serves **10**

You will need to cook 200g pumpkin for this recipe.

250g butter, softened
1 tablespoon grated orange rind
¾ cup (165g) caster sugar
2 eggs
1 cup (140g) coarsely chopped dates
½ cup (40g) coconut
½ cup cold mashed pumpkin
2 cups (300g) self-raising flour
½ cup (125ml) milk

1 Preheat oven to moderately slow (170°C/150°C fan-forced). Grease a deep 19cm square cake pan; line base with baking paper.

2 Beat butter, rind and sugar in a small bowl with electric mixer until light and fluffy. Add eggs one at a time, beating well after each addition. Transfer mixture to large bowl; stir in dates, coconut and pumpkin. Stir in flour and milk in two batches. Spread into prepared pan.

3 Bake cake for about 1¼ hours. Stand cake in pan for 5 minutes before turning onto wire rack to cool. Serve dusted with icing sugar, if desired.

Basic butter cake

preparation time **10 minutes** cooking time **40 minutes** serves **8**

125g butter, softened
1 teaspoon vanilla extract
¾ cup (165g) caster sugar
2 eggs
1½ cups (225g) self-raising flour
½ cup (125ml) milk

1 Preheat oven to moderate (180°C/160°C fan-forced). Grease a 20cm round cake pan; line base with baking paper.

2 Beat butter, extract and sugar in small bowl with electric mixer until light and fluffy. Add eggs one at a time, beating well after each addition. Stir in flour and milk, in two batches. Spread mixture into prepared pan.

3 Bake cake for about 40 minutes. Stand cake in pan about 5 minutes; turn onto wire rack to cool.

tip To marble a butter cake, place portions of cake mixture in different bowls then tint each with desired colour. Dollop spoonfuls of mixture into prepared pan, alternating colours, then gently swirl together with a skewer or spoon to create a marbled effect.

Zucchini walnut loaf

preparation time **15 minutes** cooking time **1 hour 15 minutes** serves **10**

You will need approximately 3 medium zucchinis (360g).

3 eggs
1½ cups (330g) firmly packed brown sugar
1 cup (250ml) vegetable oil
1½ cups finely grated zucchini
1 cup (110g) coarsely chopped walnuts
1½ cups (225g) self-raising flour
1½ cups (225g) plain flour

1 Preheat oven to moderate (180°C/160°C fan-forced). Grease a 15cm x 25cm loaf pan; line base and sides with baking paper.
2 Beat eggs, sugar and oil in large bowl with electric mixer until combined. Stir in zucchini, walnuts and sifted flours in batches.
3 Spread into prepared pan; bake for about 1¼ hours. Stand cake in pan for 5 minutes before turning onto a wire rack to cool. Serve with butter if desired.

Caraway seed cake

preparation time **10 minutes** cooking time **1 hour** serves **10**

180g butter
⅔ cup (150g) caster sugar
3 eggs
1 tablespoon caraway seeds
1½ cups (225g) self-raising flour
¼ cup (60ml) milk

1 Preheat oven to moderate (180°C/160°C fan-forced). Grease a 14cm x 21cm loaf pan.
2 Beat butter and sugar in small bowl with electric mixer until light and fluffy. Add eggs one at a time, beating well after each addition.
3 Transfer mixture to large bowl; stir in seeds, sifted flour and milk.
4 Spread mixture into prepared pan; bake for about 1 hour.

tip This recipe can be made two days ahead.

Cinnamon almond coffee cake

preparation time **25 minutes** cooking time **50 minutes** serves **12**

185g butter
1 cup (220g) caster sugar
2 eggs
1½ cups (225g) self-raising flour
1 cup (150g) plain flour
½ teaspoon bicarbonate of soda
1½ cups (375ml) milk

Cinnamon almond topping
90g butter
¼ cup (55g) brown sugar
¾ cup (110g) plain flour
¼ cup (35g) toasted slivered almonds
2 teaspoons ground cinnamon

1 Preheat oven to moderate (180°C/160°C fan-forced). Grease a deep 23cm square cake pan; line base with baking paper.
2 Make cinnamon almond topping.
3 Cream butter and sugar in small bowl with electric mixer until light and fluffy. Add eggs one at a time, beating well after each addition. Transfer mixture to a large bowl; stir in combined sifted flours and soda and milk, in two batches.
4 Spread into prepared pan; sprinkle with topping. Bake about 50 minutes. Stand for 5 minutes before turning onto wire rack to cool.

Cinnamon almond topping Cream butter and sugar in small bowl with electric mixer until light and fluffy. Stir in sifted flour, almonds and cinnamon.

Orange yogurt cake

preparation time **25 minutes** cooking time **2 hours** serves **10**

125g butter
1 tablespoon grated orange rind
1 cup (220g) caster sugar
3 eggs, separated
½ cup (85g) mixed peel
2 cups (300g) self-raising flour
¼ cup (60ml) orange juice
1 cup (250g) plain yogurt

Orange icing
1½ cups (240g) icing sugar
30g butter, softened
2 tablespoons orange juice, approximately

1 Preheat oven to slow (150°C/130°C fan-forced). Grease a 14cm x 21cm loaf pan; line base and sides with baking paper.
2 Beat butter, rind and sugar in small bowl with electric mixer until light and fluffy; beat in egg yolks one at a time. Transfer mixture to large bowl and stir in peel. Stir in sifted flour and combined juice and yogurt in two batches.
3 Beat egg whites in a small bowl until soft peaks form; fold gently into cake mixture in two batches. Pour into prepared pan.
4 Bake cake for about 2 hours. Stand cake in pan for 5 minutes before turning onto wire rack to cool.
5 Make orange icing; spread over cold cake.

Orange icing Combine sifted icing sugar and butter in bowl. Stir in enough juice to mix icing to a spreadable consistency.

tip This cake will keep for about four days.

Cinnamon-topped butter cake

preparation time **20 minutes** cooking time **1 hour 10 minutes** serves **12**

250g butter, softened
2 cups (440g) caster sugar
1 teaspoon vanilla extract
6 eggs
1½ cups (225g) plain flour
½ cup (75g) self-raising flour
⅔ cup (160ml) buttermilk

Cinnamon topping
¼ cup (55g) white sugar
¼ cup (35g) plain flour
1 teaspoon ground cinnamon
30g butter, chopped finely

1 Preheat oven to moderately slow (170°C/150°C fan-forced). Grease a 23cm round cake pan; line base and side with baking paper.
2 Make cinnamon topping.
3 Beat butter, sugar and extract in a medium bowl with an electric mixer until light and fluffy. Add eggs one at a time, beating until just combined after each addition. Transfer mixture to a large bowl; fold in sifted flours and buttermilk in two batches.
4 Spread mixture into prepared pan; sprinkle with cinnamon topping. Bake about 1 hour 10 minutes or until cooked. Stand for 10 minutes before turning onto wire cake rack to cool.

Cinnamon topping Combine sugar, flour and cinnamon in a small bowl; rub in butter.

Custard teacake

preparation time **30 minutes** (plus cooling time) cooking time **45 minutes**
serves **10**

125g butter
⅓ cup (75g) caster sugar
1 egg
¾ cup (110g) self-raising flour
¼ cup (35g) custard powder

Custard
1 tablespoon custard powder
1 tablespoon caster sugar
⅔ cup (160ml) milk
15g butter
2 teaspoons vanilla extract

1 Preheat oven to moderate (180°C/160°C fan-forced). Grease a deep
20cm round cake pan; line base and side with baking paper.
2 Make custard.
3 Beat butter and sugar in small bowl with electric mixer until light and fluffy;
add egg, beat until combined. Stir in sifted flour and custard powder. Spread
half the cake mixture into prepared pan, spread with cold custard. Spread
remaining cake mixture carefully on top.
4 Bake for about 35 minutes; cool cake in pan. When cake is cold, turn
out onto paper-lined wire rack. Serve dusted with sifted icing sugar.

Custard Blend custard powder and sugar with milk in saucepan. Stir
constantly over heat until mixture boils and thickens. Stir in butter and
extract; cover and cool to room temperature.

tip This teacake usually sinks slightly due to the soft custard in the centre.
Store cake for up to two days.

Moist treacle gingerbread

preparation time **25 minutes** cooking time **50 minutes** serves **10**

¾ cup (110g) plain flour
¼ cup (35g) self-raising flour
½ teaspoon bicarbonate of soda
1 teaspoon ground ginger
¼ teaspoon ground cinnamon
¼ teaspoon mixed spice
½ cup (110g) caster sugar
1 egg, beaten lightly
½ cup (125ml) milk
60g butter
½ cup (120g) treacle

Lemon frosting
60g butter
1 teaspoon grated lemon rind
1 cup (160g) icing sugar
2 teaspoons lemon juice, approximately

1 Preheat oven to moderate (180°C/160°C fan-forced). Grease 14cm x 21cm loaf pan; line base and sides with baking paper.
2 Sift flours, soda and spices into large bowl; stir in sugar and combined egg and milk. Combine butter and treacle in saucepan. Stir constantly over heat without boiling until butter is melted; stir hot mixture into flour mixture.
3 Pour into prepared pan; bake for about 50 minutes. Stand cake in pan for 5 minutes before turning onto a wire rack to cool.
4 Make lemon frosting; spread over top of cooled cake.

Lemon frosting Beat butter and lemon rind in small bowl with electric mixer until creamy. Gradually beat in sifted icing sugar and enough lemon juice to a spreadable consistency.

tip This cake will keep for up to three days.

Coconut and date loaf

preparation time **15 minutes** cooking time **40 minutes** serves **10**

1 cup (140g) chopped dates
½ cup (125ml) boiling water
125g butter
½ cup (110g) caster sugar
1 egg
⅔ cup (110g) self-raising flour
¼ cup (20g) coconut

1 Preheat oven to moderate (180°C/160°C fan-forced). Grease 14cm x 21cm loaf pan; line base with baking paper.
2 Combine dates with boiling water; cover and stand for 15 minutes.
3 Beat butter and sugar in small bowl with electric mixer until light and fluffy. Add egg; beat until combined. Transfer mixture to large bowl; stir in sifted flour, coconut and undrained dates.
4 Spread mixture into prepared pan; bake for about 40 minutes. Stand loaf in pan for 5 minutes before turning onto a wire rack to cool.

Lemon sour cream cake

preparation time **10 minutes** cooking time **1 hour 30 minutes** serves **16**

250g butter
2 teaspoons finely grated lemon rind
2 cups (440g) caster sugar
6 eggs
2 cups (300g) plain flour
¼ cup (35g) self-raising flour
200g carton sour cream

1 Preheat oven to moderately slow (170°C/150°C fan-forced). Grease a deep 27cm round cake pan; line base with baking paper.
2 Beat butter, rind and sugar in large bowl with electric mixer until light and fluffy. Add eggs one at a time, beating well after each addition. Stir in half the sifted flours with half the sour cream, then stir in remaining flours and cream.
3 Spread mixture into prepared pan; bake for about 1½ hours. Stand cake in pan for 5 minutes before turning onto wire rack to cool. Dust with icing sugar.

Madeira cake

preparation time **20 minutes** cooking time **1 hour** serves **12**

This cake does not actually contain Madeira. It is a plain cake, always topped with peel, and was served with a glass of Madeira in Victorian England.

180g butter
2 teaspoons grated lemon rind
⅔ cup caster sugar
3 eggs
¾ cup (110g) plain flour
¾ cup (110g) self-raising flour
⅓ cup (55g) mixed peel
¼ cup (35g) slivered almonds

1 Preheat oven to moderately slow (170°C/150°C fan-forced). Grease a deep 20cm round cake pan; line base with baking paper.
2 Beat butter, rind and sugar in small bowl with electric mixer until light and fluffy; add eggs one at a time, beating well after each addition.
3 Transfer mixture to large bowl, stir in sifted flours.
4 Spread mixture into prepared pan; bake for 20 minutes. Sprinkle peel and nuts evenly over cake. Bake for another 40 minutes. Stand cake in pan for 5 minutes before turning onto wire rack to cool.

tips This recipe can be made a day ahead. Store in an airtight container. This cake is suitable to freeze.

Streusel-topped caramel butter cake

preparation time **25 minutes** (plus refrigeration time)
cooking time **30 minutes** serves **12**

125g butter
1 teaspoon vanilla extract
½ cup (110g) brown sugar
2 eggs
⅔ cup (110g) self-raising flour
½ cup (75g) plain flour
2 tablespoons milk

Streusel topping
¾ cup (110g) plain flour
⅓ cup (75g) brown sugar
2 teaspoons ground cinnamon
90g butter

1 Make streusel topping.
2 Preheat oven to moderate (180°C/160°C fan-forced). Grease a 19cm x 29cm lamington pan; line base with baking paper.
3 Cream butter, extract and sugar in a small bowl with electric mixer until light and fluffy. Add eggs one at a time, beating well after each addition. Transfer mixture to large bowl; stir in sifted flours and milk in two batches.
4 Spread cake mixture into prepared pan; sprinkle with grated streusel topping. Bake for about 30 minutes. Stand cake in pan for 5 minutes before turning onto a wire rack to cool.

Streusel topping Combine flour, sugar and cinnamon in medium bowl; rub in butter. Press into a ball; refrigerate for about 30 minutes. Grate coarsely when cold.

Pecan sour cream cake

preparation time **15 minutes** cooking time **1 hour** serves **12**

250g butter
1 teaspoon vanilla extract
¾ cup (165g) caster sugar
2 eggs
300g carton sour cream
1½ cups (225g) plain flour
½ cup self-raising flour
1 teaspoon bicarbonate of soda
½ cup (60g) finely chopped pecan nuts
2 tablespoons brown sugar
½ teaspoon ground cinnamon

1 Preheat oven to moderate (180°C/160°C fan-forced). Grease a deep 23cm round cake pan.
2 Beat butter, extract and sugar in small bowl with electric mixer until light and fluffy. Add eggs one at a time, beating well after each addition. Transfer mixture to large bowl; stir in sour cream then sifted flours and soda.
3 Spread half the cake mixture into prepared pan; sprinkle with half the combined pecans, brown sugar and cinnamon. Spread evenly with remaining cake mixture. Sprinkle with remaining pecan mixture; press gently into cake mixture. Bake for about 1 hour. Stand cake in pan for 5 minutes before turning onto a wire rack to cool.

tip This cake will keep for up to three days.

Olive oil cake with blueberries

preparation time **25 minutes** cooking time **1 hour** serves **8**

3 eggs
1¼ cups (275g) caster sugar
2 tablespoons finely grated orange rind
½ cup (125ml) olive oil
⅓ cup (80ml) milk
1 cup (150g) plain flour
1 cup (150g) self-raising flour
100g frozen blueberries
⅓ cup (110g) apricot jam, warmed

1 Preheat oven to moderate (180°C/160°C fan-forced). Grease a deep 19cm square cake pan.
2 Beat eggs, sugar and rind in small bowl with electric mixer until sugar is dissolved; transfer to large bowl. Fold in combined oil and milk, and sifted dry ingredients, in two batches.
3 Pour mixture into pan; bake for about 20 minutes. Carefully remove cake from oven; sprinkle surface evenly with blueberries. Bake another 40 minutes. Stand cake in pan for 10 minutes; turn, top-side up, onto a wire rack to cool.
4 Glaze warm cake with jam.

Fresh ginger cake

preparation time **15 minutes** cooking time **1 hour** serves **12**

250g butter, chopped
½ cup (110g) firmly packed dark brown sugar
⅔ cup (230g) golden syrup
12cm piece fresh ginger (60g), grated finely
1 cup (150g) plain flour
1 cup (150g) self-raising flour
½ teaspoon bicarbonate of soda
2 eggs, beaten lightly
¾ cup (180ml) cream

Golden ginger cream
300ml whipping cream
2 tablespoons golden syrup
2 teaspoons ground ginger

1 Preheat oven to moderate (180°C/160°C fan-forced). Grease a deep
22cm round cake pan.
2 Melt butter in medium saucepan; add sugar, syrup and ginger. Stir over
low heat until sugar dissolves.
3 Whisk in combined sifted flours and soda, then egg and cream. Pour
mixture into pan; bake for about 50 minutes. Stand cake in pan for
10 minutes; turn, top-side up, onto a wire rack to cool.
4 Meanwhile, beat ingredients for golden ginger cream in a small bowl with
electric mixer until soft peaks form; serve with cake.

Lemon and lime
white chocolate mudcake

preparation time **20 minutes** cooking time **1 hour 50 minutes** (plus cooling and refrigeration time) serves **12**

250g butter, chopped
2 teaspoons finely grated lemon rind
2 teaspoons finely grated lime rind
180g white eating chocolate, chopped coarsely
1½ cups (330g) caster sugar
¾ cup (180ml) milk
1½ cups (225g) plain flour
½ cup (75g) self-raising flour
2 eggs, beaten lightly

Coconut ganache
140ml coconut cream
360g white eating chocolate, chopped finely
1 teaspoon finely grated lemon rind
1 teaspoon finely grated lime rind

1 Preheat oven to moderately slow (170°C/150°C fan-forced). Grease a deep 20cm round cake pan; line base with baking paper.
2 Combine butter, rinds, chocolate, sugar and milk in medium saucepan; stir over low heat until smooth. Transfer mixture to large bowl; cool 15 minutes.
3 Stir in sifted flours and egg; pour into pan. Bake about 1 hour 40 minutes; cool cake in pan.
4 Meanwhile, make coconut ganache.
5 Turn cake, top-side up, onto serving plate; spread ganache over cake.

Coconut ganache Bring coconut cream to a boil in small saucepan. Combine chocolate and rinds in medium bowl. Add hot cream; stir until smooth. Cover bowl; refrigerate, stirring occasionally, for about 30 minutes or until ganache is spreadable.

Spiced nut teacake

preparation time **20 minutes** cooking time **25 minutes** serves **10**

60g butter, softened
½ cup (110g) caster sugar
1 egg
1 cup (150g) self-raising flour
⅓ cup (80ml) milk
1 teaspoon vanilla extract
20g butter, melted, extra

Spiced nuts
2 tablespoons shelled pistachios, chopped finely
2 tablespoons blanched almonds, chopped finely
2 tablespoons pine nuts, chopped finely
¼ cup (40g) icing sugar
½ teaspoon ground allspice
½ teaspoon ground cardamom
1 teaspoon ground cinnamon

1 Preheat oven to moderate (180°C/160°C fan-forced). Grease a deep 20cm round cake pan.
2 Beat butter, sugar and egg in small bowl with electric mixer until light and fluffy; transfer the mixture to a medium bowl. Stir in sifted flour and combined milk and extract.
3 Spread mixture in pan; bake for about 25 minutes. Stand cake in pan for 5 minutes; turn, top-side up, onto wire rack to cool.
4 Meanwhile, make spiced nuts.
5 Brush cooled cake with melted extra butter; sprinkle with spiced nuts. Serve while still warm, cut into wedges.

Spiced nuts Place nuts in strainer; rinse under cold water. Combine wet nuts in large bowl with icing sugar and spices; spread mixture onto oven tray, toast for about 10 minutes or until nuts are dry and crisp.

Lardy cake

preparation time **30 minutes** (plus standing time) cooking time **40 minutes**
serves **12**

*This delicious flaky yeast cake originated in a number of English counties, such
as Wiltshire and Sussex, where pigs were raised. Dough left over from making
bread would be rolled with lard, sugar and currants for a baking day treat.*

15g compressed yeast
1 teaspoon caster sugar
¾ cup (180ml) warm milk
2 cups (300g) plain flour
Pinch of salt
1 egg, lightly beaten
¼ cup (40g) currants
125g lard
⅓ cup (75g) caster sugar, extra
2 teaspoons oil
1 tablespoon white sugar

1 Combine yeast and caster sugar in a small bowl; stir in milk. Cover and let
stand in a warm place for about 15 minutes, or until frothy. Grease a deep
20cm round cake pan.

2 Sift flour and salt into large bowl. Stir in yeast mixture, egg and currants;
mix to soft dough. Turn dough onto floured surface, knead about 3 minutes
or until dough is smooth and elastic.

3 Roll dough to about 15cm x 30 cm rectangle. Spread half the lard over
two-thirds of the dough; sprinkle with half the extra caster sugar. Fold the
unlarded third of the dough over, then turn dough halfway around, open end
towards you. Roll out dough and fold again using the remaining lard and extra
caster sugar. Then roll and fold twice more, without lard and sugar.

4 Shape dough into a round by turning ends under. Place into prepared
pan, press dough to fit. Brush top with oil; sprinkle with white sugar. Stand,
uncovered, in a warm place about 45 minutes, or until dough is well risen.

5 Preheat oven to moderately hot (200°C/180°C fan-forced). Slash top of
cake with a sharp knife in crisscross fashion. Bake for 40 minutes or until
cake is well browned. Turn onto wire rack, Serve warm with butter.

tips This cake is best made just before serving.

Marble cake

preparation time **25 minutes** cooking time **40 minutes** serves **8**

180g butter
1 teaspoon vanilla extract
¾ cup (110g) caster sugar
2 eggs
1½ cups (225g) self-raising flour
½ cup (125ml) milk
Pink food colouring
2 tablespoons cocoa
1 tablespoon milk, extra

Icing
90g butter
1 cup (160g) icing sugar
1½ tablespoons milk
Pink food colouring

1 Preheat oven to moderate (180°C/160°C fan-forced). Lightly grease a 20cm ring cake pan; line base with baking paper.
2 Beat butter, extract and caster sugar in small bowl with electric mixer until mixture is light and fluffy. Add eggs one at a time, beating well after each addition. Transfer mixture to large bowl; fold in sifted flour and milk in two batches. Divide mixture evenly among three bowls.
3 Tint mixture pink in one bowl; mix well. Stir sifted cocoa and extra milk into second bowl; mix well. Drop spoonfuls of each of the three mixtures into prepared pan. Run a knife through cake mixture for a marbled effect.
4 Bake cake for about 40 minutes. Stand cake in pan for 5 minutes before turning onto wire rack to cool.
5 Make icing; drop alternate spoonfuls of pink and white icing on top of cold cake. Using a spatula, swirl icing to give marbled effect.

Icing Beat butter in small bowl with electric mixer until as white as possible; beat in sifted icing sugar and milk in two batches. Divide mixture between two bowls; use pink colouring to tint mixture in one bowl.

SMALL CAKES

Coffee caramel cakes

preparation time **15 minutes** cooking time **20 minutes** makes **12**

125g butter, softened
²⁄₃ cup (150g) firmly packed brown sugar
2 tablespoons instant coffee granules
1 tablespoon boiling water
2 eggs
2 cups (300g) self-raising flour
½ cup (125ml) milk
18 (130g) jersey caramels, halved

1 Preheat oven to moderate (180°C/160°C fan-forced). Grease a 12-hole
(¹⁄₃-cup/80ml) muffin pan.
2 Beat butter and sugar in small bowl with electric mixer until light and fluffy.
Add combined coffee and the water. Add eggs, one at a time, beating until
just combined after each addition. Transfer mixture to large bowl; stir in sifted
flour and milk. Spoon mixture into prepared holes. Press three caramel halves
into the centre of each cake; cover with batter.
3 Bake cakes for about 20 minutes. Cool cakes in pan for 5 minutes before
turning onto wire racks to cool.

tip These cakes are suitable to freeze for up to one month.

Cupcakes

preparation time **15 minutes** cooking time **25 minutes** (plus cooling time)
makes **24**

125g butter, softened
1 teaspoon vanilla extract
²⁄₃ cup (150g) caster sugar
3 eggs
1½ cups (225g) self-raising flour
¼ cup (60ml) milk

Glacé icing
1½ cups (240g) icing sugar
1 teaspoon butter, softened
2 tablespoons milk, approximately
Food colouring, optional

1 Preheat oven to moderate (180°C/160°C fan-forced). Line two deep
12-hole patty pans with paper cases.
2 Beat butter, extract, sugar, eggs, flour and milk in small bowl of electric
mixer on low speed until ingredients are just combined. Increase speed to
medium, beat about 3 minutes or until mixture is smooth and pale in colour.
3 Drop slightly rounded tablespoons of mixture into paper cases; bake for
about 20 minutes. Turn cakes onto wire racks; turn top-side up to cool.
4 Make glacé icing; spread over cold cupcakes.

Glacé icing Place icing sugar in small heatproof bowl; stir in butter and
enough milk to make a firm paste. Add a few drops of food colouring, if
desired. Stir over a small saucepan of hot water until icing is a spreadable
consistency; do not overheat.

tips Cupcakes are best served on day of making. Unfilled and un-iced cakes
can be frozen for up to one month.

Banana blueberry cakes

preparation time **20 minutes** cooking time **30 minutes** (plus cooling time)
makes **12**

You will need one large (230g) overripe banana for this recipe.

125g butter
½ cup (125ml) milk
2 eggs
1 cup (220g) caster sugar
½ cup mashed banana
1½ cups (225g) self-raising flour
½ cup (75g) frozen blueberries

1 Preheat oven to moderate (180°C/160°C fan-forced). Grease 12-hole
(⅓-cup/80ml) muffin pan.
2 Place butter and milk in a small saucepan; stir over low heat until
butter melts. Cool.
3 Beat eggs in small bowl with electric mixer until thick and creamy.
Gradually add sugar, beating until dissolved between additions; stir in
banana. Fold in sifted flour and cooled butter mixture, in two batches.
Divide mixture among muffin holes.
4 Bake cakes for 10 minutes. Remove pan from oven; press frozen
blueberries into tops of cakes. Bake a further 15 minutes. Turn cakes
onto wire racks to cool.

tips Cakes can be stored in an airtight container for up to three days.
Suitable to freeze for up to one month.

Gingerbread loaves

preparation time **35 minutes** cooking time **25 minutes** makes **16**

200g butter, softened
1¼ cups (275g) caster sugar
¾ cup (270g) treacle
2 eggs
3 cups (450g) plain flour
1½ tablespoons ground ginger
3 teaspoons mixed spice
1 teaspoon bicarbonate of soda
¾ cup (180ml) milk

Vanilla icing
3 cups (500g) icing sugar
2 teaspoons butter, softened
½ teaspoon vanilla extract
⅓ cup (80ml) milk

1 Preheat oven to moderate (180°C/160°C fan-forced). Grease two 8-hole (½-cup/125ml) petite loaf pans or line 22 holes (⅓-cup/80ml) muffin pan with paper cases.
2 Beat butter and sugar in small bowl with electric mixer until light and fluffy. Pour in treacle, beat 3 minutes. Add eggs one at a time, beating until just combined after each addition. Transfer mixture to large bowl. Stir in sifted dry ingredients, then milk. Divide mixture among prepared pans.
3 Bake about 25 minutes. Stand loaves in pans for 5 minutes before turning onto wire rack to cool.
4 Make vanilla icing; spread over loaves and stand until set.

Vanilla icing Sift icing sugar into heatproof bowl; stir in butter, extract and milk to form a smooth paste. Place bowl over simmering water; stir until icing is a spreadable consistency.

tips Store cakes in airtight container for up to four days. Un-iced cakes can be frozen for up to three months. Icing may be microwaved.

Buttery apple cinnamon cakes

preparation time **10 minutes**   cooking time **25 minutes**   makes **8**

125g butter, softened
1 teaspoon vanilla extract
¾ cup (165g) caster sugar
2 eggs
¾ cup (110g) self-raising flour
¼ cup (35g) plain flour
⅓ cup (80ml) apple juice
1 small apple (130g)
1½ tablespoons demerara sugar
¼ teaspoon ground cinnamon

1 Preheat oven to moderate (180°C/160°C fan-forced). Grease an 8-hole
(½-cup/125ml) petite loaf pan.
2 Beat butter, extract and sugar in small bowl with electric mixer until light
and fluffy. Add eggs one at a time, beating until just combined after each
addition. Fold in combined sifted flours and juice in two batches. Divide
mixture into prepared pans.
3 Cut the unpeeled apple into quarters; remove core, slice thinly. Overlap
apple slices on top of cakes.
4 Combine demerara sugar and cinnamon in a small bowl; sprinkle half the
sugar mixture over cakes. Bake for about 25 minutes. Turn cakes onto wire
rack to cool. Sprinkle with remaining sugar mixture.

tips   This recipe can also be made in a 12-hole (⅓-cup/80ml) muffin pan.
Store cakes in an airtight container for up to three days. Suitable to freeze
for up to three months.

Apricot upside-down cakes

preparation time **20 minutes** cooking time **20 minutes** makes **12**

1 tablespoon brown sugar
12 canned apricot halves in syrup, drained
2 eggs
¾ cup (150g) firmly packed brown sugar, extra
¾ cup (90g) almond meal
1 teaspoon vanilla extract
⅓ cup (50g) wholemeal self-raising flour
½ cup (125ml) low-fat milk
¼ cup (80g) apricot conserve, heated

1 Preheat oven to moderate (180°C/160°C fan-forced). Grease a 12-hole
(⅓-cup/80ml) muffin pan.
2 Sprinkle sugar equally into holes of prepared pan; add one apricot half,
cut-side down, to each hole.
3 Beat eggs and extra sugar in medium bowl with electric mixer until light
and fluffy. Stir in almond meal, extract, flour and milk.
4 Divide mixture among holes of prepared pan; bake for about 20 minutes.
Stand cakes in pan for 5 minutes, then turn onto a wire rack. Brush apricot
conserve over hot cakes. Serve cakes warm or at room temperature.

Cappuccino cupcakes

preparation time **25 minutes** cooking time **25 minutes** makes **20**

125g butter, softened
3 teaspoons instant coffee granules
2 tablespoons Tia Maria
¾ cup (165g) caster sugar
2 eggs
1½ cups (225g) self-raising flour
⅓ cup (80ml) milk

Cheesecake topping
250g packaged cream cheese
1 teaspoon vanilla extract
½ cup (80g) icing sugar
1 egg

1 Preheat oven to moderate (180°C/160°C fan-forced). Line 20 holes of two 12-hole (⅓-cup/80ml) muffin pans with paper-lined foil muffin cases.
2 Beat ingredients in medium bowl with electric mixer on low speed until combined; beat on medium speed about 2 minutes, or until mixture is smooth and changed to a lighter colour. Divide mixture among muffin cases; bake for about 10 minutes.
3 Meanwhile, make cheesecake topping.
4 Remove cakes from oven. Carefully spread each cake with cheesecake topping. Return to oven and bake for about 15 minutes. Cool cakes in pans; dust with sifted drinking chocolate powder, if desired.

Cheesecake topping Beat cheese and extract in small bowl with electric mixer until fluffy. Add icing sugar and egg; beat until combined.

Wholemeal date loaf

preparation time **20 minutes** cooking time **1 hour** serves **14**

1 cup (170g) seeded dates, halved
2 tablespoons boiling water
½ teaspoon bicarbonate of soda
60g low-fat margarine
2 teaspoons finely grated lemon rind
¾ cup (150g) firmly packed brown sugar
200g low-fat cottage cheese
2 eggs
2 cups (320g) wholemeal self-raising flour
2 tablespoons wheatgerm

1 Preheat oven to moderately slow (170°C/150°C fan-forced). Grease 14cm x 21cm loaf pan; line base and two long sides with baking paper, extending paper 5cm above edge.
2 Combine dates, the water and bicarbonate of soda in small bowl; cover and let stand for 5 minutes.
3 Beat margarine, rind and sugar in small bowl with electric mixer until light and fluffy. Add cheese; beat until smooth. Add eggs one at a time, beating well after each addition. Stir in flour, wheatgerm and date mixture; spread into prepared pan.
4 Bake loaf for about 1 hour. Stand loaf in pan for 10 minutes; turn onto wire rack to cool.

English malt loaf

preparation time **15 minutes** cooking time **1 hour 45 minutes** serves **12**

4 cups (640g) wholemeal plain flour
½ cup (100g) firmly packed brown sugar
1½ cups (250g) sultanas
1 teaspoon bicarbonate of soda
1 tablespoon hot water
1¼ cups (310ml) milk
1 cup (250ml) liquid malt
½ cup (125ml) treacle

1 Preheat oven to moderately slow (170°C/150°C fan-forced). Grease 15cm x 25cm loaf pan; line base with baking paper.
2 Sift flour into a large heatproof bowl; add sugar and sultanas. Add bicarbonate of soda to water in a medium jug; add milk.
3 Stir malt and treacle in a medium pan over low heat until mixture begins to bubble; add milk mixture. Stir foaming milk mixture into flour mixture.
4 Spread cake mixture into prepared pan; bake for about 1¾ hours. Stand loaf in pan for 5 minutes; turn onto wire rack to cool.

Mini choc chip almond cakes

preparation time **20 minutes** cooking time **20 minutes** makes **18**

3 egg whites
90g butter, melted
½ cup (60g) almond meal
¾ cup (120g) icing sugar
¼ cup (35g) plain flour
100g dark eating chocolate, chopped finely
¼ cup (60ml) cream
100g dark eating chocolate, extra

1 Preheat oven to moderate (180°C/160°C fan-forced). Grease two
12-hole mini (1 tablespoon/20ml) muffin pans.
2 Place egg whites in a medium bowl; whisk lightly with a fork until
combined. Add butter, almond meal, sifted icing sugar and flour to bowl;
using a wooden spoon, stir until just combined. Stir in the chopped chocolate.
Spoon tablespoons of mixture into pan holes.
3 Bake almond cakes for about 15 minutes or until browned lightly and
cooked through. Turn onto wire racks to cool.
4 Combine cream and extra chocolate in a medium heatproof bowl over a
pan of simmering water. Stir until just melted; stand until thickened. Spoon
chocolate mixture over tops of cakes.

Strawberries and cream powder puffs

preparation time **25 minutes** cooking time **10 minutes** makes **12**

2 eggs
⅓ cup (75g) caster sugar
2 tablespoons cornflour
2 tablespoons plain flour
2 tablespoons self-raising flour
⅔ cup (160ml) cream
⅓ cup (55g) icing sugar
250g strawberries, chopped coarsely

1 Preheat oven to moderate (180°C/160°C fan-forced). Grease and flour two 12-hole shallow patty pans.
2 Beat eggs in small bowl with electric mixer until thick and creamy. Gradually add caster sugar, 1 tablespoon at a time, beating until sugar dissolves after each addition. Sift flours together three times onto baking paper; fold into egg mixture.
3 Divide mixture among prepared pans; bake, uncovered, about 8 minutes. Turn out immediately onto wire rack to cool.
4 Beat cream and half of the icing sugar in small bowl with electric mixer until soft peaks form; fold in strawberries. Divide cream mixture among half of the sponges; top with remaining sponges. Serve powder puffs dusted with remaining icing sugar.

Butterfly cakes

preparation time **30 minutes** cooking time **20 minutes** makes **24**

Butterfly cakes are made by removing a small circle of cake from the top of each patty cake, filling the cavity with your favourite jam and some cream, then topping the cream with the two halves of the circle to create 'wings'.

125g butter, softened
1 teaspoon vanilla extract
²⁄₃ cup (150g) caster sugar
3 eggs
1½ cups (225g) self-raising flour
¼ cup (60ml) milk
½ cup (160g) jam
300ml whipping cream

1 Preheat oven to moderate (180°C/160°C fan-forced). Line two deep 12-hole patty pans with paper cases.
2 Combine butter, extract, sugar, eggs, flour and milk in small bowl of electric mixer; beat on low speed until ingredients are just combined. Increase speed to medium, beat for about 3 minutes, or until mixture is smooth and changed to a lighter colour.
3 Drop slightly rounded tablespoons of mixture into paper cases; bake for about 20 minutes. Turn cakes onto wire racks; turn top-side up to cool.
4 Using a small, sharp-pointed knife, cut a circle from the top of each cake; cut the circle in half to make two 'wings'. Fill cake cavities with jam and whipped cream. Place the wings in position on top of the cakes; top with strawberry pieces and dust with a little sifted icing sugar, if desired.

Spiced coffee cakes

preparation time **25 minutes** cooking time **25 minutes** makes **12**

125g butter
¾ cup (180ml) milk
3 eggs
¾ cup (165g) caster sugar
1½ cups (225g) self-raising flour
2 tablespoons instant coffee granules
2 teaspoons hot water

Icings
60g butter
¾ cup (120g) icing sugar
1 tablespoon milk
1 tablespoon cocoa powder
¼ teaspoon ground cardamom
1 tablespoon instant coffee granules
1 teaspoon hot water

1 Preheat oven to moderate (180°C/160°C fan-forced). Line 12-hole (⅓-cup/80ml capacity) muffin pan with paper-lined foil muffin cases.
2 Place butter and milk in small pan; stir over low heat until butter melts.
3 Beat eggs in small bowl with an electric mixer until thick and creamy; gradually add sugar, beating until dissolved between additions. Transfer mixture to large bowl; fold in sifted flour and cooled butter mixture, in two batches. Fold in combined coffee and hot water.
4 Divide mixture among muffin cases; bake for about 25 minutes. Turn onto wire rack to cool.
5 Make icings; swirl both icings over each cooled cake.

Icings Beat butter with wooden spoon in small bowl until pale. Gradually beat in half the icing sugar. Beat in milk and remaining icing sugar. Divide mixture between two bowls. Stir sifted cocoa powder and cardamom into one bowl. Stir combined coffee and hot water into remaining bowl.

White chocolate mudcakes

preparation time **45 minutes** cooking time **40 minutes** makes **24**

250g butter, chopped coarsely
150g white eating chocolate, chopped coarsely
2 cups (440g) caster sugar
1 cup (250ml) milk
1½ cups (225g) plain flour
½ cup (75g) self-raising flour
1 teaspoon vanilla extract
2 eggs, beaten lightly

Fluffy frosting
1 cup (220g) caster sugar
⅓ cup (80ml) water
2 egg whites

1 Preheat the oven to moderately slow (170°C/150°C fan-forced). Line two 12-hole (⅓-cup/80ml) muffin pans with patty cases.
2 Combine butter, chocolate, sugar and milk in a medium pan; with a wooden spoon, stir over low heat, without boiling, until smooth. Transfer mixture to a bowl; cool for 15 minutes.
3 Whisk in sifted flours, then extract and eggs. Pour mixture evenly into prepared pans. Bake cakes for about 35 minutes or until cooked when tested. Cool.
4 Make fluffy frosting; spread over cakes.

Fluffy frosting Combine sugar and water in a small pan; stir with a wooden spoon over low heat, without boiling, until sugar dissolves. Boil, uncovered, without stirring, for 3–5 minutes or until syrup is slightly thick. (Syrup should not colour; if it does, discard it and start again.) Meanwhile, beat egg whites in a small bowl with an electric mixer until firm. When the syrup is ready, allow bubbles to subside. With electric mixer operating on medium speed, pour syrup in a thin stream onto egg whites – if syrup is added too quickly, frosting will not thicken. Continue to beat on high speed for about 5 minutes or until thick. Frosting should be barely warm. Tint frosting with a few drops of food colouring, if desired.

Strawberry jelly cakes

preparation time **45 minutes** cooking time **25 minutes** (plus refrigeration time) makes **36**

125g butter, softened
½ teaspoon vanilla extract
½ cup (110g) caster sugar
2 eggs
1½ cups (225g) self-raising flour
⅓ cup (80ml) milk
80g packet strawberry jelly crystals
3 cups (150g) flaked coconut
½ cup (125ml) whipping cream

1 Preheat oven to moderate (180°C/160°C fan-forced). Grease a deep 23cm-square cake pan; line base with baking paper.
2 Beat butter, extract and sugar in small bowl with electric mixer until light and fluffy. Beat in eggs one at a time, until just combined after each addition. Stir in flour and milk until smooth; spread mixture into prepared pan. Bake for about 25 minutes. Stand cake in pan for 5 minutes; turn, top-side up, onto a wire rack to cool.
3 Meanwhile, make jelly according to manufacturer's instructions. Refrigerate until set to the consistency of unbeaten egg white.
4 Cut cooled cake into 36 squares; dip each square into jelly, then coconut. Cover; refrigerate for 30 minutes.
5 Meanwhile, beat cream in a small bowl with electric mixer until firm peaks form. Serve cakes with cream.

Currant cakes with orange glaze

preparation time **20 minutes** cooking time **45 minutes** makes **24**

¼ cup (55g) caster sugar
¼ cup (35g) dried currants
2 teaspoons grated orange rind
½ cup (125g) orange juice
125g butter
2 teaspoons grated orange rind, extra
½ cup (110g) caster sugar, extra
2 eggs
1½ cups (225g) self-raising flour
⅓ cup (80ml) milk

1 Preheat oven to moderate (180°C/160°C fan-forced). Grease two deep 12-hole patty pans.
2 Combine sugar, currants, rind and juice in a small pan; stir over heat, without boiling, until sugar dissolves. Bring to a boil, then reduce heat and simmer, uncovered, without stirring, for 2 minutes. Remove from heat; stand for 30 minutes. Strain mixture into jug; reserve currants and syrup.
3 Beat butter, extra rind and extra sugar in medium bowl with electric mixer until light and fluffy; add eggs one at a time, beating until just combined after each addition. Stir in reserved currants, then flour and milk, in two batches. Divide mixture among holes of prepared pans; bake for about 45 minutes.
4 Turn cake onto a wire rack over a tray; brush the tops of the hot cakes with reserved syrup.

Strawberry and almond cakes

preparation time **20 minutes** cooking time **25 minutes** makes **12**

6 egg whites
185g butter, melted
1 cup (125g) almond meal
1½ cups (240g) icing sugar
½ cup (75g) plain flour
100g strawberries, sliced thinly

1 Preheat oven to moderately hot (200°C/180°C fan-forced). Grease a 12-hole (⅓-cup/80ml) muffin pan; stand on oven tray.

2 Place egg whites in medium bowl; whisk lightly with a fork until combined. Add butter, almond meal, icing sugar and flour to bowl; using a wooden spoon, stir until just combined. Divide mixture among prepared pans; top with strawberry slices.

3 Bake cakes for about 25 minutes. Stand cakes in pan for 5 minutes then turn onto wire rack; turn top-side up to cool.

4 Serve cakes warm, or at room temperature, dusted with a little extra sifted icing sugar, if desired.

tip Individual oval or rectangular cake pans with the same capacity can also be used for this recipe.

Little lime almond cakes

preparation time **20 minutes** cooking time **15 minutes** (plus cooling time)
makes **30**

6 egg whites
185g butter, melted
1 cup (125g) almond meal
1 ½ cups (240g) icing sugar
½ cup (75g) plain flour
1 tablespoon finely grated lime rind
1 tablespoon lime juice
30 whole blanched almonds (60g)

1 Preheat oven to moderately hot (200°C/180°C fan-forced). Grease 30 mini
(1 ½-tablespoon/30ml) muffin pan holes.
2 Place egg whites in a medium bowl; whisk lightly until combined. Add
butter, almond meal, sifted icing sugar and flour, then rind and juice. Whisk
until just combined. Divide mixture among prepared pans; top mixture in
each hole with an almond.
3 Bake cakes for about 15 minutes. Turn onto wire racks to cool, top-side up.
Serve warm or at room temperature.

tips This recipe can be made up to two days ahead; suitable to freeze.

Pear and hazelnut almond cakes

preparation time **15 minutes** cooking time **20 minutes** makes **12**

6 egg whites
185g butter, melted
1 cup (100g) hazelnut meal
1½ cups (240g) icing sugar
½ cup (75g) plain flour
1 small corella pear (100g)
12 shelled toasted hazelnuts (10g), skinned and halved

1 Preheat oven to moderately hot (200°C/180°C fan-forced). Grease a 12-hole (⅓-cup/80ml) muffin pan; stand on an oven tray.
2 Place egg whites in medium bowl; whisk lightly with fork until combined. Add butter, meal, sugar and flour; using a wooden spoon, stir until ingredients are just combined.
3 Core the pear; cut lengthways into 12 even slices.
4 Divide cake mixture among prepared holes; top each with one pear slice and two nut halves. Bake, uncovered, for about 20 minutes. Stand cakes in pan for 5 minutes; turn, top-side up, onto a wire rack to cool.

tip Individual oval or rectangular cake pans with the same capacity can also be used for this recipe.

Coffee almond cakes

preparation time **15 minutes** cooking time **20 minutes** makes **12**

6 egg whites
2 teaspoons instant coffee granules
2 teaspoons hot water
185g butter, melted
1 cup (100g) hazelnut meal
1½ cups (240g) icing sugar
½ cup (75g) plain flour
24 whole coffee beans

1 Preheat oven to moderately hot (200°C/180°C fan-forced). Grease 12
½-cup (125ml) rectangular or oval individual cake pans; stand on oven tray.
2 Place egg whites in a medium bowl; whisk lightly with fork until combined.
Dissolve coffee granules in the hot water; add to egg-white mixture.
3 Add butter, hazelnut meal, sugar and flour to egg-white mixture; using a
wooden spoon, stir until just combined.
4 Divide the mixture among prepared pans; top each cake with two coffee
beans. Bake, uncovered, for about 25 minutes. Stand cakes in pans for
5 minutes; turn, top-side up, onto a wire rack to cool.

tip A 12-hole muffin pan with the same capacity can also be used.

Citrus poppy seed loaves

preparation time **35 minutes** cooking time **30 minutes** serves **8**

125g butter, softened
2 teaspoons finely grated orange rind
2 teaspoons finely grated lemon rind
¾ cup (165g) caster sugar
2 eggs
1 cup (150g) self-raising flour
¼ cup (30g) almond meal
1 tablespoon poppy seeds
⅓ cup (80ml) fresh orange juice

Glacé icing
¾ cup (120g) icing sugar
1 tablespoon orange juice

1 Preheat oven to moderate (180°C/160°C fan-forced). Grease an 8-hole (½-cup/125ml) mini loaf pan; line bases with baking paper.
2 Beat butter, rinds and sugar in small bowl with an electric mixer until light and fluffy. Add eggs one at a time, beating until just combined after each addition. Transfer mixture to a large bowl; fold in combined sifted flour, almond meal, poppy seeds and juice in two batches. Divide mixture among prepared pans.
3 Bake loaves for about 25 minutes. Stand cakes in pan for 5 minutes before turning onto a wire rack to cool.
4 Make glacé icing; spread immediately over cold cakes. Serve topped with glacé oranges, if desired.

Glacé icing Sift icing sugar into a small heatproof bowl; add juice and mix to a firm paste. Stir over a small pan of simmering water until icing is a spreadable consistency; do not overheat.

Choc-chip butterfly cakes

preparation time **25 minutes** cooking time **20 minutes** makes **12**

60g butter
1 teaspoon vanilla extract
⅓ cup (75g) caster sugar
¾ cup (110g) self-raising flour
¼ cup (60ml) milk
1 egg
¼ cup (45g) dark choc chips, chopped
⅔ cup (160ml) cream
1 tablespoon icing sugar
2 red glacé cherries

1 Preheat oven to moderate (180°C/160°C fan-forced). Line a deep 12-hole patty pan with paper patty cases.
2 Beat butter, extract, sugar, flour, milk and egg in small bowl with electric mixer on low speed until combined; beat on medium speed until mixture is smooth and changed to a lighter colour. Stir in chocolate. Divide mixture among patty cases; bake for about 20 minutes. Turn onto wire rack to cool.
3 Using the point of a small knife, cut shallow 4cm rounds from tops of cold cakes; cut each round in half.
4 Beat cream and icing sugar in a small bowl until soft peaks form. Cut each cherry into six slices. Spoon cream into holes in cakes; place halved cake and cherry pieces on top to resemble butterflies.

SPONGES

Best-ever sponge cake

preparation time **25 minutes** cooking time **25 minutes** serves **10**

4 eggs
¾ cup (165g) caster sugar
1 cup (150g) self-raising flour
1 tablespoon cornflour
10g butter, softened
⅓ cup (80ml) hot water
⅓ cup (110g) lemon butter
¾ cup (180ml) whipping cream, whipped
1 tablespoon icing sugar

1 Preheat oven to moderate (180°C/160°C fan-forced). Grease two deep 20cm round cake pans.
2 Beat eggs in large bowl with electric mixer until thick and foamy. Gradually add sugar, 1 tablespoon at a time, beating until sugar is dissolved between additions. Total beating time should be about 10 minutes.
3 Sift flour and cornflour together three times onto paper. Sift flour mixture over egg mixture; gently fold ingredients together. Pour combined butter and hot water down side of bowl; fold through egg mixture. Pour mixture evenly into prepared pans; using a metal spatula, spread mixture to edges of pans.
4 Bake about 25 minutes. Turn onto baking paper-covered wire racks; turn top-side up to cool.
5 Place one sponge on a plate and spread with lemon butter and whipped cream. Top with remaining cake; dust with sifted icing sugar.

tip When folding flour into egg mixture, you can use a large metal spoon, a rubber spatula or a whisk, or use one hand like a rake.

Chocolate sponge

preparation time **25 minutes** cooking time **25 minutes** serves **10**

3 eggs
½ cup (110g) caster sugar
¼ cup (35g) cornflour
¼ cup (35g) plain flour
¼ cup (35g) self-raising flour
2 tablespoons cocoa powder
300ml whipping cream, whipped

Coffee icing
3 teaspoons instant coffee granules
2 tablespoons milk
1½ cups (240g) icing sugar
10g butter, softened

1 Preheat oven to moderate (180°C/160°C fan-forced). Grease a deep 22cm round cake pan; line base with baking paper.
2 Beat eggs in small bowl with electric mixer for 8 minutes or until thick and creamy. Gradually add sugar, beating until dissolved between each addition. Transfer mixture to a large bowl; gently fold in triple-sifted dry ingredients. Spread mixture into prepared pan; bake for 25 minutes. Turn sponge immediately onto a wire rack to cool.
3 Make coffee icing.
4 Split sponge in half; join with cream. Spread top with coffee icing; leave to set before cutting.

Coffee icing Combine coffee and milk in asmall bowl; stir until dissolved. Sift icing sugar into a small bowl; stir in butter and enough of the coffee mixture to give a firm paste. Stir over hot water until icing is a spreadable consistency.

tips This cake is best made on the day of serving. The unfilled and un-iced cake is suitable to freeze.

Jam roll

preparation time **20 minutes** cooking time **8 minutes** serves **8**

3 eggs, separated
½ cup (110g) caster sugar
¾ cup (110g) self-raising flour
2 tablespoons hot milk
¼ cup (110g) caster sugar, extra
½ cup (160g) jam, warmed

1 Preheat oven to moderately hot (200°C/180°C fan-forced). Grease a 25cm x 30cm swiss roll pan; line base and short sides of pan with baking paper, extending paper 5cm over edges.

2 Beat egg whites in small bowl with electric mixer until soft peaks form; gradually add sugar, 1 tablespoon at a time, beating until sugar is dissolved between additions.

3 With motor operating, add egg yolks, one at a time, beating until mixture is pale and thick; this will take about 10 minutes.

4 Meanwhile, sift flour three times onto baking paper.

5 Pour hot milk down side of bowl; add triple-sifted flour. Working quickly, gently fold ingredients together. Spread into prepared pan, gently spreading mixture evenly into corners.

6 Bake for about 8 minutes or until top of cake feels soft and springy when touched lightly with fingertips.

7 Meanwhile, place a piece of baking paper cut the same size as the cake on a board or bench; sprinkle evenly with extra sugar. When cake is cooked, immediately turn it onto the sugared paper, quickly peeling away the lining paper. Working rapidly, use a serrated knife to cut crisp edges from all sides of the cake.

8 Gently roll the cake loosely from one of the short sides; unroll and spread evenly with jam. Roll cake again, from same short side, by lifting the paper and using it to guide the roll into shape.

Wendy's sponge cake

preparation time **20 minutes** cooking time **20 minutes** serves **10**

4 eggs
¾ cup (165g) caster sugar
⅔ cup (100g) wheaten cornflour
¼ cup (30g) custard powder
1 teaspoon cream of tartar
½ teaspoon bicarbonate of soda
300ml whipping cream
1 tablespoon icing sugar
½ teaspoon vanilla extract
¼ cup (80g) strawberry jam, warmed
250g strawberries, sliced thinly
1 tablespoon icing sugar, extra

1 Preheat oven to moderate (180°C/160°C fan-forced). Grease and flour two deep 22cm-round cake pans.
2 Beat eggs and caster sugar in small bowl with electric mixer for about 5 minutes, or until thick and creamy; transfer to a large bowl.
3 Sift dry ingredients twice onto paper; sift over egg mixture and gently fold ingredients together.
4 Divide mixture evenly between prepared pans; bake for about 20 minutes. Turn sponges immediately onto baking paper-covered wire rack; turn top-side up to cool.
5 Beat cream, icing sugar and extract in small bowl with electric mixer until firm peaks form. Place one sponge on serving plate; spread first with jam, then with cream mixture. Top with strawberry slices, then with remaining sponge. Dust with sifted extra icing sugar.

tip When folding flour into egg mixture, you can use a large metal spoon, a rubber spatula or a whisk, or use one hand like a rake.

Honey roll with mocha cream

preparation time **25 minutes** cooking time **18 minutes** serves **8**

60g butter
¾ cup golden syrup
¾ cup (110g) plain flour
½ cup (75g) self-raising flour
2 teaspoons ground ginger
1 teaspoon ground cinnamon
¾ teaspoon ground nutmeg
¼ teaspoon ground cloves
2 eggs, beaten lightly
1 teaspoon bicarbonate of soda
¼ cup (60ml) boiling water
½ cup coconut

Mocha cream
125g butter
1 teaspoon vanilla extract
½ cup (110g) caster sugar

1 Preheat oven to moderate (180°C/160°C fan-forced). Grease a 25cm x 30cm swiss roll pan; line base with baking paper.
2 Beat butter in small bowl with electric mixer until smooth and creamy; gradually beat in golden syrup. Stir in sifted flours and spices, then eggs. Quickly stir in combined soda and water. Spread mixture evenly into prepared pan.
3 Bake cake for about 18 minutes. Stand cake a few minutes. Line a wire cooling rack with baking paper; sprinkle with coconut. Turn cake onto paper and roll up loosely. Let stand for a few minutes; unroll and cool to room temperature.
4 Meanwhile, make mocha cream; spread over cake and roll up.

Mocha cream Cream butter, extract and sugar in a small bowl with electric mixer until light and fluffy. Cover mixture with cold water, swirl around bowl for 1 minute, then pour off water. Return bowl to electric mixer, beat mixture well. Repeat washing and beating about six times, or until mixture is white in colour and sugar has dissolved.

Grated chocolate roll

preparation time **25 minutes** cooking time **12 minutes** serves **8**

4 eggs, separated
½ cup (110g) caster sugar
2 tablespoons hot water
60g dark cooking chocolate, grated
½ cup (75g) self-raising flour
2 tablespoons caster sugar, extra

Vanilla cream
¾ cup (180ml) whipping cream
2 teaspoons icing sugar
1 teaspoon vanilla extract

1 Preheat oven to moderate (180°C/160°C fan-forced). Grease a 25cm x 30cm swiss roll pan; line base and sides with baking paper, extending paper 5cm over long sides.

2 Beat egg yolks and sugar in a small bowl with electric mixer for 5 minutes, or until thick and creamy. Transfer mixture to large bowl, fold in hot water and chocolate, then fold in sifted flour.

3 Beat egg whites in small bowl with electric mixer until soft speaks form; fold into chocolate mixture. Pour into prepared pan; bake for 12 minutes. Turn immediately onto baking paper which has been sprinkled with extra sugar. Trim crisp edges from sides of cake, roll up in paper from the long side. Let stand for 2 minutes, then unroll; cool.

4 Meanwhile, beat ingredients for vanilla cream in small bowl with electric mixer until soft peaks form; spread over cake and roll up.

5 Serve topped with extra whipped cream and chocolate curls if desired.

Hazelnut coffee roll

preparation time **25 minutes** cooking time **12 minutes** serves **8**

4 eggs
¾ cup (165g) caster sugar
¼ cup (35g) self-raising flour
1 tablespoon plain flour
⅓ cup (35g) ground hazelnuts
2 tablespoons warm water
¼ teaspoon bicarbonate of soda
30g dark cooking chocolate, melted
2 tablespoons caster sugar, extra

Coffee cream
2 teaspoons instant coffee granules
1 teaspoon water
300ml whipping cream
1 tablespoon icing sugar

1 Preheat oven to moderate (180°C/160°C fan-forced). Grease a 25cm x 30cm swiss roll pan; line base and long sides with baking paper, extending paper 5cm over edges.

2 Beat eggs and sugar in medium bowl with electric mixer for 10 minutes or until mixture is thick and creamy. Fold in sifted flours and ground hazelnuts. Stir water and soda into chocolate; fold into flour mixture. Pour into prepared pan; bake for about 12 minutes.

3 Turn cake immediately onto baking paper sprinkled with extra sugar. Trim crisp edges from cake, roll up in paper from the long side. Stand for 2 minutes, then unroll; cool.

4 Meanwhile, make coffee cream. Spread half the coffee cream over cake, roll up, cover and decorate with remaining cream. Top with chocolate-dipped hazelnuts, if desired.

Coffee cream Dissolve coffee in water. Place in small bowl with water, cream and icing cugar; beat with electric mixer until firm peaks form.

Coffee liqueur roll

preparation time **25 minutes** cooking time **15 minutes** serves **8**

5 eggs
¾ cup (165g) caster sugar
1 cup (150g) self-raising flour
90g butter, melted
1 tablespoon instant coffee granules
1 tablespoon hot water
1 tablespoon cocoa
1 tablespoon caster sugar, extra

Liqueur cream
2 teaspoons dry instant coffee
1 tablespoon hot water
1 tablespoon coffee-flavoured liqueur
300ml whipping cream

1 Preheat oven to moderately hot (200°C/180°C fan-forced). Grease a 25cm x 30cm swiss roll pan; line base and long sides with baking paper, extending paper 5cm over edges.
2 Beat eggs in medium bowl with electric mixer for about 3 minutes, or until thick and creamy. Gradually beat in sugar, about a tablespoon at a time; beat until dissolved. Fold in sifted flour, then combined butter, coffee and water. Spread mixture into prepared pan.
3 Bake cake for about 15 minutes. Turn immediately onto baking paper sprinkled with combined sifted cocoa and extra sugar. Trim edges from cake. Roll up with paper from long side. Let stand for 2 minutes, then unroll; cool.
4 Make liqueur cream; spread over cake and roll up.

Liqueur cream Dissolve coffee in water; cool. Place coffee mixture, liqueur and cream in a small bowl; beat with electric mixer until soft peaks form.

Apple sponge

preparation time **30 minutes**   cooking time **35 minutes**   serves **6**

4 large apples (800g)
¼ cup (55g) caster sugar
¼ cup (60ml) water

Sponge topping
2 eggs
⅓ cup (75g) caster sugar
2 tablespoons cornflour
2 tablespoons plain flour
2 tablespoons self-raising flour

1 Preheat oven to moderate (180°C/160°C fan-forced).
2 Peel, core, quarter and slice apples. Place in saucepan with sugar and water; cook, covered, for about 10 minutes or until apples are tender.
3 Meanwhile, make sponge topping.
4 Spoon hot apple mixture into a deep 14cm round ovenproof dish (6-cup); spread sponge topping over. Bake, uncovered, about 25 minutes.

Sponge topping   Beat eggs in small bowl with electric mixer for about 7 minutes or until thick and creamy. Gradually add sugar, beating until dissolved between additions. Fold in sifted flours.

tip   Ensure apple mixture is as hot as possible before topping with sponge.

Ginger sponge

preparation time **20 minutes**   cooking time **18 minutes**   serves **10**

5 eggs, separated
¾ cup (165g) caster sugar
1 tablespoon golden syrup
⅓ cup (50g) self-raising flour
⅓ cup (50g) cornflour
3 teaspoons ground ginger
1 teaspoon ground cinnamon
2 teaspoons cocoa
¾ cup (180ml) whipping cream

1 Preheat oven to moderately hot (200°C/180°C fan-forced). Grease two deep 20cm round cake pans.

2 Beat egg whites in medium bowl with electric mixer until soft peaks form; gradually add sugar, beating until dissolved after additions. Beat in egg yolks and golden syrup. Sift dry ingredients three times onto paper; fold into mixture.

3 Pour mixture into prepared pans; bake for about 18 minutes. Turn sponges immediately onto wire racks to cool.

4 Beat cream until soft peaks form; join cakes with cream. Dust top with a little sifted icing sugar, if desired.

Chocolate fluff sponge

preparation time **20 minutes** cooking time **35 minutes** serves **10**

3 eggs
1 teaspoon vanilla extract
²⁄₃ cup (150g) caster sugar
½ cup (75g) self-raising flour
¼ cup (25g) cocoa
2 tablespoons arrowroot
1 tablespoon honey
1 tablespoon boiling water
300ml whipping cream

Coffee cream
300ml whipping cream
1 tablespoon icing sugar
1 teaspoon instant coffee granules
1 tablespoon coffee-flavoured liqueur

1 Preheat oven to moderate (180°C/160°C fan-forced). Grease a deep 20cm round cake pan; line base with baking paper.

2 Beat eggs and extract in small bowl with electric mixer until thick and creamy; gradually add sugar and beat until dissolved between additions. Transfer to a large bowl. Fold in sifted dry ingredients, then combined honey and water. Pour into prepared pan; bake for about 35 minutes. Turn immediately onto a wire rack to cool. Split cold cake into three layers.

3 Beat ingredients for coffee cream in small bowl with electric mixer until firm peaks form. Join layers of sponge with coffee cream. Cover with whipped cream and decorate with chocolate curls and raspberries, if desired.

Passionfruit sponge roll

preparation time **40 minutes** cooking time **25 minutes** (plus cooling time)
serves **8**

You will need about 4 passionfruit. Curd can be made three days ahead.

3 eggs
½ cup (110g) caster sugar
1 teaspoon vanilla extract
¾ cup (100g) wheaten cornflour
¾ teaspoon cream of tartar
½ teaspoon bicarbonate of soda
¼ cup (10g) flaked coconut
¼ cup (55g) caster sugar, extra
½ cup (125ml) whipping cream
1 teaspoon icing sugar

Passionfruit curd
⅓ cup (80ml) passionfruit pulp
⅔ cup (150g) caster sugar
2 eggs, beaten lightly
125g unsalted butter, chopped

1 Preheat oven to moderate (180°C/160°C fan-forced). Grease 25cm x 30cm swiss roll pan; line base with baking paper, extending it 5cm over long sides.
2 Beat eggs and sugar in a small bowl with electric mixer until the mixture is thick and creamy; add extract.
3 Sift cornflour, cream of tartar and bicarbonate of soda three times onto baking paper; lightly fold into egg mixture. Pour mixture into pan, spreading it into corners; sprinkle with coconut. Bake for about 12 minutes or until the top springs back when touched lightly.
4 Place a damp tea towel on a bench. Top towel with a sheet of greaseproof paper; sprinkle with extra sugar. Immediately turn cake onto sugared paper; remove lining paper. Using a serrated knife, trim cake edges from short sides. Roll cake firmly from short side with paper inside; cover with a tea towel. Cool.
5 Meanwhile, make passionfruit curd.
6 Whip cream and icing sugar in small bowl with electric mixer until soft peaks form; unroll sponge, spread with half the passionfruit curd and top with cream. Roll cake again by lifting paper and using it to guide the roll into shape.

Passionfruit curd Combine ingredients in a heatproof bowl. Stir over pan of simmering water for about 10 minutes or until thickened slightly; cool.

Spicy sponge cake

preparation time **20 minutes** cooking time **40 minutes** serves **8**

3 eggs
¾ cup (165g) caster sugar
1½ cups (225g) self-raising flour
1 teaspoon ground cinnamon
1 teaspoon ground ginger
1 teaspoon ground cloves
1 teaspoon ground cardamom
125g butter, melted
⅓ cup (80ml) milk

1 Preheat oven to moderate (180°C/160°C fan-forced). Grease 15cm x 25cm loaf pan; line base with baking paper.
2 Beat eggs and sugar in small bowl with electric mixer on high speed for about 10 minutes or until mixture is thick and creamy. Gently fold in remaining ingredients. Pour mixture into prepared pan.
3 Bake for 40 minutes. Turn onto wire rack to cool.
4 Serve with whipped cream and dusted with icing sugar, if desired.

Coconut sponge cake

preparation time **15 minutes** cooking time **30 minutes** serves **10**

185g butter, chopped
¾ cup (165g) caster sugar
3 eggs
⅔ cup (60g) desiccated coconut
1½ cups (225g) self-raising flour
1 teaspoon baking powder
⅓ cup (80ml) milk

1 Preheat oven to moderate (180°C/160°C fan-forced). Grease a 20cm x 30cm lamington pan; line base with baking paper.
2 Beat ingredients in medium bowl with electric mixer on low speed until combined; beat on medium speed until mixture is smooth and has changed colour. Spread mixture into prepared pan. Bake for about 30 minutes. Turn onto a wire rack to cool.
3 Serve cake with whipped cream and passionfruit icing (page 297), if desired.

Genoise sponge

preparation time **35 minutes** cooking time **30 minutes** serves **8**

4 eggs
½ cup (110g) caster sugar
⅔ cup (100g) plain flour
60g butter, melted
300ml whipping cream
1 tablespoon icing sugar
¼ cup (80g) strawberry jam, warmed
500g strawberries, sliced thinly
1 tablespoon icing sugar, extra

1 Preheat oven to moderate (180°C/160°C fan-forced). Grease a deep 20cm-round cake pan; line base with baking paper.

2 Combine eggs and sugar in large heatproof bowl. Place over a saucepan of simmering water; do not allow water to touch the base of the bowl. beat mixture with electric mixer until thick and creamy. Remove bowl from pan; beat mixture until it returns to room temperature.

3 Sift half the flour over the egg mixture; carefully fold in flour. Sift the remaining flour; fold in. Quickly and carefully fold in cooled melted butter. Pour mixture into prepared pan; bake about 20 minutes, or until sponge feels springy to touch. Turn immediately onto a wire rack to cool.

4 Beat cream and icing sugar in a small bowl with an electric mixer until soft peaks form. Split the sponge in half; place one half, cut-side up, on a serving plate. Spread with jam and cream; top with strawberries, then remaining sponge half. Decorate cake with extra icing sugar and strawberries, if desired.

tip This cake can be frozen, unfilled, for up to one month.

Raspberries and cream sponge cake

preparation time **30 minutes** cooking time **25 minutes** serves **12**

4 eggs
¾ cup (165g) caster sugar
⅔ cup (100g) wheaten cornflour
2 tablespoons custard powder
1 teaspoon cream of tartar
½ teaspoon bicarbonate of soda
1 medium pomegranate (320g)
300ml whipping cream
1 tablespoon icing sugar
½ teaspoon vanilla extract
240g fresh raspberries

1 Preheat oven to moderate (180°C/160°C fan-forced). Grease and flour a deep 23cm square cake pan.

2 Beat eggs and sugar in a small bowl with an electric mixer until thick and creamy; transfer to a large bowl.

3 Sift cornflour, custard powder, cream of tartar and soda twice onto baking paper; sift over egg mixture, gently fold together.

4 Pour mixture into prepared pan; bake for about 25 minutes, or until sponge springs back when touched lightly in the centre. Turn immediately onto a backing paper-lined wire rack lined; turn top-side up to cool.

5 Remove seeds from pomegranate; discard flesh.

6 Beat cream, icing sugar and extract in small bowl with an electric mixer until firm peaks form. Place the sponge on a serving plate; top with cream mixture, raspberries and pomegranate seeds.

Lime cream sponge

preparation time **45 minutes** (plus cooling time) cooking time **25 minutes**
serves **8**

2 eggs
4 egg whites
1 cup (220g) caster sugar
½ cup (75g) plain flour
1 cup (150g) self-raising flour
½ cup (125ml) buttermilk
½ cup (110g) caster sugar, extra
2 tablespoons lime juice
¼ cup (60ml) water

Lime cream filling
¼ cup (75g) cornflour
½ cup (110g) caster sugar
½ cup (125ml) lime juice
¾ cup (180ml) water
¼ cup (60ml) cream

1 Preheat oven to moderate (180°C/160°C fan-forced). Grease two 20cm
sandwich pans; line bases with baking paper.
2 Make lime cream filling.
3 Beat eggs and egg whites in medium bowl with an electric mixer until thick.
Gradually add sugar, beating until dissolved. Transfer mixture to a large bowl.
Gently fold in combined sifted flours and buttermilk, in two batches.
4 Divide mixture between prepared pans; bake for about 15 minutes. Stand
cakes for 5 minutes, then turn onto wire racks to cool.
5 Combine extra sugar, juice and water in small saucepan. Stir over a low heat
until sugar dissolves, bring to the boil; boil, uncovered, for 1 minute. Cool.
6 Split each cake in half. Place one layer on a serving plate, cut-side up.
Brush with a third of the lime syrup, then spread with a third of the lime
cream filling. Repeat layering, finishing with a cake, cut-side down.Dust top
with icing sugar and sprinkle with finely shredded lime rind, if desired.

Lime cream filling Combine cornflour, sugar and juice in a small saucepan
to form a smooth paste. Add water; cook, stirring, until mixture boils and
thickens. Remove from heat; whisk in cream. Cover surface of filling with
plastic wrap to prevent a skin forming; cool.

Little chocolate and coconut sponges

preparation time **35 minutes** (plus cooling time) cooking time **15 minutes**
makes **18**

4 eggs
¾ cup (165g) caster sugar
⅔ cup (100g) self-raising flour
⅓ cup (35g) cocoa powder
90g butter, melted
1 tablespoon hot water
⅔ cup (160ml) whipping cream
2 tablespoons caster sugar, extra
⅓ cup (15g) flaked coconut

Chocolate ganache
200g dark eating chocolate, chopped coarsely
⅔ cup (160ml) cream

1 Preheat the oven to moderate (180°C/160°C fan-forced). Grease two
9-hole (½-cup/125ml) individual oval cake pans.
2 Beat eggs in small bowl with an electric mixer for about 8 minutes or until
thick and creamy. Beat in sugar, 1 tablespoon at a time, until dissolved.
Transfer mixture to a large bowl. Fold in sifted flour, cocoa, then butter and
hot water. Spoon into prepared pans.
3 Bake cakes for about 12 minutes until sponges spring back when touched
lightly. Turn out immediately onto wire racks to cool.
4 Make ganache.
5 Beat cream and extra sugar in a small bowl with an electric mixer until
soft peaks form.
6 Split cooled sponges in half. Spread the bases with cream; replace tops.
Spread ganache over cakes; sprinkle with coconut.

Chocolate ganache Combine the chocolate and cream in a small
saucepan; stir over a low heat until smooth. Remove from heat; let stand
until thickened.

Honey sponge

preparation time **15 minutes** cooking time **25 minutes** serves **10**

3 large eggs
½ cup (180g) honey
1 cup (150g) self-raising flour
300ml whipping cream

1 Preheat oven to moderate (180°C/160°C fan-forced). Grease 20cm x 30cm lamington pan.
2 Beat eggs in small bowl with electric mixer until thick and creamy. With electric mixer operating, add honey in thin stream; continue beating on high speed for another 5 minutes. Transfer mixture to a large bowl. Sift flour over egg mixture, then fold in gently. Spread mixture into prepared pan.
3 Bake about 25 minutes. Turn onto a wire rack to cool. When cold, split in half, fill with whipped cream and dust top with sifted icing sugar.

Victoria sponge sandwich

preparation time **20 minutes** cooking time **30 minutes** serves **10**

250g butter
1 teaspoon vanilla extract
1 cup (220g) caster sugar
4 eggs
⅓ cup (80ml) milk
2 cups (300g) self-raising flour
Strawberry or raspberry jam
Icing sugar, for dusting

1 Preheat oven to moderate (180°C/160°C fan-forced). Grease two deep 20cm round cake pans; line bases with baking paper.
2 Beat butter, extract and sugar in small bowl with electric mixer until light and fluffy. Add eggs one at a time, beating well after each addition. Add milk and beat well. Transfer mixture to large bowl. Stir in half the sifted flour, then remaining sifted flour; stir until the mixture is smooth.
3 Divide mixture evenly between prepared pans; bake for about 30 minutes.
4 Turn cakes onto a wire rack to cool. Join cakes together with jam; dust with icing sugar.

Brown sugar sponge

Preparation time **30 minutes** cooking time **20 minutes** (plus cooling time)
serves **10**

4 eggs
¾ cup (165g) firmly packed dark brown sugar
1 cup (150g) wheaten cornflour
1 teaspoon cream of tartar
½ teaspoon bicarbonate of soda
300ml whipping cream
1 tablespoon icing sugar

Praline
⅓ cup (75g) white sugar
¼ cup (60ml) water
½ teaspoon malt vinegar
⅓ cup (45g) roasted hazelnuts

1 Preheat oven to moderate (180°C/160°C fan-forced). Grease two deep
22cm-round cake pans.
2 Beat eggs and brown sugar in small bowl with electric mixer for about
10 minutes or until thick and creamy; transfer to large bowl.
3 Sift cornflour, cream of tartar and soda twice onto baking paper, then sift
over egg mixture; gently fold dry ingredients into egg mixture.
4 Divide mixture between pans; bake for about 20 minutes. Turn sponges
immediately onto baking paper-lined wire racks to cool.
5 Meanwhile, make praline.
6 Beat cream in a small bowl with electric mixer until firm peaks form; fold in
praline. Place one sponge on serving plate; spread with cream mixture. Top
with remaining sponge; dust with sifted icing sugar.

Praline Stir sugar, water and vinegar in a small saucepan over heat, without
boiling, until sugar dissolves; bring to a boil. Reduce heat; simmer, uncovered,
without stirring, for about 10 minutes or until syrup is golden brown. Add
hazelnuts. Pour praline mixture onto a baking paper-lined tray. Cool for about
15 minutes or until set. Break praline into pieces, then blend or process until
mixture is as fine (or coarse) as desired.

CHOCOLATE CAKES

Rich truffle mudcake

preparation time **15 minutes** (plus refrigeration time) cooking time **1 hour**
serves **12**

This very rich cake is perfect for the grand finale to a dinner party, and should be made a day ahead and served cold. It has a truffle-like texture – note that there is no flour in the recipe.

6 eggs
½ cup (110g) firmly packed brown sugar
400g dark eating chocolate, melted
1 cup (250ml) double cream
⅓ cup (80ml) cointreau

1 Preheat oven to moderate (180°C/160°C fan-forced). Grease a deep 22cm-round cake pan; line base and side with baking paper.
2 Beat eggs and sugar in large bowl with electric mixer about 5 minutes or until thick and creamy. With motor operating, gradually beat in barely warm chocolate; beat until combined.
3 Using a metal spoon, gently fold in combined cream and liqueur. Pour mixture into prepared pan. Place pan in baking dish; pour enough boiling water into dish to come halfway up side of pan.
4 Bake cake, uncovered, for 30 minutes. Cover loosely with foil; bake for another 30 minutes. Discard foil; cool cake in pan.
5 Turn cake onto serving plate, cover; refrigerate overnight. Serve dusted with a little sifted cocoa powder, if desired.

tips Any liqueur can be substituted for the citrus-flavoured cointreau, if you prefer; try rum or frangelico. This cake will keep for up to four days in an airtight container in the refrigerator.

Family chocolate cake

preparation time **25 minutes** (plus refrigeration time) cooking time **1 hour**
serves **20**

3 cups (660g) caster sugar
250g butter, chopped
2 cups (500ml) water
⅓ cup (35g) cocoa powder
1 teaspoon bicarbonate of soda
3 cups (450g) self-raising flour
4 eggs, beaten lightly

Fudge frosting
90g butter
⅓ cup (80ml) water
½ cup (110g) caster sugar
1½ cups (240g) icing sugar
⅓ cup (35g) cocoa powder

1 Preheat oven to moderate (180°C/160°C fan-forced). Grease deep
26.5cm x 33cm (3.5-litre/14-cup) baking dish; line base with baking paper.
2 Combine sugar, butter, the water and combined sifted cocoa powder
and soda in medium saucepan; stir over heat, without boiling, until sugar
dissolves. Bring to a boil, then reduce heat and simmer, uncovered, for
5 minutes. Transfer mixture to large bowl; cool to room temperature.
3 Add flour and egg to bowl; beat with electric mixer until mixture is smooth
and paler in colour. Pour mixture into prepared dish. Bake for 50 minutes.
Stand cake in baking dish for 10 minutes before turning onto a wire rack;
turn cake top-side up to cool.
4 Meanwhile, make fudge frosting; spread over cold cake.

Fudge frosting Combine butter, the water and the caster sugar in a small
saucepan; stir over heat, without boiling, until sugar dissolves. Sift icing sugar
and cocoa powder into small bowl then gradually stir in hot butter mixture.
Cover; refrigerate for about 20 minutes or until frosting thickens. Beat with
a wooden spoon until of a spreadable consistency.

tips Choose a perfectly level-bottomed baking dish; one made from cast
aluminium is best, but almost any type will work.

Chocolate buttermilk cake

preparation time **35 minutes** cooking time **1 hour** serves **10**

180g butter, chopped
1 teaspoon vanilla extract
1½ cups (330g) caster sugar
4 eggs, separated
¾ cup (110g) self-raising flour
⅓ cup (35g) cocoa powder
¾ cup (180ml) buttermilk

Chocolate filling
400g dark eating chocolate, melted
250g butter, melted
½ cup (80g) icing sugar

1 Preheat oven to moderate (180°C/160°C fan-forced). Grease a deep 20cm round cake pan; line base with baking paper.
2 Beat butter, extract and sugar in small bowl with electric mixer until light and fluffy; beat in egg yolks one at a time, until just combined after each addition. Transfer the mixture to a large bowl; stir in sifted dry ingredients and buttermilk.
3 Beat egg whites in a clean small bowl with electric mixer until soft peaks form; fold into cake mixture in two batches. Pour into prepared pan.
4 Bake cake for about 1 hour. Cool cake in pan.
5 Make chocolate filling; reserve about 1 cup to cover cake.
6 Split cake into three layers. Place one cake layer onto serving plate; spread thinly with some of the remaining chocolate filling. Repeat layering with remaining cake layers and filling. Spread reserved filling all over cake. Refrigerate for 3 hours before serving.

Chocolate filling Combine chocolate and butter in a medium bowl; stir in sifted icing sugar. Cool filling to room temperature; beat with a wooden spoon until thick and of a spreadable consistency.

tip This cake can be made a day ahead and kept, covered, in the refrigerator.

Sacher torte

preparation time **35 minutes** (plus standing time) cooking time **35 minutes**
serves **12**

150g dark eating chocolate, chopped
1 tablespoon warm water
150g butter, chopped
½ cup (110g) caster sugar
3 eggs, separated
1 cup (150g) plain flour
2 tablespoons caster sugar, extra
⅔ cup (220g) apricot jam

Chocolate icing
125g dark eating chocolate, chopped
125g butter

1 Preheat oven to moderate (180°C/160°C fan-forced). Grease a deep
22cm round cake pan; line base with baking paper.
2 Melt chocolate in heatproof bowl over hot water, stir in the water; cool to
room temperature.
3 Beat butter and sugar in small bowl with electric mixer until pale in colour.
Add egg yolks one at a time, beating until combined after each addition.
Transfer mixture to large bowl; stir in chocolate mixture, then sifted flour.
4 Beat egg whites in small bowl until soft peaks form. Gradually add extra
sugar, beating until dissolved between each addition; fold lightly into
chocolate mixture. Spread mixture into prepared pan.
5 Bake cake for about 30 minutes. Stand cake in pan for 5 minutes before
turning onto wire rack to cool; leave cake upside down.
6 Meanwhile, make chocolate icing.
7 Split cold cake in half and place one half onto serving plate. Heat and
strain jam; brush over half of the cake. Top with remaining half of cake,
brush cake all over with remaining jam. Stand cake for about 1 hour at room
temperature to allow jam to set.
8 Spread top and side of cake with chocolate icing; set at room temperature.

Chocolate icing Melt ingredients in medium bowl over hot water; stir until
smooth. Cool to room temperature, stirring occasionally, until spreadable
– this may take up to 2 hours.

Upside-down chocolate caramel nut cake

preparation time **25 minutes** cooking time **1 hour 20 minutes** serves **10**

Use unsalted nuts for this recipe.

2 tablespoons chopped roasted macadamias
2 tablespoons chopped roasted pistachios
2 tablespoons chopped roasted walnuts
125g butter, chopped
1 cup (220g) firmly packed brown sugar
3 eggs
1 cup (150g) self-raising flour
¼ cup (35g) plain flour
¼ teaspoon bicarbonate of soda
⅓ cup (35g) cocoa powder
100g dark eating chocolate, melted
¾ cup (180ml) milk

Caramel topping
40g butter
¼ cup (55g) firmly packed brown sugar
2 tablespoons cream

1 Preheat oven to moderately slow (170°C/150°C fan-forced). Grease deep 20cm round cake pan; line base with baking paper.

2 Make caramel topping; pour over base of prepared pan and sprinkle with combined nuts. Freeze while preparing cake mixture.

3 Beat butter and sugar in small bowl with electric mixer until light and fluffy. Add eggs one at a time, beating until just combined after each addition.

4 Stir in sifted flours, bicarbonate of soda and cocoa powder, then chocolate and milk. Spread cake mixture over caramel nut topping. Bake for about 1 hour 10 minutes. Stand cake in pan for 15 minutes before turning onto a wire rack to cool.

Caramel topping Combine ingredients in small saucepan; stir over low heat, without boiling, until sugar dissolves. Bring to a boil; remove from heat.

tip This cake can be made a day ahead and kept in an airtight container.

White chocolate mudcake

preparation time **25 minutes** (plus refrigeration time)
cooking time **2 hours 10 minutes** serves **12**

250g butter, chopped
150g white cooking chocolate, chopped
2 cups (440g) caster sugar
1 cup (250ml) milk
1½ cups (225g) plain flour
½ cup (75g) self-raising flour
1 teaspoon vanilla extract
2 eggs, beaten lightly

White chocolate ganache
½ cup (125ml) cream
300g white cooking chocolate, chopped

1 Preheat oven to moderately slow (170°C/150°C fan-forced). Grease deep 20cm round cake pan; line base and side with baking paper.
2 Combine butter, chocolate, sugar and milk in medium saucepan; using wooden spoon, stir over low heat, without boiling, until smooth. Transfer mixture to large bowl; cool for 15 minutes. Whisk in flours, then extract and egg; pour mixture into prepared pan.
3 Bake cake, uncovered, for 1 hour. Cover pan loosely with foil; bake for another hour. Discard foil, stand cake in pan for 10 minutes then turn onto a wire rack; turn top-side up to cool.
4 Meanwhile, make white chocolate ganache.
5 Place cooled cake on a serving plate and spread all over with white chocolate ganache.

White chocolate ganache Bring cream to a boil in a small saucepan; pour over chocolate in small bowl and stir with wooden spoon until chocolate melts. Cover bowl; refrigerate, stirring occasionally, for about 30 minutes or until ganache is of a spreadable consistency.

tips Cover the cake loosely with foil about halfway through the baking time if it starts to brown too much. The un-iced cake will keep for up to one week in an airtight container at room temperature. The iced cake will keep for up to one week in an airtight container in the refrigerator.

Mississippi mudcake

preparation time **25 minutes** cooking time **1 hour 30 minutes**
(plus standing time) serves **10**

250g butter, chopped
150g dark eating chocolate, chopped
2 cups (440g) caster sugar
1 cup (250ml) hot water
⅓ cup (80ml) coffee-flavoured liqueur
1 tablespoon instant coffee granules
1½ cups (225g) plain flour
¼ cup (35g) self-raising flour
¼ cup (25g) cocoa powder
2 eggs, beaten lightly

1 Preheat oven to moderately slow (170°C/150°C fan-forced). Grease deep 20cm round cake pan; line base and side with baking paper.
2 Combine butter, chocolate, sugar, the water, liqueur and coffee granules in a medium saucepan. Using wooden spoon, stir over low heat until chocolate melts. Transfer mixture to a large bowl; cool for 15 minutes. Whisk in combined sifted flours and cocoa powder, then egg. Pour mixture into prepared pan.
3 Bake cake for about 1½ hours. Stand cake in pan for 30 minutes before turning onto a wire rack; turn cake top-side up to cool.

tips Any coffee- or chocolate-flavoured liqueur (tia maria, kahlua or crème de cacao) can be used in this recipe. Cover the cake loosely with foil about halfway through the baking time if it starts to brown too much. This cake will keep for up to one week in an airtight container in the refrigerator.

Low-fat chocolate fudge cake

preparation time **20 minutes** cooking time **40 minutes** serves **8**

85g dark eating chocolate, chopped finely
½ cup (50g) cocoa powder
1 cup (200g) firmly packed brown sugar
½ cup (125ml) boiling water
2 egg yolks
¼ cup (30g) almond meal
⅓ cup (50g) wholemeal plain flour
4 egg whites

1 Preheat oven to moderate (180°C/160°C fan-forced). Grease a deep 20cm round cake pan; line base and side with baking paper.
2 Combine chocolate, cocoa and sugar with the water in large bowl; stir until smooth. Add egg yolks; whisk to combine. Fold in almond meal and flour.
3 Beat egg whites in small bowl with electric mixer until firm peaks form. Gently fold egg white mixture into chocolate mixture, in two batches; pour into prepared pan.
4 Bake cake for about 40 minutes. Stand cake in pan for 5 minutes. Turn onto a wire rack to cool.

Cream cheese chocolate cake

Preparation time **20 minutes** cooking time **50 minutes** serves **8**

125g packaged cream cheese
60g butter
½ cup (110g) caster sugar
½ cup (100g) firmly packed brown sugar
1 egg
½ cup (60g) chopped walnuts or pecans
¾ cup (180ml) milk
1 cup (150g) plain flour
⅓ cup (50g) self-raising flour
2 tablespoons cocoa powder
½ teaspoon bicarbonate of soda

1 Preheat oven to moderate (180°C/160°C fan-forced). Grease a deep 20cm round cake pan; line base with baking paper.
2 Beat cheese, butter, sugars and egg in medium bowl with electric mixer until light and fluffy. Stir in nuts, milk and sifted dry ingredients, in two batches.
3 Spoon mixture into prepared pan; bake for about 50 minutes. Stand cake in pan for 5 minutes; turn onto wire rack to cool.
4 Spread cake with chocolate fudge frosting (see p272), if desired.

Sticky chocolate date pudding

preparation time **25 minutes** cooking time **1 hour 10 minutes** serves **10**

1 ⅓ cups (200g) seeded dried dates, chopped
1 ¾ cups (430ml) water
1 teaspoon bicarbonate of soda
80g butter, chopped
⅔ cup (150g) caster sugar
2 eggs
1 cup (150g) self-raising flour
⅓ cup (35g) cocoa powder
⅔ cup (70g) pecans, toasted, chopped

Butterscotch sauce
1 ¼ cups (280g) firmly packed brown sugar
80g butter
300ml cream

1 Preheat oven to moderate (180°C/160°C fan-forced). Grease a deep 22cm round cake pan; line base with baking paper.
2 Combine dates and the water in small saucepan; bring to a boil. Remove from heat, add soda; cover and stand for 5 minutes. Blend or process until the mixture is smooth.
3 Beat butter and sugar in small bowl with electric mixer until combined; beat in eggs quickly, one at a time (mixture will curdle at this stage). Transfer mixture to large bowl; fold in sifted flour and cocoa powder, then add nuts and warm date mixture, in two batches. Pour mixture into prepared pan.
4 Bake pudding for about 1 hour. Stand pudding in pan for 10 minutes before turning onto a serving plate.
5 Make butterscotch sauce; serve pudding with hot sauce and whipped· cream, if desired.

Butterscotch sauce Combine ingredients in a medium saucepan; stir over heat, without boiling, until sugar is dissolved. Simmer, without stirring, for 3 minutes.

Chocolate fleck cake

preparation time **20 minutes** cooking time **45 minutes** serves **16**

185g butter
1 teaspoon vanilla extract
1 ¼ cups (275g) caster sugar
3 eggs
1 cup (150g) plain flour
1 cup (150g) self-raising flour
¼ cup (30g) custard powder
½ cup (125ml) milk
90g dark chocolate, grated

1 Preheat oven to moderate (180°C/160°C fan-forced). Grease a 23cm square slab cake pan; line base with baking paper.
2 Combine butter, extract, sugar, eggs, flours, custard powder and milk in large bowl; beat on low speed with electric mixer until ingredients are combined. Beat on medium speed for about 3 minutes, or until mixture is smooth and changed to a lighter colour. Stir in chocolate; spread mixture into prepared pan.
3 Bake for about 45 minutes. Stand cake in pan for 5 minutes; turn onto a wire rack to cool.

Double-decker mudcake

preparation time **30 minutes** (plus cooling time) cooking time **1 hour**
serves **10**

250g butter, chopped
150g white eating chocolate, chopped coarsely
2 cups (440g) caster sugar
1 cup (250ml) milk
1½ cups (225g) plain flour
½ cup (75g) self-raising flour
1 teaspoon vanilla extract
2 eggs, beaten lightly
2 tablespoons cocoa powder
600g milk eating chocolate, chopped coarsely
1 cup (250ml) cream

1 Preheat oven to slow (150°C/130°C fan-forced). Grease two deep 20cm round cake pans; line base and side with baking paper.
2 Combine butter, white chocolate, sugar and milk in a medium saucepan; stir over heat, without boiling, until smooth. Transfer mixture to large bowl; cool for 15 minutes.
3 Whisk sifted flours into white chocolate mixture, then whisk in extract and egg; pour half of the mixture into one of the prepared pans. Whisk sifted cocoa into remaining mixture; pour into other prepared pan.
4 Bake for about 50 minutes. Stand cakes for 5 minutes, then turn, top-side up, onto a wire rack to cool.
5 Combine milk chocolate and cream in medium saucepan; stir over low heat until smooth. Transfer to medium bowl and cover; refrigerate, stirring occasionally, until mixture is a spreadable consistency. Reserve 1 cup of the chocolate mixture for spreading over cake.
6 Split each cooled cake in half. Centre one layer of cake on serving plate; spread with ½ cup of the remaining milk chocolate mixture. Repeat layering, alternating colours. Cover the top and sides of the cake with the reserved chocolate mixture.

Low-fat chocolate cake

preparation time **15 minutes** cooking time **50 minutes** (plus cooling time)
serves **12**

½ cup (160g) plum jam
½ cup (110g) firmly packed brown sugar
½ cup (50g) cocoa powder
¾ cup (180ml) skim evaporated milk
2 teaspoons instant coffee granules
50g butter
2 eggs
½ cup (110g) caster sugar
1 cup (150g) self-raising flour
⅓ cup (50g) plain flour
2 teaspoons icing sugar

1 Preheat oven to moderate (180°C/160°C fan-forced). Spray a 21cm baba
cake pan with cooking-oil spray.
2 Combine jam, brown sugar, sifted cocoa, milk, coffee and butter in a
medium saucepan. Stir over low heat until butter is melted and mixture
is smooth – do not boil. Cool.
3 Beat eggs and caster sugar in a small bowl with electric mixer until thick
and pale. Transfer mixture to large bowl. Stir in sifted flours and chocolate
mixture. Pour mixture into prepared pan.
4 Bake for about 45 minutes. Stand cake in pan for 5 minutes before turning
onto wire rack to cool.
5 Serve cake dusted with sifted icing sugar, if desired.

Dark chocolate and almond torte

preparation time **20 minutes** cooking time **55 minutes** (plus cooling and standing time) serves **14**

Candied (vienna) almonds are whole almonds coated in toffee. They are available from selected supermarkets, nut shops, and gourmet food and specialty confectionery stores.

160g dark eating chocolate, chopped coarsely
160g unsalted butter
5 eggs, separated
¾ cup (165g) caster sugar
1 cup (125g) almond meal
⅔ cup (50g) toasted flaked almonds, chopped coarsely
⅓ cup (35g) coarsely grated dark eating chocolate
1 cup (140g) candied (vienna) almonds

Dark chocolate ganache
125g dark eating chocolate, chopped coarsely
⅓ cup (80ml) cream

1 Preheat oven to moderate (180°C/160°C fan-forced). Grease a deep 22cm round cake pan; line base and side with two layers of baking paper.
2 Stir chopped chocolate and butter in small saucepan over low heat until smooth; cool to room temperature.
3 Beat egg yolks and sugar in small bowl with electric mixer until thick and creamy. Transfer to large bowl; fold in chocolate mixture, almond meal, flaked almonds and grated chocolate.
4 Beat egg whites in small bowl with electric mixer until soft peaks form; fold into chocolate mixture, in two batches. Pour mixture into prepared pan.
5 Bake for about 45 minutes. Stand cake in pan for 15 minutes before turning onto wire rack; turn top-side up to cool.
6 Meanwhile, stir ingredients for dark chocolate ganache in small saucepan over low heat until smooth.
7 Spread ganache over cake and decorate cake with candied almonds. Let stand for 30 minutes before serving.

Triple choc brownies

preparation time **15 minutes** cooking time **40 minutes** makes **9**

125g cold butter, chopped
200g dark eating chocolate, chopped finely
¾ cup (165g) caster sugar
2 eggs, beaten lightly
1 cup (150g) plain flour
150g white eating chocolate, chopped
100g milk eating chocolate, chopped

1 Preheat oven to moderate (180°C/160°C fan-forced). Grease a deep 19cm square pan; line base and sides with baking paper.
2 Combine butter and dark chocolate in a large saucepan; stir over a very low heat until melted. Remove from heat.
3 Stir in sugar, then eggs. Stir in sifted flour, then chopped chocolate. Spread mixture into prepared pan.
4 Bake cake for about 35 minutes or until the brownie is firm to touch. Cool in pan. Cut into squares. Dust with sifted cocoa or icing sugar, if desired.

tip Store in an airtight container for up to four days.

Raspberry and white chocolate brownies

preparation time **20 minutes** cooking time **40 minutes** makes **16**

150g butter, chopped
200g dark eating chocolate, chopped
1 cup (220g) caster sugar
2 teaspoons vanilla extract
3 eggs, beaten lightly
½ cup (75g) plain flour
½ cup (75g) self-raising flour
100g white eating chocolate, chopped
150g frozen raspberries

1 Preheat oven to moderate (180°C/160°C fan-forced). Grease a deep 19cm square cake pan; line base and two opposite sides with baking paper, extending paper 5cm over edge.
2 Melt butter and dark chocolate in medium heatproof bowl over saucepan of simmering water. Stir in sugar and extract; add eggs, sifted flours, white chocolate and raspberries, stir until well combined.
3 Spread mixture into prepared pan; bake about 35 minutes or until just firm. Cool brownies in pan. Turn out; cut into squares.

tip These brownies can be stored in an airtight container for up to five days.

Chocolate peppermint cake

preparation time **20 minutes** (plus refrigeration time) cooking time **1 hour** serves **20**

125g unsalted butter, chopped
2 teaspoons instant coffee granules
100g dark cooking chocolate, chopped coarsely
1 cup (220g) caster sugar
¾ cup (180ml) water
1 egg, beaten lightly
¾ cup (110g) self-raising flour
½ cup (75g) plain flour
2 tablespoons cocoa powder

Peppermint cream
125g unsalted butter, chopped
3 cups (480g) icing sugar
2 tablespoons milk
½ teaspoon peppermint essence
Green food colouring

Chocolate ganache
300g dark eating chocolate, chopped coarsely
1 cup (250ml) cream

1 Preheat oven to slow (150°C/130°C fan-forced). Grease two 8cm x 25cm bar cake pans; line base and sides with baking paper.
2 Stir butter, coffee, chocolate, sugar and the water in a medium saucepan over heat until smooth. Transfer mixture to a medium bowl. Whisk in egg with sifted flours and cocoa.
3 Pour mixture equally between prepared pans; bake about 45 minutes. Stand cakes for 5 minutes; turn, top-side up, onto a wire rack to cool.
4 Make peppermint cream.
5 Using a serrated knife, split cooled cakes in half. Place bottom layers on wire rack over tray. Spread each with about a quarter of the peppermint cream; top with cake tops. Place remaining peppermint cream in a piping bag fitted with 2cm fluted tube. Pipe remaining cream along the centre of each cake top; refrigerate for 1 hour.
6 Meanwhile, stir ingredients for chocolate ganache in saucepan over low heat until smooth.

6 Using a metal spatula and working quickly, pour chocolate ganache over cakes, smoothing sides. Stand at room temperature until ganache sets.

Peppermint cream Beat butter in small bowl with electric mixer until as pale as possible. Gradually beat in icing sugar, milk, essence, and enough of the colouring to tint to the desired shade of green.

Rich chocolate cake

Preparation time **15 minutes** cooking time **45 minutes** serves **10**

1 ⅓ cups (200g) self-raising flour
½ cup (50g) cocoa powder
125g butter, softened
1 teaspoon vanilla extract
1 ¼ cups (275g) caster sugar
2 eggs
⅔ cup (160ml) water

1 Preheat the oven to moderate (180°C/160°C fan-forced). Grease and line a 20cm round cake pan.
2 Sift flour and cocoa into a medium bowl; add remaining ingredients. Beat on low speed with electric mixer until ingredients are combined. Increase speed to medium; beat about 3 minutes or until mixture is smooth and changed to a lighter colour.
3 Spread into prepared pan; bake for about 45 minutes. Stand cake in pan for about 5 minutes; turn onto a wire rack to cool.

Lamington roll

preparation time **30 minutes** cooking time **12 minutes** serves **10**

3 eggs
½ cup (110g) caster sugar
¾ cup (110g) self-raising flour
2 tablespoons hot milk
¾ cup (65g) desiccated coconut

Filling
90g unsalted butter
1 teaspoon vanilla extract
1 cup (160g) icing sugar
1 tablespoon milk

Icing
1 cup (160g) icing sugar
¼ cup (25g) cocoa powder
1 teaspoon butter
2 tablespoons milk

1 Preheat oven to moderate (180°C/160°C fan-forced). Grease a 26cm x 32cm swiss roll pan; line base with baking paper.
2 Beat eggs in small bowl with electric mixer until thick and creamy; gradually add sugar, beating until sugar dissolves between additions. Fold in sifted flour and milk, in two batches; pour into prepared pan. Bake for about 12 minutes.
3 Meanwhile, sprinkle 2 tablespoons of coconut over baking paper-lined wire cooling rack. Turn cake onto paper; remove lining paper. Roll up from short side, using paper to lift and guide roll. Let stand for 2 minutes, then unroll; cool.
4 Make filling. Make icing.
5 Spread the filling over cake; re-roll cake. Place on wire rack over a tray; pour icing over roll. Press remaining coconut onto roll; refrigerate until set.

Filling Beat butter and extract in small bowl with electric mixer until pale and creamy. Gradually beat in icing sugar and milk until light and fluffy.

Icing Sift icing sugar and cocoa into small heatproof bowl; stir in butter and milk and place over small pan of simmering water. Stir icing until it reaches pouring consistency.

Mocha truffle cake

preparation time **35 minutes** (plus refrigeration time)
cooking time **30 minutes** serves **12**

3 eggs
½ cup (110g) caster sugar
¼ cup (35g) cornflour
¼ cup (35g) self-raising flour
¼ cup (35g) plain flour
2 tablespoons cocoa
2 tablespoons coffee-flavoured liqueur
2 tablespoons milk
600ml whipping cream
100g white eating chocolate, melted
200g dark eating chocolate, melted

Milk chocolate topping
200g milk eating chocolate, melted
90g unsalted butter, melted

1 Preheat the oven to moderate (180°C/160°C fan-forced). Grease a deep 23cm round cake pan; line base with baking paper.
2 Beat eggs in a small bowl with electric mixer until thick and creamy. Gradually add sugar; beat until dissolved between each addition. Transfer mixture to large bowl; lightly fold in sifted flours and cocoa. Spread into prepared pan.
3 Bake cake about 30 minutes or until firm. Turn onto a wire rack to cool. Split cake in half; brush with combined liqueur and milk.
4 Beat cream until soft peaks form; divide into two bowls. Quickly stir cooled white chocolate into one bowl of the cream and cooled dark chocolate into the remaining bowl of cream.
5 Place strips of foil over the base of a deep cake pan and extend over the edges, or use a 23cm springform tin. Place one cake half into pan, spread cake with half the white chocolate cream, top with dark chocolate cream, then the remaining white chocolate cream. Top with the other cake. Refrigerate assembled cake for several hours or overnight, until firm. Carefully remove from pan to a serving plate.
6 Make milk chocolate topping; spread over cake before serving.

Milk chocolate topping Combine hot chocolate and butter in bowl; stir until smooth. Cool to room temperature, then stir until spreadable.

Devilishly dark chocolate torte

preparation time **30 minutes** cooking time **1 hour 25 minutes** serves **16**

185g butter
3 teaspoons instant coffee granules
1 cup (250ml) hot water
150g dark eating chocolate, chopped
1½ cup (330g) caster sugar
1 cup (150g) self-raising flour
¾ cup (110g) plain flour
2 tablespoons cocoa
2 eggs
1 teaspoon vanilla extract
2 teaspoons raspberry jam
2½ tablespoons crème de cacao
¾ cup (20g) flaked toasted almonds, chopped coarsely
15g dark eating chocolate, melted, extra

Dark chocolate filling
200g dark eating chocolate, melted
125g unsalted butter, melted
¼ cup icing sugar

1 Preheat oven to slow (150°C/130°C fan-forced). Grease a deep 23cm square cake pan; line base with baking paper.
2 Melt butter in saucepan, then remove from heat. Stir in combined coffee and hot water, then chocolate and sugar; stir until smooth. Place into large bowl of electric mixer, then beat in sifted dry ingredients in three batches. Beat in eggs and extract.
3 Pour into prepared pan; bake for about 1¼ hours, or until firm. Stand cake for 5 minutes before turning onto a wire rack to cool.
4 Meanwhile, make dark chocolate filling; reserve ⅔ cup to spread over cake.
5 Split cake in half, split each half into 3 layers. Place one layer onto serving plate; spread thinly with jam then a thin layer of filling. Top with another cake layer, sprinkle with a little liqueur, then spread thinly with filling. Repeat with remaining cake, liqueur and filling. Refrigerate several hours or until firm.
6 Spread reserved filling all over cake, then press almonds onto sides. While the top of the cake is soft, pipe lines of extra chocolate on cake crossways, about 2cm apart. Pull a skewer through the chocolate lines at 2cm intervals in alternate directions to give a feathered effect.

Dark chocolate filling Combine hot chocolate and butter in a bowl; stir in sifted icing sugar. Cool to room temperature, then beat with a wooden spoon until thick and spreadable.

tip Crème de cacao is a chocolate-flavoured liqueur. This torte can be made two days ahead; keep, covered, in refrigerator. The plain cake can be frozen for up to two months.

Chocolate fruit cake

preparation time **20 minutes** cooking time **1 hour** serves **12**

125g butter, chopped
¾ cup (150g) firmly packed brown sugar
50g dark cooking chocolate, chopped coarsely
½ cup (125ml) water
¼ cup (60ml) dark rum
¼ cup (30g) coarsely chopped walnuts
2½ cups (475g) mixed dried fruit
¾ cup (110g) plain flour
2 tablespoons cocoa powder
2 tablespoons self-raising flour
½ teaspoon mixed spice
2 eggs, beaten lightly
80g dark cooking chocolate, melted, extra
¼ cup (60g) sour cream

1 Preheat oven to slow (150°C/130°C fan-forced). Grease a 20cm ring pan; line base with baking paper.
2 Combine butter, sugar, chocolate and the water in a medium saucepan; stir over heat until sugar dissolves. Remove from heat; stir in rum, nuts and fruit. Add sifted dry ingredients and egg; stir until combined.
3 Spoon mixture into prepared pan; bake about 1 hour. Cool cake in pan.
4 Just before serving, combine cooled extra chocolate and sour cream in a small bowl; stir until smooth. Turn cake onto a serving plate, top-side up; spread chocolate mixture over top of cake.

tip This cake can be baked in a 14cm x 21cm loaf pan, if desired. Bake in a slow oven for about 1½ hours.

Chocolate poppy seed cake

preparation time **20 minutes** cooking time **1 hour 15 minutes** serves **12**

125g butter
½ cup (110g) caster sugar
8 eggs, separated
¾ cup (45g) stale breadcrumbs
1 cup (160g) poppy seeds
300g dark cooking chocolate, melted
¼ cup (80g) plum jam

Rich cream glaze
⅔ cup (160ml) cream
200g dark cooking chocolate, melted

1 Preheat oven to moderately slow (170°C/150°C fan-forced). Grease base and side of a deep 23cm round cake pan; line base with baking paper.
2 Beat butter and sugar in small bowl with electric mixer until light and fluffy. Add yolks one at a time, beating until combined after each addition. Transfer to large bowl; stir in breadcrumbs, poppy seeds and cooled chocolate.
3 Beat egg whites in large bowl with electric mixer until soft peaks form. Fold into chocolate mixture in two batches; pour into prepared pan.
4 Bake for about 1¼ hours, or until firm; cool in pan.
5 Place ingredients for rich cream glaze in small bowl; stir until mixture is smooth and pourable.
6 Trim top of cake to make a flat surface, then split cake into two layers. Place one layer onto a serving plate, spread with sieved jam, then top with remaining layer of cake. Spread glaze all over cake; refrigerate until set.

Chocolate walnut log

preparation time **30 minutes** (plus refrigeration time)
cooking time **50 minutes** serves **16**

125g butter
¾ cup (165g) caster sugar
2 eggs
½ cup (75g) plain flour
¾ cup (110g) self-raising flour
¼ cup (25g) cocoa
⅓ cup (80ml) milk
½ cup (50g) walnuts, chopped

Chocolate brandy cream
125g unsalted butter
¼ cup (40g) icing sugar
200g white eating chocolate, melted
2 tablespoons brandy

1 Preheat oven to moderate (180°C/160°C fan-forced). Grease two
nut roll tins.
2 Beat butter and sugar in small bowl with electric mixer until light and fluffy;
add eggs one at a time, beating until combined after each addition. Transfer
mixture to large bowl; stir in sifted flours and cocoa with milk and walnuts
in two batches.
3 Divide mixture between prepared tins; bake for 50 minutes. Stand the rolls
in tins with lids on for 10 minutes; remove lids and turn rolls onto a wire rack
to cool. Trim the ends from the rolls, then trim the side of each so rolls sit flat.
4 Make chocolate brandy cream.
5 Cut roll into 1cm slices, join with thin layer of chocolate brandy cream.
Place roll on serving plate; refrigerate for 2 hours. Spread roll with remaining
chocolate brandy cream. Serve sliced diagonally. Decorate with chocolate
leaves, if desired.

Chocolate brandy cream Cream butter and sifted icing sugar in a small
bowl with electric mixer until light and fluffy; beat in cooled chocolate and
brandy. Refrigerate, stirring occasionally until spreadable.

tip This cake can be prepared up to a day ahead; store, covered, in the
refrigerator. The plain log can be frozen for up to two months.

Choc-chip orange sour cream cake

preparation time **20 minutes** cooking time **1 hour** serves **10**

185g butter
2 teaspoons grated orange rind
1¼ cups (275g) caster sugar
4 eggs
100g choc chips
¾ cup (180g) sour cream
2 cups (300g) plain flour
½ teaspoon bicarbonate of soda

Orange syrup
½ cup (110g) sugar
¼ cup (60ml) orange juice

1 Preheat oven to moderately slow (170°C/150°C fan-forced). Grease a 20cm baba pan; sprinkle with flour, then shake out excess flour.
2 Beat butter, rind and sugar in medium bowl with electric mixer until light and fluffy. Add eggs one at a time, beating after each addition until combined. Fold in choc chips and sour cream, then sifted flour and soda.
3 Spread into prepared pan; bake for about 55 minutes or until firm. Stand cake for 5 minutes before turning onto a wire rack.
4 Meanwhile, make orange syrup.
5 Place cake on rack over an oven tray; pour hot syrup evenly over hot cake.

Orange syrup Combine sugar and juice in saucepan; stir over heat, without boiling, until sugar dissolves. Bring to boil, then remove from heat.

tip This cake can be made up to four days ahead; store, covered, in refrigerator until required.

Chocolate cake with whipped chocolate frosting

preparation time **25 minutes** (plus refrigeration time)
cooking time **1 hour 30 minutes** serves **about 30**

1½ cups (150g) cocoa
1½ cups (375ml) boiling water
500g butter, softened
4½ cups (1kg) caster sugar
2 teaspoons vanilla extract
8 eggs
4 cups (600g) self-raising flour
1 cup (150g) plain flour
1 teaspoon bicarbonate of soda
2½ cups (625ml) buttermilk

Whipped chocolate frosting
300g dark eating chocolate, chopped
200g milk eating chocolate, chopped
180g butter, chopped
2 teaspoons vegetable oil

1 Preheat the oven to moderately slow (170°C/150°C fan-forced). Grease a deep 30cm square cake pan; line base and sides with two layers of baking paper, extending the paper 5cm above the edges.
2 Whisk cocoa and the water in a medium bowl until smooth; allow to cool.
3 Beat butter, sugar and extract in large bowl with electric mixer until light and fluffy. Add eggs one at a time, beating until just combined after each addition. Transfer mixture to a very large bowl.
4 Stir combined sifted flours and soda into butter and egg mixture. Add buttermilk in three batches until well combined. Stir in cocoa mixture; mix well. Spread mixture into prepared pan; bake for 1½ hours. Cool cake in pan for 20 minutes before turning onto a wire rack to cool.
5 Make whipped chocolate frosting; spread over top and sides of cold cake.

Whipped chocolate frosting Place both chocolates and butter in medium heatproof bowl; stir over saucepan of simmering water until chocolate and butter melts. Stir in oil. Refrigerate until mixture is thick. Beat with electric mixer for about 3 minutes.

Chocolate mocha dacquoise terrine

preparation time **20 minutes** (plus refrigeration time)
cooking time **45 minutes** serves **12**

4 egg whites
1 cup (220g) caster sugar
2 tablespoons cocoa powder
200g dark eating chocolate, chopped coarsely
¾ cup (180ml) cream
2 teaspoons cocoa powder, extra

Mocha butter cream
1 tablespoon instant coffee granules
2 tablespoons boiling water
100g unsalted butter
2¼ cups (360g) icing sugar

1 Preheat oven to slow (150°C/130°C fan-forced). Line three oven trays with baking paper; draw a 10cm x 25cm rectangle on paper.
2 Beat egg whites in medium bowl with electric mixer until soft peaks form. Gradually add sugar, beating after each addition until sugar dissolves; fold in sifted cocoa.
3 Spread meringue evenly over rectangles; bake, uncovered, 45 minutes, or until meringue is dry. Turn off oven; cool meringues in oven with door ajar.
4 Meanwhile, stir chocolate and cream in small saucepan over low heat until smooth; transfer to small bowl and refrigerate until firm. Beat with electric mixer about 20 seconds or until just changed in colour.
5 Make mocha butter cream.
6 Place one meringue layer on serving plate; spread with half the chocolate mixture, then top with half of the butter cream. Top with another meringue layer; spread with remaining chocolate mixture, then with remaining butter cream. Top with last meringue layer, cover; refrigerate for 3 hours, or overnight. To serve, dust with sifted extra cocoa powder.

Mocha butter cream Dissolve coffee with the water in small bowl; cool 10 minutes. Beat butter in small bowl with electric mixer until pale; gradually add sugar, beating until combined. Add coffee mixture; beat until combined.

Chocolate ganache and raspberry cake

preparation time **15 minutes** cooking time **1 hour 15 minutes** (plus standing time) serves **12**

⅓ cup (35g) cocoa powder
⅓ cup (80ml) hot water
150g dark eating chocolate, chopped
150g butter, chopped
1 ⅓ cups (300g) firmly packed brown sugar
1 cup (125g) almond meal
4 eggs, separated
240g fresh raspberries

Chocolate ganache
200g dark eating chocolate, chopped
⅔ cup (160ml) cream

1 Preheat oven to moderately slow (170°C/150°C fan-forced). Grease a deep 22cm round cake pan; line base and side with baking paper.
2 Blend cocoa powder with the water in a small bowl until smooth.
3 Combine chocolate and butter in medium heatproof bowl over a saucepan of simmering water; stir until melted. Remove from heat; stir in cocoa mixture, sugar, almond meal and egg yolks.
4 Beat egg whites in a clean small bowl with electric mixer until soft peaks form; fold into chocolate mixture in two batches.
5 Pour mixture into prepared pan; bake for about 1 ¼ hours. Stand cake in pan for 15 minutes before turning onto a wire rack to cool.
6 Stir ingredients for chocolate ganache in small saucepan over low heat until smooth.
7 Place raspberries on top of cake; pour chocolate ganache over cake to partially cover raspberries. Stand at room temperature until set.

tip The cake can be made up to three days ahead; store in an airtight container. Top with raspberries and chocolate ganache on day of serving.

FRUIT CAKES

Moist whole orange cake

preparation time **30 minutes** cooking time **2 hours 45 minutes** (plus cooling time) serves **10**

2 medium oranges (480g)
²/₃ cup (110g) blanched almonds, toasted
1 cup (220g) caster sugar
1 teaspoon baking powder
6 eggs
2 cups (250g) almond meal
2 tablespoons plain flour

1 Place unpeeled oranges in medium saucepan; cover with cold water, bring to a boil. Boil, covered, for 30 minutes; drain. Repeat process with fresh water and boil about 1 hour or until oranges are tender; cool.
2 Preheat oven to moderate (180°C/160°C fan-forced). Grease a deep 22cm round cake pan; line base and side with baking paper.
3 Process almonds with 2 tablespoons of the sugar until finely chopped.
4 Trim ends off oranges and discard. Halve oranges; remove and discard seeds. Process oranges, including rind, with baking powder until mixture is pulpy.
5 Beat eggs and remaining sugar in medium bowl with electric mixer for about 3 minutes or until fluffy and pale in colour. Fold in almond mixture, almond meal, flour and orange pulp.
6 Pour mixture into prepared pan; bake for about 1 hour or until cooked when tested. Cool cake in pan. Turn cake onto a serving plate and dust with sifted icing sugar, if desired.

tips This cake can be stored in an airtight container for up to two days. It can be frozen for up to three months.

Banana cake with passionfruit icing

preparation time **35 minutes** cooking time **50 minutes** (plus cooling time) serves **10**

You need approximately 2 large overripe bananas (460g) for this recipe.

125g butter, softened
¾ cup (150g) firmly packed brown sugar
2 eggs
1½ cups (225g) self-raising flour
½ teaspoon bicarbonate of soda
1 teaspoon mixed spice
1 cup mashed banana
½ cup (120g) sour cream
¼ cup (60ml) milk

Passionfruit icing
1½ cups (240g) icing sugar
1 teaspoon soft butter
2 tablespoons passionfruit pulp, approximately

1 Preheat oven to moderate (180°C/160°C fan-forced). Grease a 15cm x 25cm loaf pan; line base with baking paper.
2 Beat butter and sugar in small bowl with electric mixer until light and fluffy. Add eggs one at a time, beating until combined after each addition. Transfer mixture to large bowl; using a wooden spoon, stir in sifted dry ingredients, banana, sour cream and milk. Spread mixture into prepared pan.
3 Bake cake for about 50 minutes. Stand cake in pan for 5 minutes before turning onto a wire rack; turn cake top-side up to cool.
4 Make passionfruit icing; spread onto cold cake.

Passionfruit icing Place icing sugar in small heatproof bowl; stir in butter and enough pulp to make a firm paste. Stir over hot water until icing is of a spreadable consistency, taking care not to overheat.

tips It is important that the bananas are overripe for this recipe – if they are underripe the cake will be too heavy. This cake will keep for up to three days in an airtight container. Un-iced, it can be frozen for up to three months.

Glacé peach and almond cake

preparation time **20 minutes** cooking time **1 hour** (plus cooling time)
serves **6**

185g butter, softened
½ teaspoon almond essence
¾ cup (165g) caster sugar
3 eggs
1 cup (250g) finely chopped glacé peaches
⅓ cup (40g) almond meal
1½ cups (225g) self-raising flour
½ cup (75g) plain flour
½ cup (125ml) milk
2 tablespoons brandy

1 Preheat oven to moderate (180°C/160°C fan-forced). Grease a 21cm
baba cake pan.
2 Beat butter, essence and sugar in medium bowl with electric mixer until
light and fluffy. Add eggs one at a time, beating after each addition until
just combined.
3 Transfer mixture to a large bowl; stir in peaches, almond meal, sifted flours,
milk and brandy, in two batches. Spread cake mixture into prepared pan.
4 Bake cake for about 1 hour. Stand cake in pan for 5 minutes before turning
top-side up onto a wire rack to cool.

tips This cake can be made two days ahead; store in an airtight container.

Apricot loaf

preparation time **15 minutes** cooking time **1 hour 25 minutes**
(plus cooling time) serves **8**

200g dried apricots, chopped coarsely
½ cup (125ml) apricot nectar
½ cup (110g) caster sugar
½ cup (110g) firmly packed brown sugar
250g butter, chopped
3 eggs, beaten lightly
1 cup (150g) plain flour
¾ cup (110g) self-raising flour

1 Preheat oven to slow (150°C/130°C fan-forced). Grease a 14cm x 21cm loaf pan; line base and sides with baking paper, extending paper 2cm above edges.

2 Place apricots, nectar and sugars in medium saucepan. Bring to a boil then reduce heat; simmer, covered, for 5 minutes, stirring occasionally. Remove from heat; add butter, stir until melted. Transfer mixture to large bowl; cover, then cool to room temperature.

3 Stir egg and sifted flours into apricot mixture; spread into prepared pan. Bake for about 1¼ hours. Cover hot cake tightly with foil; cool in pan.

tips This cake can be made two days ahead and stored in an airtight container. It can be frozen for up to three months.

Lemon fruit twist

preparation time **30 minutes** cooking time **25 minutes** serves **8**

2¼ cups (335g) self-raising flour
60g butter
1 tablespoon caster sugar
2 tablespoons sultanas
2 teaspoons grated lemon rind
1 egg, lightly beaten
½ cup milk, approximately
2 tablespoons mixed peel
2 tablespoons chopped glacé cherries

Sugar glaze
1 tablespoon sugar
2 tablespoons boiling water

Lemon icing
¾ cup (165g) icing sugar
1 tablespoon lemon juice
15g butter
1 tablespoon boiling water, approximately

1 Preheat oven to moderately hot (200°C/180°C fan-forced). Lightly grease an oven tray.

2 Sift flour into bowl; rub in butter. Stir in sugar, sultanas and lemon rind, then egg and enough milk to mix to a soft pliable dough. Knead on a lightly floured surface until smooth. Divide mixture into three portions and roll each into a roll about 40cm long. Plait the three rolls firmly together. Place onto prepared tray, then press ends of plait together to form a round shape. Bake for about 20 minutes.

3 Meanwhile, stir ingredients for sugar glaze in a medium bowl until sugar is completely dissolved.

4 Make lemon icing.

5 Brush twists with sugar glaze, then bake for a further 5 minutes. Lift onto a wire rack to cool. Drizzle with lemon icing; sprinkle with peel and cherries.

Lemon icing Sift icing sugar into bowl; stir in lemon juice, butter and enough water to mix to a pouring consistency.

Fig, walnut and ginger cake

preparation time **20 minutes** cooking time **1 hour 15 minutes** serves **10**

185 g butter
¾ cup (165g) caster sugar
3 eggs
½ cup (95g) finely chopped dried figs
⅓ cup (65g) finely chopped glacé ginger
½ cup (50g) finely chopped walnuts
½ cup (75g) plain four
½ cup (75g) self-raising flour
⅓ cup (65g) sour cream

1 Preheat oven to moderately slow (170°C/150°C fan-forced). Grease a 14cm x 21cm loaf pan; line base with baking paper.

2 Beat butter and sugar in small bowl with electric mixer until light and fluffy. Add eggs one at a time, beating until combined after each addition. Transfer mixture to large bowl. Stir in figs, ginger and walnuts, then sifted flours and sour cream.

3 Spread mixture into pan; bake about 1¼ hours. Stand cake in pan for 5 minutes before turning onto a wire rack to cool.

Raspberry hazelnut cake

preparation time **30 minutes** cooking time **1 hour 30 minutes** serves **12**

250g butter, softened
2 cups (440g) caster sugar
6 eggs
1 cup (150g) plain flour
½ cup (75g) self-raising flour
1 cup (110g) hazelnut meal
⅔ cup (160g) sour cream
300g fresh or frozen raspberries

Mascarpone cream
250g mascarpone
¼ cup (40g) icing sugar
2 tablespoons frangelico
½ cup (120g) sour cream
½ cup (75g) roasted hazelnuts, chopped finely

1 Preheat oven to moderate (180°C/160°C fan-forced). Grease a deep 22cm round cake pan; line base and side with baking paper.
2 Beat butter and sugar in medium bowl with electric mixer until light and fluffy; add eggs one at a time, beating until just combined after each addition (mixture will curdle at this stage, but will come together later).
3 Transfer to a large bowl; using a wooden spoon, stir in flours, hazelnut meal, sour cream and raspberries. Spread mixture into prepared pan.
4 Bake about 1½ hours. Stand cake for 10 minutes; turn onto a wire rack, top-side up, to cool.
5 Meanwhile, make mascarpone cream.
6 Place cake on serving plate; using a metal spatula, spread cake all over with mascarpone cream.

Mascarpone cream Combine mascarpone, icing sugar, liqueur and sour cream in medium bowl. Using a wooden spoon, stir until smooth; stir in nuts.

tips In cooler weather the unfrosted cake will keep for up to three days in an airtight container at room temperature. Unfrosted, it can also be frozen for up to three months.

Orange and passionfruit swirl cake

preparation time **30 mins** cooking time **1 hour** serves **10**

Only half the passionfruit curd is required for this cake; use the rest on toast or scones, in a sponge cake or to fill small sweet pastry shells.

150g butter
2 teaspoons grated orange rind
²⁄₃ cup (150g) caster sugar
3 eggs
1 cup (150g) self-raising flour
¼ cup (60ml) orange juice
Icing sugar, for dusting

Passionfruit curd
60g butter, chopped
²⁄₃ cup (150g) caster sugar
2 eggs, beaten lightly
¼ cup (60ml) orange juice
2 teaspoons cornflour
½ cup passionfruit pulp

1 Preheat oven to moderate (180°C/160°C fan-forced). Grease a 21cm baba pan; lightly flour pan and tap out excess flour.
2 Make passionfruit curd.
3 Beat butter, rind and sugar in a small bowl with an electric mixer until light and fluffy. Add eggs, one at a time, beating well after each addition. Add flour and juice; beat for 3 minutes.
4 Spoon half the cake mixture into prepared pan; add half the passionfruit curd and top with remaining cake mixture. Using a knife or metal skewer, swirl the curd through the cake. Bake for about 45 minutes. Turn onto a wire rack to cool.
5 Serve cake dusted with sifted icing sugar.

Passionfruit curd Combine ingredients in a heatproof bowl; stir over a pan of simmering water for about 10 minutes, or until the mixture thickens slightly; cool.

Hummingbird cake

preparation time **35 minutes** cooking time **40 minutes** serves **12**

You will need approximately 2 large overripe bananas (460g) for this recipe.

450g can crushed pineapple in syrup
1 cup (150g) plain flour
½ cup (75g) self-raising flour
½ teaspoon bicarbonate of soda
½ teaspoon ground cinnamon
½ teaspoon ground ginger
1 cup (200g) firmly packed brown sugar
½ cup (45g) desiccated coconut
1 cup mashed banana
2 eggs, beaten lightly
¾ cup (180ml) vegetable oil

Cream cheese frosting
30g butter, softened
60g cream cheese, softened
1 teaspoon vanilla extract
1½ cups (240g) icing sugar

1 Preheat oven to moderate (180°C/160°C fan-forced). Grease a deep 23cm-square cake pan; line base with baking paper.
2 Drain pineapple over a medium bowl, pressing with a spoon to extract as much syrup as possible. Reserve ¼ cup (60ml) syrup.
3 Sift flours, soda, spices and sugar into a large bowl. Using wooden spoon, stir in reserved syrup, coconut, banana, egg and oil; pour into prepared pan.
4 Bake cake for about 40 minutes. Stand for 5 minutes pan then turn onto wire rack; turn cake top-side up to cool.
5 Make cream cheese frosting; spread over cold cake.

Cream cheese frosting Beat butter, cream cheese and extract in a small bowl with electric mixer until light and fluffy; gradually beat in icing sugar.

Wholemeal fruit and coconut loaf

preparation time **20 minutes** (plus standing time) cooking time **50 minutes**
serves **10**

⅔ cup (110g) chopped dates
⅓ cup (50g) chopped dried apricots
¼ cup (20g) desiccated coconut
2 tablespoons brandy
⅔ cup (150g) firmly packed brown sugar
125g butter, chopped
½ teaspoon bicarbonate of soda
¾ cup (180ml) boiling water
2 eggs, lightly beaten
¾ cup (120g) wholemeal self-raising flour
¾ cup (120g) wholemeal plain flour
1 teaspoon mixed spice

1 Combine dates in medium bowl with apricots, coconut and brandy; let stand overnight.
2 Preheat oven to moderate (180°C/160°C fan-forced). Grease a 15cm x 25cm loaf pan; line base with baking paper.
3 Add sugar, butter and soda to date mixture, then stir in the water; cool for 10 minutes. Stir in eggs, then sifted dry ingredients. Pour into prepared pan.
4 Bake loaf for about 50 minutes. Stand loaf in pan for 5 minutes before turning onto a wire rack to cool.

tip This loaf can be stored in an airtight container for up to three days.

Fig fudge cake with milk chocolate icing

preparation time **30 minutes** (plus cooling and refrigeration time)
cooking time **1 hour** serves **8**

¾ cup (195g) chopped dried figs
½ cup (125ml) brandy
1½ cups (160g) roasted hazelnuts
¼ cup (25g) packaged breadcrumbs
125g butter
⅔ cup (150g) caster sugar
3 eggs
125g dark eating chocolate, melted

Milk chocolate icing
⅓ cup (75g) sugar
100g milk eating chocolate, chopped
½ cup (125ml) cream

1 Combine figs and brandy in saucepan, bring to boil; boil, uncovered, until brandy has evaporated. Transfer figs to bowl; cool to room temperature.
2 Preheat oven to moderate (180°C/160°C fan-forced). Grease deep 20cm round cake pan; line base with baking paper.
3 Blend or process hazelnuts and breadcrumbs until hazelnuts are finely chopped (not ground). Combine butter and sugar in small bowl, beat with electric mixer until light and fluffy; add eggs, one at a time, beating well after each addition. Stir in hazelnut and fig mixtures and cooled chocolate. Pour mixture into prepared pan, bake about 45 minutes or until firm; cool in pan.
4 Meanwhile, make milk chocolate icing. Turn cooled cake onto a serving plate; spread with icing. Refrigerate for several hours before serving.

Milk chocolate icing Cook sugar in small heavy-based saucepan until completely melted and golden brown. Add chopped chocolate and cream, stirring constantly over heat, without boiling, until mixture is smooth. Cool to room temperature.

tip This cake will keep for three days, covered, in the refrigerator. The plain cake can be frozen for up to two months

Banana bread

preparation time **10 minutes** cooking time **30 minutes** (plus cooling time)
makes **8 slices**

You will need 1 large overripe banana (230g) for this recipe.

1 ¼ cups (185g) self-raising flour
1 teaspoon ground cinnamon
20g butter
½ cup (110g) firmly packed brown sugar
1 egg, beaten lightly
¼ cup (60ml) milk
½ cup mashed banana

1 Preheat oven to hot (220°C/200°C fan forced). Grease a 14cm x 21cm loaf pan; line base with baking paper.
2 Sift flour and cinnamon into a large bowl, then rub in butter. Stir in sugar, egg, milk and banana — do not overmix, the batter should be lumpy. Spoon mixture into prepared pan.
3 Bake for about 30 minutes. Stand cake in pan for 5 minutes before turning onto a wire rack; turn cake top-side up to cool.
4 Cut banana bread into eight slices. Toast lightly on both sides and spread with butter, if desired.

tips Unsliced banana bread will keep in an airtight container for up to two days. The loaf is suitable for freezing for up to three months.

Upside-down toffee and banana cake

preparation time **15 minutes** cooking time **55 minutes** serves **8**

You will need approximately 2 large overripe bananas (460g) for the mashed banana in this recipe.

1 cup (220g) caster sugar
1 cup (250ml) water
2 medium bananas (400g), sliced thinly
2 eggs, beaten lightly
⅔ cup (160ml) vegetable oil
¾ cup (165g) firmly packed brown sugar
1 teaspoon vanilla extract
⅔ cup (100g) plain flour
⅓ cup (50g) wholemeal self-raising flour
2 teaspoons mixed spice
1 teaspoon bicarbonate of soda
1 cup mashed banana

1 Preheat oven to moderate (180°C/160°C fan-forced). Grease a deep 22cm round cake pan; line base with baking paper.
2 Stir caster sugar and the water in a medium saucepan over heat, without boiling, until sugar dissolves; bring to a boil. Boil, uncovered, without stirring, for about 10 minutes or until caramel in colour. Pour toffee into prepared pan; top with sliced banana.
3 Combine egg, oil, brown sugar and extract in a medium bowl. Stir in sifted dry ingredients, then mashed banana; pour mixture into prepared pan.
4 Bake for about 40 minutes. Stand cake in pan for 5 minutes before turning onto a wire rack covered with baking paper; turn cake top-side up. Serve warm or at room temperature with thick cream, if desired.

tip Store this cake in the refrigerator for up to two days. It is not suitable to freeze.

Fig jam and raisin rolls

preparation time **20 minutes** cooking time **50 minutes** (plus cooling time)
serves **20**

125g butter
½ cup (100g) firmly packed brown sugar
2 eggs
1½ cups (225g) self-raising flour
½ cup (160g) fig jam
1 cup (170g) chopped raisins
½ cup (125ml) milk

1 Preheat oven to moderate (180°C/160°C fan-forced). Grease two
8cm x 19cm nut roll tins; line base with baking paper. Place tins upright
on oven tray.

2 Beat butter and sugar in small bowl with electric mixer until light and
fluffy. Add eggs one at a time, beating until just combined after each addition
(mixture may curdle); transfer to medium bowl. Stir in flour, jam, raisins and
milk, in two batches. Spoon mixture into prepared tins; replace lids.

3 Bake rolls, tins standing upright, for about 50 minutes. Stand rolls in tins
for 5 minutes, remove ends (top and bottom); shake tins gently to release
rolls onto wire rack to cool.

tips Nut roll tins are available from cookware shops and department stores.
Store fruit rolls in an airtight container for up to three days. Fruit rolls can be
frozen for up to three months.

Date and walnut rolls

preparation time **15 minutes** cooking time **50 minutes** (plus cooling time)
serves **20**

60g butter
1 cup (250ml) boiling water
1 cup (180g) finely chopped seeded dried dates
½ teaspoon bicarbonate of soda
1 cup (220g) firmly packed brown sugar
2 cups (300g) self-raising flour
½ cup (60g) coarsely chopped walnuts
1 egg, beaten lightly

1 Preheat oven to moderate (180°C/160°C fan-forced). Grease two
8cm x 19cm nut roll tins; line bases with baking paper. Place tins upright
on an oven tray.
2 Combine butter and the water in a medium saucepan; stir over low heat
until butter melts. Transfer mixture to large bowl; stir in dates and soda, then
sugar, flour, nuts and egg. Spoon mixture into prepared tins; replace lids.
3 Bake rolls, tins standing upright, for about 50 minutes. Stand rolls for
5 minutes in tins, then remove ends (top and bottom); shake tins gently to
release nut rolls onto a wire rack to cool.

tips Nut roll tins are available from cookware shops and department stores.
Store the rolls in an airtight container for up to three days. They can be frozen
for up to three months.

Rhubarb and coconut cake

preparation time **25 minutes** cooking time **1 hour 30 minutes** serves **8**

1½ cups (225g) self-raising flour
1¼ cups (275g) caster sugar
1¼ cups (110g) desiccated coconut
125g butter, melted
3 eggs, beaten lightly
½ cup (125ml) milk
½ teaspoon vanilla extract
1 cup (110g) finely chopped rhubarb
5 trimmed rhubarb stalks (300g)
2 tablespoons demerara sugar

1 Preheat oven to slow (150°C/130°C fan-forced). Grease a 14cm x 21cm loaf pan; line base with baking paper.

2 Combine flour, caster sugar and coconut in a medium bowl; stir in the butter, eggs, milk and extract until combined.

3 Spread half the mixture into prepared pan; sprinkle evenly with chopped rhubarb. Spread remaining cake mixture over rhubarb.

4 Cut rhubarb stalks into 12cm lengths. Place rhubarb pieces over top of cake; sprinkle with demerara sugar.

5 Bake cake for about 1½ hours. Stand cake in pan for 5 minutes; turn, top-side up, onto a wire rack to cool.

Raspberry yogurt cake

preparation time **30 minutes** cooking time **1 hour 5 minutes** serves **12**

½ cup (125g) margarine
¾ cup (165g) firmly packed brown sugar
2 eggs
1¼ cups (200g) wholemeal self-raising flour
½ cup (140g) low-fat yogurt
100g frozen raspberries

Cream cheese frosting
80g light cream cheese, softened
⅓ cup (55g) icing sugar
1 teaspoon lemon juice

1 Preheat oven to moderate (180°C/160°C fan-forced). Grease a 14cm x 21cm loaf pan; line base and two long sides with baking paper, extending paper 5cm above edges.
2 Beat margarine and sugar in medium bowl with electric mixer until light and fluffy. Add eggs one at a time, beating until combined after each addition. Transfer mixture to medium bowl; stir in flour, yogurt and raspberries. Spread mixture into prepared pan.
3 Bake for about 1 hour 5 minutes. Stand cake in pan for 10 minutes, then turn onto a wire rack; turn top-side up to cool.
4 Whisk ingredients for cream cheese frosting in small bowl until smooth. Place cake on a serving plate; using a spatula, spread top of cake with cream cheese frosting.

Plum and cinnamon cake

preparation time **15 minutes** cooking time **30 minutes** serves **12**

½ cup (125g) margarine
1 teaspoon vanilla extract
½ cup (100g) firmly packed brown sugar
3 eggs, separated
½ cup (75g) white self-raising flour
½ cup (80g) wholemeal self-raising flour
1 teaspoon ground cinnamon
4 whole canned plums in syrup, drained, halved, seeded

1 Preheat oven to moderate (180°C/160°C fan-forced). Grease a 20cm ring pan; line base and side with baking paper.
2 Beat margarine, extract, sugar and egg yolks in small bowl with electric mixer until light and fluffy. Transfer mixture to medium bowl; stir in flours and cinnamon.
3 Beat egg whites in small bowl with electric mixer until soft peaks form; gently fold whites into cake mixture. Spread mixture into prepared pan; place plums on top, cut-side down.
4 Bake cake for about 30 minutes. Stand cake in pan for 10 minutes; turn onto a wire rack, then top-side up to cool. Serve cake dusted with icing sugar, if desired.

Citrus olive oil cake

preparation time **25 minutes** cooking time **50 minutes** serves **12**

3 medium (720g) mandarins or oranges, peeled, sliced thinly
⅓ cup (80ml) sauterne
3 eggs
1¼ cups (275g) caster sugar
1 tablespoon finely grated lemon rind
½ cup (125ml) extra light olive oil
⅓ cup (80ml) sauterne, extra
1 cup (150g) plain flour
1 cup (150g) self-raising flour
Icing sugar, for dusting

1 Preheat oven to moderate (180°C/160°C fan-forced). Grease a deep 22cm round cake pan; line base with baking paper.
2 Place mandarins and sauterne in medium bowl; cover and refrigerate until required.
3 Beat eggs, sugar and rind in small bowl with electric mixer for about 5 minutes, or until thick and creamy; transfer mixture to a large bowl. Fold in oil and extra sauterne, then sifted combined flours.
4 Pour mixture into prepared pan; bake for about 50 minutes, or until cooked when tested. Stand cake for 10 minutes, then turn onto a wire rack; turn top-side up to cool.
5 Dust cake with sifted icing sugar; serve with macerated mandarin slices and thick cream, if desired.

tip Any dessert wine can be used instead of sauterne in this recipe.

Glacé fruit and chocolate cake

preparation time **20 minutes** cooking time **10 minutes** serves **12**

125g butter, chopped
¾ cup (150g) firmly packed brown sugar
100g dark chocolate, chopped coarsely
½ cup (125ml) water
¼ cup (60ml) cointreau
¼ cup (30g) coarsely chopped pecans
1 cup (250g) finely chopped glacé figs
1 cup (250g) finely chopped glacé apricots
1 cup (170g) coarsely chopped raisins
¾ cup (110g) plain flour
2 tablespoons cocoa powder
2 tablespoons self-raising flour
2 eggs, beaten lightly
80g dark chocolate, melted, extra
¼ cup (60ml) cream

1 Preheat oven to slow (150°C/130°C fan-forced). Grease 20cm round cake pan; line base with baking paper.
2 Combine butter, sugar, chocolate and the water in medium saucepan; stir over heat until sugar dissolves. Remove from heat; stir in liqueur, nuts and fruit. Add sifted dry ingredients and egg; stir until combined.
3 Spoon mixture into prepared pan; bake for about 10 minutes. Cool in pan.
4 Just before serving, combine cooled extra chocolate and cream in small bowl; stir until smooth. Turn cake onto serving plate, top-side up; spread chocolate mixture over top of cake.

tip This cake can be baked in a 14cm x 21cm loaf pan; bake in a slow oven for about 1½ hours.

Banana raisin cake

preparation time **20 minutes** cooking time **1 hour 15 minutes** serves **12**

You will need about 3 large overripe bananas (690g) for this recipe.

125g butter
¾ cup (165g) caster sugar
2 eggs
1 cup (170g) chopped raisins
1½ cups mashed banana
2 cups (300g) self-raising flour
½ teaspoon bicarbonate of soda
1 tablespoon milk

1 Preheat oven to moderate (180°C/160°C fan-forced). Grease a 15cm x 25cm loaf pan; line base with baking paper.
2 Beat butter and sugar in a medium bowl with electric mixer until light and fluffy. Add eggs one at a time, beating until just combined after each addition. Stir in raisins and banana, then flour and combined soda and milk.
3 Spread mixture into prepared pan. Bake for about 1¼ hours. Stand cake in pan for 5 minutes; turn onto wire rack to cool.

Raspberry buttercake

preparation time **15 minutes** cooking time **1 hour** serves **8**

125g butter
¾ cup (165g) caster sugar
2 eggs
1½ cups (225g) self-raising flour
½ cup (125ml) milk
¾ cup raspberries

1 Preheat oven to moderate (180°C/160°C fan-forced). Grease deep 20cm round cake pan; line base with baking paper.
2 Beat butter and sugar in medium bowl with electric mixer until light and fluffy. Add eggs one at a time, beating until just combined after each addition. Stir in flour and milk, in two batches; fold ¼ cup raspberries into mixture.
3 Spread three-quarters of cake mixture into prepared pan; sprinkle with remaining raspberries. Spread with remaining cake mixture; bake about 1 hour. Stand cake in pan for 5 minutes; turn onto wire rack to cool.

Tropical papaya and banana cake

preparation time **20 minutes** cooking time **1 hour** serves **10**

You will need 1 large (230g) overripe banana for this recipe.

125g butter
¾ cup (165g) caster sugar
2 eggs
½ cup mashed banana
½ cup (100g) roughly chopped fresh, just-ripe papaya
1½ cups (225g) self-raising flour
½ cup (45g) desiccated coconut
¼ cup (60ml) milk

1 Preheat oven to moderate (180°C/160°C fan-forced). Grease deep 20cm round cake pan; line base with baking paper.
2 Beat butter and sugar in medium bowl with electric mixer until pale. Add eggs one at a time, beating until just combined after each addition. Stir in banana and papaya. Stir in flour, coconut and milk, in two batches; spread mixture into prepared pan.
3 Bake cake for about 1 hour. Stand cake in pan for 5 minutes; turn onto wire rack to cool.

Whole mandarin cake

preparation time **25 minutes** (plus cooling time)
cooking time **1 hour 20 minutes** serves **10**

2 medium (400g) mandarins, unpeeled
2 eggs
1 cup (220g) caster sugar
125g butter
½ cup (45g) desiccated coconut
⅓ cup (35g) hazelnut meal
2 cups (300g) self-raising flour

1 Preheat oven to moderate (180°C/160°C fan-forced). Grease 21cm baba pan.
2 Place mandarins in medium saucepan, cover with cold water and bring to boil; drain. Repeat process twice more, then cool to room temperature.
3 Cut mandarins in half, discard seeds. Blend or process mandarins until

smooth. Measure mandarin pulp; put 1 cup of mandarin pulp back into the
food processor (discard remaining pulp) with remaining ingredients. Process
until ingredients are combined and mixture is smooth; pour into prepared pan.
4 Bake cake for about 1 hour. Stand cake in pan for 5 minutes; turn onto a
wire rack to cool.

Apple buttermilk cake

preparation time **15 minutes** cooking time **45 minutes** serves **16**

150g butter
¾ cup (150g) firmly packed brown sugar
2 eggs
2 cups (300g) self-raising flour
½ cup (125ml) buttermilk
2 large (400g) apples, peeled, sliced thinly
40g butter, melted, extra
1 tablespoon brown sugar, extra
1 tablespoon golden syrup

1 Preheat oven to moderate (180°C/160°C fan-forced). Grease deep 23cm
square cake pan; line base with baking paper.
2 Beat butter and sugar in medium bowl with electric mixer until light and
fluffy. Add eggs one at a time, beating until just combined after each addition.
Stir in flour and buttermilk, in two batches. Spread mixture into prepared
pan; top with apple, brush with extra butter and sprinkle with extra sugar.
3 Bake for about 45 minutes. Stand cake in pan 10 minutes; turn onto wire
rack, then invert onto another wire rack and brush apples with golden syrup.

Frosted carrot and ginger cake

preparation time **30 minutes** cooking time **1 hour 5 minutes** serves **10**

450g can crushed pineapple in natural juice
1 cup (160g) wholemeal plain flour
²⁄₃ cup (100g) self-raising flour
1 teaspoon bicarbonate of soda
1 teaspoon ground cinnamon
¾ cup (150g) firmly packed brown sugar
200g butter, melted
3 eggs, beaten lightly
2 tablespoons finely grated fresh ginger
1½ cups coarsely grated carrot
¾ cup (90g) coarsely chopped walnuts

Ginger cream cheese frosting
2 tablespoons finely grated fresh ginger
30g soft butter
125g cream cheese, softened
2 teaspoons lemon juice
½ cup (80g) icing sugar

1 Preheat oven to moderate (180°C/160°C fan-forced). Grease a deep 19cm square cake pan; line base with baking paper.
2 Place pineapple in sieve over medium bowl; leave to drain for 5 minutes. Sift flours, soda and cinnamon into a large bowl. Stir in sugar, butter and eggs, then ginger, carrot, nuts and pineapple.
3 Pour mixture into prepared pan; bake about 1 hour 5 minutes. Stand cake in pan for 5 minutes; turn onto a wire rack to cool.
4 Make ginger cream cheese frosting; spread over cold cake.

Ginger cream cheese frosting Press ginger between two spoons to extract juice (you will need 1 tablespoon of juice). Beat butter and cream cheese in a small bowl with an electric mixer until light and fluffy. Stir combined juices and icing sugar into cheese mixture until smooth.

Rich fruit and nut brownies

preparation time **20 minutes** cooking time **50 minutes** serves **15**

½ cup (140g) dried figs, chopped finely
½ cup (90g) raisins, chopped coarsely
2 tablespoons rum
125g butter, chopped
200g dark chocolate, chopped
1 ¼ cups (275g) firmly packed brown sugar
3 eggs, beaten lightly
¾ cup (110g) plain flour
⅓ cup (80g) sour cream
⅓ cup (50g) toasted hazelnuts, chopped coarsely
⅓ cup (50g) toasted walnuts, chopped coarsely

1 Preheat oven to moderate (180°C/160°C fan-forced). Grease a 20cm x 30cm lamington pan; line base and two opposite sides with baking paper, extending paper 5cm above edge.
2 Combine figs, raisins and rum in a heatproof bowl. Cover; microwave on HIGH (100%) for 30 seconds. Stand, covered, for 5 minutes.
3 Meanwhile, stir butter and chocolate in a medium pan over a low heat until the mixture is smooth. Transfer the mixture to a medium bowl.
4 Stir sugar and eggs into the chocolate mixture, then stir in the sifted flour, sour cream, nuts and the fruit mixture. Spread into prepared pan. Bake for about 30 minutes. Cool in pan.

tip This cake can be stored in an airtight container for up to a week.

Rum and citrus fruit cake

preparation time **25 minutes** (plus standing time) cooking time **2 hours**
serves **10**

1½ cup (250g) quartered red glacé cherries
½ cup (125g) chopped glacé apricots
¾ cup (165g) sultanas
¾ cup (135g) currants
½ cup (80g) chopped blanched almonds
1 tablespoon grated orange rind
2 teaspoons grated lemon rind
2 tablespoons rum
250g butter
¾ cup (165g) caster sugar
5 eggs
1½ cups (225g) plain flour
¼ cup (35g) self-raising flour

1 Combine fruit, almonds, rinds and rum in a large bowl; cover and let
stand overnight.
2 Preheat oven to moderately slow (170°C/150°C fan-forced). Grease deep
20cm round cake pan; line base and side with paper, grease paper well.
3 Beat butter and sugar in large bowl with electric mixer until just combined.
Add eggs one at a time, beating until combined after each addition. Stir in
sifted flours and fruit mixture in two batches.
4 Spread mixture into prepared pan. Bake for about 2 hours. Cover cake
with foil; cool in pan.

tip This cake can be stored in an airtight container for up to two weeks.

Norwegian apple cake

preparation time **25 minutes** cooking time **35 minutes** serves **12**

2 eggs
1 cup (220g) caster sugar
125g butter, chopped
²/₃ cup (160ml) milk
1½ cups (225g) self-raising flour
3 medium (450g) granny smith apples, sliced
1 tablespoon cinnamon sugar

1 Preheat oven to moderate (180°C/160°C fan-forced). Grease a 20cm x 30cm lamington pan; line base with baking paper.
2 Beat eggs and sugar in small bowl with electric mixer until mixture is thick and creamy.
3 Meanwhile, combine butter and milk in small saucepan; bring to the boil, then remove immediately from heat.
4 Add butter mixture gradually to egg mixture, beating continuously. Transfer to a large bowl; fold in sifted flour. Spread mixture into prepared pan. Overlap apple slices over mixture; sprinkle with cinnamon sugar.
5 Bake cake for 35 minutes or until cooked when tested. Cool cake in pan.

tip This cake is suitable to freeze.

Boiled passionfruit and orange fruit cake

preparation time **20 minutes** (plus cooling time)
cooking time **1 hour 35 minutes** serves **10**

You will need about 7 large passionfruit for this recipe.

½ cup (125ml) strained passionfruit pulp
500g mixed fruit
¼ cup (60ml) orange juice
1 cup (220g) caster sugar
125g butter, chopped
3 eggs, beaten lightly
¾ cup (110g) plain flour
¾ cup (110g) self-raising flour
1 teaspoon mixed spice

1 Preheat oven to moderately slow (170°C/150°C fan-forced). Grease a deep 20cm round cake pan; line base and side with baking paper.
2 Combine passionfruit pulp, mixed fruit, juice, sugar and butter in saucepan; stir constantly over heat, without boiling, until sugar is dissolved. Bring to a boil, reduce heat; simmer, uncovered, for 3 minutes. Remove from heat; transfer mixture to large bowl, then cool to room temperature.
3 Stir eggs and sifted dry ingredients into cold fruit mixture. Pour into prepared pan. Bake for about 1½ hours. Cover cake with foil; cool in pan.

Buttery banana cake with lime cream cheese frosting

preparation time **25 minutes** cooking time **1 hour 10 minutes** serves **25**

You will need about 5 large overripe bananas (1kg) for this recipe.

500g butter, softened
2 cups (400g) firmly packed brown sugar
6 eggs
2 cups mashed overripe bananas
4 cups (600g) self-raising flour, sifted

Lime cream cheese frosting
50 g butter, softened
250g cream cheese
2 teaspoons finely grated lime rind
1 ¼ cups (200g) icing sugar
2 tablespoons lime juice

1 Preheat oven to moderately slow (170°C/150°C fan-forced). Grease a 25cm x 35cm baking dish; line base and side with baking paper.
2 Beat butter and sugar in large bowl with electric mixer until well combined. Add eggs one at a time, beating until just combined after each addition. Transfer mixture to very large bowl; stir in sifted flour and banana in two batches. Spread mixture into prepared dish.
3 Bake cake for about 1 hour 10 minutes. Stand cake in baking dish for 20 minutes, before turning onto a wire rack to cool.
4 Meanwhile, make lime cream cheese frosting, spread over cold cake, marking the top with a cake comb or fork, if desired.

Lime cream cheese frosting Beat butter, cream cheese and rind in medium bowl with electric mixer until light and fluffy. Gradually beat in sifted icing sugar, then juice.

tips This recipe can be made two days ahead; store in an airtight container in the refrigerator. Not suitable to freeze.

Pear crumble cake

preparation time **25 minutes** cooking time **1 hour 10 minutes** serves **8**

It is important to slice the pears as thinly as possible in this recipe – if the slices are too thick, the cake will sink in the centre.

1 cup (220g) caster sugar
2 cinnamon sticks
2 cups (500ml) water
2 small (360g) pears, sliced thinly
125g butter
²/₃ cup (150g) caster sugar, extra
2 eggs
1 ½ cups (225g) self-raising flour

Crumble topping
½ cup (75g) plain flour
⅓ cup (75g) caster sugar
60g butter
½ cup (45g) desiccated coconut

1 Preheat oven to moderate (180°C/160°C fan-forced). Line base and side of 22cm springform tin with foil.
2 Combine sugar, cinnamon and the water in medium pan; stir over heat, without boiling, until sugar dissolves. Add pears, simmer about 5 minutes or until just tender; drain on absorbent paper.
3 Meanwhile, blend or process ingredients for crumble topping until fine and crumbly.
4 Beat butter and extra sugar in small bowl with electric mixer until light and fluffy. Add eggs one at a time, beating well after each addition. Add flour, beat until combined. Spread mixture into prepared pan, top with half the pears; sprinkle with half the crumble topping. Repeat with remaining pears and topping.
5 Bake cake for about 1 hour. Cool cake in pan.

tip This cake can be stored in an airtight container for up to a week.

Petite orange coconut loaves

preparation time **25 minutes** cooking time **20 minutes** makes **8**

60g butter, chopped
½ cup (110g) caster sugar
2 eggs, separated
½ cup (75g) self-raising flour
¼ cup (35g) plain flour
2 tablespoons desiccated coconut
¼ cup (60 ml) fresh orange juice
¼ cup (60ml) milk
⅓ cup (75g) caster sugar, extra
1 ¼ cups (85g) shredded coconut
1 tablespoon cornflour

1 Preheat oven to moderate (180°C/160°C fan-forced). Grease an eight-hole petite loaf cake pan; line base with baking paper.
2 Beat butter, sugar and egg yolks in small bowl with electric mixer until light and fluffy. Stir in combined sifted flours, desiccated coconut, juice and milk in two batches. Divide mixture among prepared pan holes.
3 Beat egg whites in a clean small bowl with an electric mixer until soft peaks form; gradually add extra sugar, beating until sugar is dissolved. Stir in shredded coconut and sifted cornflour. Divide coconut topping over top of cake mixture in pans.
4 Bake loaves for about 20 minutes or until cooked through. Cool loaves in pans for 5 minutes; transfer to a wire rack to cool.

Vanilla pear almond cake

preparation time **30 minutes** (plus cooling time)
cooking time **2 hours 15 minutes** serves **8**

Corellas are miniature dessert pears with pale flesh and a sweet, mild flavour.

8 corella pears (800g)
1 strip lemon rind
1 ¾ cups (385g) caster sugar
2 ½ cups (625ml) water
1 vanilla bean
125g butter, chopped
3 eggs
⅔ cup (160g) sour cream
⅔ cup (100g) plain flour
⅔ cup (100g) self-raising flour
¼ cup (40g) blanched almonds, toasted, chopped coarsely
40g dark eating chocolate, chopped coarsely
½ cup (60g) almond meal

1 Peel pears, leaving stems intact.
2 Combine rind, 1 cup of the sugar and the water in medium saucepan. Split vanilla bean in half lengthways; scrape seeds into saucepan, then add pod. Stir over heat, without boiling, until sugar dissolves. Add pears, bring to a boil, then reduce heat; simmer, covered, about 30 minutes or until pears are just tender. Transfer pears to medium bowl; bring syrup to a boil. Boil, uncovered, until syrup reduces by half. Cool completely.
3 Preheat oven to moderately slow (170°C/150°C fan-forced). Insert base of 23cm springform tin upside down in tin to give a flat base; grease tin.
4 Beat butter and remaining sugar in medium bowl with electric mixer until light and fluffy. Add eggs one at a time, beating until just combined after each addition. Add sour cream; beat until just combined. (Mixture may curdle at this stage but will come together later.) Stir in 2 tablespoons of the syrup, then flours, nuts, chocolate and almond meal.
5 Spread cake mixture into prepared tin; place pears upright around edge of tin, gently pushing to the bottom. Bake about 1 hour 35 minutes. Stand cake in pan for 10 minutes; remove from tin.
6 Serve cake warm, brushed with remaining syrup.

Vanilla bean cherry financier

preparation **20 minutes** cooking **1 hour 30 minutes** serves **12**

1 vanilla bean
150 butter, melted
6 egg whites
1 tablespoon milk
1 teaspoon vanilla extract
1½ cups (185g) almond meal
1½ cups (240g) pure icing sugar
½ cup (75g) self-raising flour
1 cup (150g) frozen cherries

1 Preheat the oven to moderately slow (170°C/150°C fan-forced). Grease a deep 20cm round cake pan; line base with baking paper.
2 Split vanilla bean in half lengthways; scrape seeds from bean. Stir seeds into melted butter until seeds are dispersed.
3 Place egg whites in a medium bowl; whisk lightly with a fork until combined. Add butter mixture, milk, extract, almond meal, sifted icing sugar and flour; stir until just combined.
4 Pour mixture into prepared pan; drop cherries on top of mixture. Bake for about 1½ hours. Stand cake in pan for 5 minutes before turning onto a wire rack to cool.
5 Serve dusted with extra sifted icing sugar, if desired.

Carrot and banana cake

preparation time **20 minutes** cooking time **1 hour 15 minutes** serves **12**

You will need 4 medium carrots (480g) and 2 large overripe bananas (460g).

1 ¼ **cups (185g) plain flour**
½ **cup (75g) self-raising flour**
1 **teaspoon bicarbonate of soda**
1 **teaspoon mixed spice**
½ **teaspoon ground cinnamon**
1 **cup (220g) firmly packed brown sugar**
¾ **cup (90g) chopped walnuts or pecans**
3 **eggs, beaten lightly**
2 **cups finely grated carrot**
1 **cup mashed banana**
1 **cup (250ml) vegetable oil**

1 Preheat oven to moderately slow (170°C/150°C fan-forced). Grease 24cm springform tin; line base with baking paper.
2 Sift flours, soda, spices and sugar into large bowl; stir in remaining ingredients. Pour mixture into prepared tin.
3 Bake cake about 1 ¼ hours. Cool cake in pan.

Mango cake

preparation time **20 minutes** cooking time **1 hour 15 minutes** serves **10**

185g **butter**
1 **cup (220g) caster sugar**
3 **eggs, beaten lightly**
½ **cup (125ml) mango puree**
⅓ **cup (80ml) sour cream**
1 ¾ **cups (260g) self-raising flour**
½ **cup (100g) chopped dried mango**

1 Preheat oven to moderately slow (170°C/150°C fan-forced). Grease a 15cm x 25cm loaf pan; line base and two long sides with baking paper, extending paper 2cm above edge.
2 Beat butter and sugar in medium bowl with electric mixer until light and fluffy. Add eggs one at a time, beating until just combined after each addition

(mixture may curdle). Stir in mango puree, cream, flour and dried mango; pour mixture into prepared pan.

3 Bake cake about 1¼ hours. Stand cake in pan for 5 minutes, before turning onto wire rack to cool.

Lime poppy seed yogurt cake

preparation time **25 minutes** cooking time **1 hour** serves **8**

250g butter, softened
1 tablespoon finely grated lime rind
1½ cups (330g) caster sugar
3 eggs
1¾ cups (260g) self-raising flour
2 tablespoons poppy seeds
1 cup (280g) yogurt

Lime icing
2 limes
1½ cups (240g) icing sugar
10g soft butter

1 Preheat oven to moderate (180°C/160°C fan-forced). Liberally grease a 21cm baba cake pan.

2 Beat butter, rind and sugar in small bowl with electric mixer until light and fluffy. Add eggs one at a time, beating after each addition until combined.

3 Transfer mixture to large bowl; stir in sifted flour, poppy seeds, then yogurt. Spoon mixture into prepared pan; smooth top.

4 Bake cake for about 55 minutes. Stand cake in pan for 5 minutes, then turn onto a wire rack set over an oven tray to cool.

5 Make lime icing; pour over cold cake just before serving.

Lime icing Remove rind from one lime with a zester (or peel rind thinly from lime, avoiding the white pith; cut rind into long, thin strips.) Squeeze limes – you will need about 2½ tablespoons juice. Sift icing sugar into a small heatproof bowl; stir in butter and enough juice to form a firm paste. Place bowl over small saucepan of simmering water, then stir until icing is a thin consistency; add lime rind.

Pineapple teacake

preparation time **20 minutes** cooking time **1 hour 5 minutes** serves **8**

450g can crushed pineapple in syrup
125g butter
1½ cups (225g) self-raising flour
½ cup (110g) caster sugar
1 egg, beaten lightly
¼ cup (60ml) honey
¼ cup (20g) desiccated coconut

1 Preheat oven to moderate (180°C/160°C fan-forced). Grease deep 20cm round cake pan; line base with baking paper.
2 Drain pineapple over a jug; reserve ⅔ cup (160ml) of the syrup.
3 Melt half the butter. Combine flour and sugar in medium bowl; stir in reserved syrup, melted butter and egg. Spread mixture into prepared pan.
4 Beat remaining butter and honey in small bowl with electric mixer until light and fluffy; stir in pineapple (mixture may curdle). Spread over cake mixture in pan; sprinkle with coconut.
5 Bake cake about 1 hour. Stand cake in pan 5 minutes; turn onto wire rack, invert onto another rack to cool.

Glacé fruit loaf

preparation time **20 minutes** cooking time **2 hours** serves **8**

⅔ cup (150g) chopped glacé ginger
¼ cup (60g) chopped glacé cherries
¼ cup (55g) chopped glacé pineapple
¼ cup (60g) chopped glacé apricots
⅓ cup (55g) mixed peel
⅓ cup (80ml) grand marnier
125g butter
½ cup (110g) caster sugar
2 eggs
1¼ cups (185g) plain flour

1 Preheat oven to slow (150°C/130°C fan-forced). Grease 8cm x 26cm bar cake pan; line base and two long sides with baking paper, extending paper 5cm above edge of pan.

2 Combine fruit and ¼ cup (60ml) of the liqueur in large bowl.

3 Beat butter and sugar in small bowl with electric mixer until light and fluffy. Add eggs one at a time, beating until just combined after each addition (mixture may curdle). Stir into fruit mixture with flour; spread cake mixture into prepared pan.

4 Bake cake about 2 hours. Brush top of cake with remaining liqueur; cover tightly with foil. Cool in pan.

Orange macaroon cake

preparation time **20 minutes** cooking time **30 minutes** serves **12**

125g butter
2 teaspoons finely grated orange rind
¾ cup (165g) caster sugar
2 egg yolks
2 cups (300g) self-raising flour
¾ cup (180ml) milk

Topping
2 egg whites
2 tablespoons caster sugar
½ teaspoon vanilla extract
½ cup (45g) desiccated coconut

1 Preheat oven to moderate (180°C/160°C fan-forced). Grease 20cm x 30cm lamington pan; line base with baking paper.

2 Beat butter, rind, sugar and egg yolks in medium bowl with electric mixer until light and fluffy; stir in flour and milk, in two batches. Spread mixture into prepared pan.

3 Make topping; spread over cake mixture.

4 Bake cake about 30 minutes. Stand cake in pan 5 minutes; turn onto wire rack; invert onto another rack to cool.

Topping Beat egg whites in small bowl with electric mixer until soft peaks form; gradually add sugar, beating until dissolved. Stir in extract and coconut.

Little blueberry oat loaves

preparation time **10 minutes** cooking time **25 minutes** serves **8**

2 cups (300g) self-raising flour
¾ cup (165g) firmly packed brown sugar
½ cup (45g) rolled oats
2 eggs, beaten lightly
½ cup (140g) yogurt
⅓ cup (80ml) orange juice
½ cup (125ml) vegetable oil
¾ cup (120g) frozen blueberries
½ cup (50g) walnuts, toasted, chopped coarsely

Crunchy topping
1 cup (90g) rolled oats
½ teaspoon ground cinnamon
2 tablespoons honey

1 Preheat oven to moderately hot (200°C/180°C fan-forced). Lightly grease an 8-hole petite loaf pan.
2 Make crunchy topping.
3 Combine sifted flour with sugar and oats in a large bowl. Stir in combined eggs, yogurt, juice and oil. Add blueberries and walnuts; stir gently until just combined. Divide mixture evenly among prepared pans. Sprinkle with crunchy topping.
4 Bake for about 25 minutes. Turn onto a wire rack to cool.

Crunchy topping Blend or process oats until chopped coarsely. Place in small bowl with cinnamon and honey; mix well.

tip This cake is suitable to freeze.

Orange marmalade cake

preparation time **15 minutes** cooking time **1 hour** serves **8**

125g butter
2 teaspoons finely grated orange rind
½ cup (110g) caster sugar
2 eggs
2 tablespoons orange marmalade
⅓ cup (55g) dried mixed peel
½ cup (45g) desiccated coconut
1½ cups (225g) self-raising flour
½ cup (125ml) milk

1 Preheat oven to moderate (180°C/160°C fan-forced). Grease 14cm x 21cm loaf pan; line base and two long sides with a strip of baking paper, extending paper 2cm above edge of pan.
2 Beat butter, rind and sugar in medium bowl with electric mixer until light and fluffy. Add eggs one at a time, beating until combined after each addition. Stir in marmalade and peel, then coconut, flour and milk, in two batches.
3 Spread cake mixture into prepared pan; bake in moderate oven about 1 hour. Stand cake in pan 5 minutes; turn onto wire rack to cool.

Moist date cake

preparation time **25 minutes** (plus standing time)
cooking time **1 hour 15 minutes** serves **10**

500g dates
1 cup (250ml) water
½ teaspoon bicarbonate of soda
185g butter
⅔ cup (150g) caster sugar
3 eggs
1½ (225g) cups self-raising flour
¼ cup (35g) plain flour

1 Combine the dates, water and soda in a medium bowl; cover, then allow to stand overnight.
2 Preheat oven to moderate (180°C/160°C fan-forced). Grease a deep 19cm square cake pan, line base and side with paper; grease paper well.

3 Beat butter and sugar in small bowl with electric mixer until light and fluffy. Add eggs one at a time, beating until well combined after each addition. Transfer mixture to large bowl, stir in sifted flours and undrained date mixture in two batches. Spread mixture into prepared pan.

4 Bake cake for about 1 ¼ hours. Stand cake in pan for 5 minutes before turning onto wire rack to cool.

Date and nut cakes

preparation time **25 minutes**   cooking time **1 hour 15 minutes**   serves **12**

⅔ **cup (110g) seeded dates, halved**
½ **cup (95g) dried figs, quartered**
⅓ **cup (55g) mixed peel**
½ **cup (105g) red glacé cherries, halved**
½ **cup (105g) green glacé cherries, halved**
½ **cup (85g) raisins**
⅓ **cup (75g) glacé ginger, chopped**
1 ½ **cups (240g) blanched almonds**
1 ½ **cups (150g) pecans**
1 ¼ **cups (155g) almond meal**
½ **teaspoon baking powder**
4 eggs
¼ **cup (60ml) honey**
2 tablespoons dark rum

1 Preheat oven to slow (150°C/130°C fan-forced). Grease two 8cm x 26cm bar cake pans; line base and sides with three layers of baking paper, extending paper 5cm above edges.

2 Place fruit, ginger and whole nuts in large bowl; stir in almond meal and baking powder.

3 Beat eggs in small bowl with electric mixer until thick and creamy; beat in honey. Stir egg mixture into fruit mixture; spread cake mixture into prepared pans. Using slightly wet hands, press mixture firmly into pans.

4 Bake cakes for about 1 ¼ hours. Brush hot cakes with rum; cover tightly with foil. Cool in pans.

tip These cakes will slice easily if refrigerated for several hours.

Fruit chews

preparation time **15 minutes** cooking time **45 minutes** makes **about 18**

⅓ cup (75g) firmly packed brown sugar
90g butter
1¼ cups (185g) plain flour
1 egg yolk

Topping
2 eggs
1 cup (220g) firmly packed brown sugar
⅓ cup (50g) self-raising flour
½ cup (85g) raisins
¾ cup (120g) sultanas
1¼ cups (185g) roasted unsalted peanuts
1 cup (90g) desiccated coconut

1 Preheat oven to moderate (180°C/160°C fan-forced). Grease 20cm x 30cm lamington pan; line base and two long sides with baking paper, extending paper 2cm above edge.
2 Combine sugar and butter in medium saucepan; stir over medium heat until butter is melted. Stir in sifted flour and egg yolk. Press mixture over base of prepared pan. Bake about 10 minutes or until browned lightly; cool.
3 Meanwhile, make topping.
4 Spread topping over cold cake base; bake a further 30 minutes or until browned lightly. Cool cake in pan before cutting into pieces.

Topping Beat eggs and sugar in small bowl with electric mixer until changed to a lighter colour and thickened slightly; fold in sifted flour. Transfer mixture to large bowl; stir in remaining ingredients.

tip This recipe can be made a week ahead; store in an airtight container.

Quince and blackberry crumble cake

Preparation time **30 minutes** cooking time **2 hours 15 minutes** (plus cooling time) serves **16**

185g unsalted butter, softened
¾ cup (165g) caster sugar
2 eggs
2¼ cups (335g) self-raising flour
¾ cup (180ml) milk
2 cups (300g) frozen blackberries
2 teaspoons cornflour

Poached quince
3 cups (750ml) water
¾ cup (165g) caster sugar
1 cinnamon stick
1 tablespoon lemon juice
3 medium quinces (1kg), each cut into 8 wedges

Cinnamon crumble
¾ cup (110g) plain flour
2 tablespoons caster sugar
½ cup (110g) firmly packed brown sugar
100g cold unsalted butter, chopped
1 teaspoon ground cinnamon

1 Make poached quince.
2 Preheat oven to moderate (180°C/160°C fan-forced). Grease a deep 23cm square cake pan; line base and sides with baking paper.
3 Beat butter and sugar in small bowl with electric mixer until light and fluffy. Add eggs one at a time, beating until just combined after each addition; transfer to a large bowl. Stir in sifted flour and milk, in two batches.
4 Spread mixture into pan; bake for about 25 minutes.
5 Meanwhile, make cinnamon crumble.
6 Remove cake from oven. Working quickly, toss frozen blackberries in cornflour to coat. Top cake with drained quince then blackberries; sprinkle with cinnamon crumble. Bake for another 20 minutes. Stand cake in pan for 5 minutes; turn, top-side up, onto baking paper-lined wire rack.
7 Serve cake warm or cold with reserved quince syrup.

Poached quince Stir the water, sugar, cinnamon stick and juice in medium saucepan over low heat until sugar dissolves. Add quince. Bring to a boil, then reduce heat; simmer, covered, about 1 ½ hours or until quince is tender and rosy in colour. Cool quince in syrup to room temperature; strain quince over medium bowl. Reserve syrup.

Cinnamon crumble Blend or process ingredients, pulsing until ingredients just come together.

Mandarin, polenta and macadamia cake

Preparation time **20 minutes** (plus cooling time) cooking time **2 hours** (plus standing time) serves **12**

4 small mandarins (400g), unpeeled
2 cups (280g) toasted macadamias
250g butter, softened
1 teaspoon vanilla extract
1 cup (220g) caster sugar
3 eggs
1 cup (170g) polenta
1 teaspoon baking powder
1 tablespoon icing sugar

1 Cover whole mandarins in medium saucepan with cold water; bring to a boil. Drain then repeat process two more times. Cool to room temperature.
2 Preheat oven to moderately slow (170°C/150°C fan-forced). Grease deep 22cm round cake pan; line base with baking paper.
3 Blend or process nuts until mixture forms a coarse meal. Halve mandarins; discard seeds. Blend or process mandarins until pulpy.
4 Beat butter, extract and sugar in small bowl with electric mixer until light and fluffy. Add eggs, one at a time, beating until just combined after each addition; transfer to large bowl. Stir in polenta, baking powder, macadamia meal and mandarin pulp. Pour mixture into prepared pan.
5 Bake cake for about 1 hour. Stand cake in pan for 15 minutes; turn, top-side up, onto wire rack to cool. Serve cake dusted with sifted icing sugar.

Date squares

preparation time **30 minutes** (plus refrigeration time)
cooking time **35 minutes** makes **about 16**

1 ¼ cups (185g) plain flour
1 ¼ cups (200g) wholemeal plain flour
200g butter, chopped
½ cup (110g) caster sugar
1 egg, beaten lightly
1 tablespoon water, approximately
1 tablespoon milk
1 tablespoon raw sugar
2 teaspoons caster sugar, extra

Apple date filling
1 medium apple (150g), peeled, sliced finely
1 ½ cups (225g) seeded dried dates, chopped coarsely
½ cup (125ml) water

1 Preheat oven to moderately hot (200°C/180°C fan-forced). Grease a 25cm x 30cm swiss roll pan; line base and two long sides with baking paper, extending paper 2cm above edge.
2 Sift flours into large bowl; rub in butter, stir in caster sugar. Add egg and enough water to mix to a firm dough. Knead on floured surface until smooth, cover; refrigerate for 30 minutes.
3 Meanwhile, make apple date filling.
4 Roll out half the dough until large enough to cover base of prepared pan; spread with cold apple date filling. Roll out remaining dough until large enough to cover filling; brush with milk, then sprinkle with raw sugar.
5 Bake for about 25 minutes; cool in pan before cutting. Sprinkle with extra caster sugar.

Apple date filling Combine ingredients in small saucepan; simmer, covered, for about 5 minutes or until mixture is pulpy. Blend or process until smooth; cool.

tip This recipe can be made a week ahead; store in an airtight container.

Siena cake

preparation time **30 minutes** cooking time **1 hour** (plus cooling time)
serves **8**

¾ cup (120g) blanched almonds, toasted, chopped coarsely
1 cup (125g) coarsely chopped roasted hazelnuts
¼ cup (60g) finely chopped glacé apricots
¼ cup (55g) finely chopped glacé pineapple
⅓ cup (55g) mixed peel, chopped finely
⅔ cup (100g) plain flour
2 tablespoons cocoa powder
1 teaspoon ground cinnamon
⅓ cup (75g) caster sugar
½ cup (175g) honey
60g dark chocolate, melted

1 Preheat oven to moderately slow (170°C/150°C fan-forced). Lightly grease
a 20cm round sandwich pan; line base and side with baking paper.
2 Combine nuts, apricots, pineapple, peel, flour, cocoa and cinnamon in large
bowl; mix well.
3 Place sugar and honey in medium saucepan; stir over low heat until sugar
dissolves, brushing down side of pan to dissolve any sugar crystals. Bring to
a boil, then reduce heat; simmer, uncovered, about 5 minutes or until syrup
forms a soft ball when a few drops are dropped into a glass of cold water.
4 Add syrup and chocolate to fruit and nut mixture; mix well. Spread mixture
quickly and evenly into prepared pan.
5 Bake cake for 35 minutes; cool in pan. Turn out; remove paper. Wrap cake
in foil. Leave at least one day before cutting.

tips This recipe can be made three weeks ahead and wrapped tightly in foil.
Siena cake is a perfect accompaniment to after-dinner coffee. Cut into thin
wedges or slices about 1cm thick, then into small pieces.

SYRUP CAKES

Mocha syrup cake

preparation time **25 minutes** cooking time **50 minutes** serves **8**

3 teaspoons instant coffee granules
1 tablespoon hot water
3 eggs
¾ cup (165g) caster sugar
1 cup (150g) self-raising flour
1 tablespoon cocoa powder
150g butter, melted

Coffee syrup
¾ cup (165g) caster sugar
¾ cup (180ml) water
3 teaspoons instant coffee granules

1 Preheat oven to moderate (180°C/160°C fan-forced). Grease a 21cm baba cake pan.
2 Combine coffee and the water; stir until dissolved.
3 Beat eggs in small bowl with electric mixer about 8 minutes or until thick and creamy. Gradually add sugar; beat until dissolved between each addition.
4 Transfer to large bowl, fold in sifted flour and cocoa powder, then butter and coffee mixture. Pour mixture into prepared pan.
5 Bake cake about 40 minutes. Stand cake in pan 5 minutes, before turning onto baking paper-covered wire rack; stand wire rack over a tray.
6 Make coffee syrup; reserve ¼ cup of the hot syrup. Pour remaining syrup over hot cake. Serve drizzled with reserved syrup.

Coffee syrup Combine ingredients in small saucepan; stir over heat, without boiling, until sugar is dissolved. Bring to a boil, then remove from heat; transfer syrup to heatproof jug.

Mixed berry cake with vanilla bean syrup

preparation time **20 minutes** cooking time **50 minutes** serves **8**

125g butter, softened
1 cup (220g) caster sugar
3 eggs
½ cup (75g) plain flour
¼ cup (35g) self-raising flour
½ cup (60g) almond meal
⅓ cup (80g) sour cream
1½ cups (225g) frozen mixed berries
½ cup (100g) drained canned seeded black cherries

Vanilla bean syrup
½ cup (125ml) water
½ cup (110g) caster sugar
2 vanilla beans

1 Preheat oven to moderate (180°C/160°C fan-forced). Grease a 21cm baba cake pan well.

2 Beat butter and sugar in small bowl with electric mixer until light and fluffy. Add eggs one at a time, beating until just combined after each addition (mixture may curdle at this stage, but will come together later).

3 Transfer mixture to large bowl; stir in sifted flours, almond meal, sour cream, berries and cherries. Pour mixture into prepared pan.

4 Bake about 40 minutes. Stand cake in pan 5 minutes before turning onto wire rack placed over a large tray.

5 Make vanilla bean syrup; pour hot syrup over hot cake.

Vanilla bean syrup Combine the water and sugar in small saucepan. Split vanilla beans in half lengthways; scrape seeds into pan then add pods. Stir over heat, without boiling, until sugar dissolves. Simmer, uncovered, without stirring, for 5 minutes. Using tongs, remove pods from syrup.

Orange poppy seed syrup cake

preparation time **25 minutes** (plus standing time) cooking time **1 hour**
serves **16**

⅓ cup (50g) poppy seeds
¼ cup (60ml) milk
185g butter, softened
1 tablespoon finely grated orange rind
1 cup (220g) caster sugar
3 eggs
1½ cups (225g) self-raising flour
½ cup (75g) plain flour
½ cup (60g) almond meal
½ cup (125ml) orange juice

Orange syrup
1 cup (220g) caster sugar
⅔ cup (160ml) orange juice
⅓ cup (80ml) water

1 Preheat oven to moderate (180°C/160°C fan-forced). Grease a deep
22cm round cake pan; line base and side with baking paper.
2 Combine seeds and milk in a small bowl; let stand for 20 minutes.
3 Meanwhile, beat butter, rind and sugar in a small bowl with electric mixer
until light and fluffy. Add eggs one at a time, beating until just combined after
each addition. Transfer mixture to large bowl; using a wooden spoon, stir in
flours, almond meal, juice and poppy-seed mixture.
4 Spread mixture into prepared pan; bake for about 1 hour. Stand cake in
pan for 5 minutes before turning onto a wire rack over oven tray.
5 Make orange syrup.
6 Turn cake top-side up; pour hot syrup over hot cake. Return any syrup that
drips onto tray to jug; pour over cake.

Orange syrup Using a wooden spoon, stir combined ingredients in a small
saucepan over heat, without boiling, until sugar dissolves. Bring to a boil,
reduce heat; simmer, uncovered, without stirring, for 2 minutes. Pour syrup
into a heatproof jug.

tips This cake, with or without syrup, can be kept in an airtight container for
up to two days. Without syrup, it can be frozen for up to three months.

Banana butterscotch syrup cake

preparation time **30 minutes** cooking time **1 hour 10 minutes** serves **9**

You will need 2 large overripe bananas (460g) for this recipe.

125g butter
¾ cup (165g) caster sugar
2 eggs
1 cup mashed banana
¾ cup (110g) self-raising flour
¾ cup (110g) plain flour
½ teaspoon bicarbonate of soda
¾ cup (110g) hazelnuts, toasted, chopped finely

Butterscotch syrup
½ cup (100g) firmly packed brown sugar
30g butter
¾ cup (180ml) water

1 Preheat oven to moderate (180°C/160°C fan-forced). Grease a deep 19cm square cake pan; line base with baking paper.
2 Beat butter and sugar in medium bowl with electric mixer until light and fluffy. Add eggs one at a time, beating until combined after each addition. Stir in banana, then combined sifted flours and soda, and nuts.
3 Spread mixture into prepared pan; bake for about 1 hour. Stand cake in pan for 5 minutes; turn onto wire rack over tray.
4 Make butterscotch syrup; slowly drizzle hot syrup over hot cake.

Butterscotch syrup Combine sugar and butter in small saucepan; stir over heat until butter melts. Add the water and bring to a boil, stirring; transfer to a heatproof jug.

Lime coconut syrup cake

preparation time **30 minutes** cooking time **55 minutes** serves **10**

125g butter
1 tablespoon finely grated lime rind
1 cup (220g) caster sugar
3 eggs
1¾ cups (260g) self-raising flour
1 cup (90g) desiccated coconut
½ cup (125ml) yogurt
½ cup (125ml) milk

Tangy lime syrup
⅓ cup (80ml) lime juice
¾ cup (165g) caster sugar
¼ cup (60ml) water

1 Preheat oven to moderate (180°C/160°C fan-forced). Grease a 21cm baba pan.
2 Beat butter, rind and sugar in medium bowl with electric mixer until light and fluffy. Add eggs one at a time, beating until just combined after each addition (mixture may curdle at this point). Stir in remaining ingredients, in two batches; spread mixture into prepared pan.
3 Bake cake for about 45 minutes. Stand cake in pan for 5 minutes; turn onto a wire rack over oven tray.
4 Make tangy lime syrup; drizzle hot syrup over hot cake.

Tangy lime syrup Combine ingredients in small saucepan; stir over heat, without boiling, until sugar dissolves. Simmer, uncovered, without stirring, for 3 minutes; transfer to a heatproof jug.

Espresso syrup cake

preparation time **25 minutes** cooking time **55 minutes** serves **10**

3 teaspoons instant espresso coffee granules
1 tablespoon hot water
3 eggs
¾ cup (165g) caster sugar
1 cup (150g) self-raising flour
1 tablespoon cocoa powder
150g butter, melted

Espresso syrup
¾ cup (165g) caster sugar
¾ cup (180ml) water
3 teaspoons instant espresso coffee granules

1 Preheat oven to moderate (180°C/160°C fan-forced). Grease a 21cm baba pan.
2 Combine coffee and water in small jug; stir until dissolved.
3 Beat eggs in small bowl with electric mixer about 8 minutes or until thick and creamy. Gradually add sugar, beating until dissolved between additions. Fold in sifted flour and cocoa, then butter and coffee mixture; pour mixture into prepared pan.
4 Bake cake for about 40 minutes. Stand cake in pan for 5 minutes; turn onto wire rack over oven tray.
5 Make espresso syrup; reserve ¼ cup (60ml) espresso syrup. Drizzle remaining hot syrup over hot cake. Serve with reserved syrup.

Espresso syrup Combine ingredients in small saucepan; stir over heat, without boiling, until sugar dissolves. Bring to a boil, then transfer to a heatproof jug.

Orange syrup cake

preparation time **25 minutes** cooking time **1 hour 10 minutes** serves **12**

1 large orange (300g)
2 cups (500ml) water
2 cups (440g) caster sugar
²/₃ cup (160ml) brandy
250g unsalted butter, softened
1 cup (220g) caster sugar, extra
4 eggs
1½ cups (225g) self-raising flour
2 tablespoons cornflour

1 Preheat oven to moderately slow (170°C/150°C fan-forced). Grease a deep 22cm round cake pan; line base and side with baking paper.
2 Peel orange. Finely chop rind and flesh; discard seeds.
3 Stir flesh and rind in medium saucepan with the water, sugar and brandy over medium heat until sugar dissolves. Bring to a boil, then reduce heat; simmer, uncovered, for about 15 minutes or until rind is tender. Strain syrup into jug; reserve orange solids separately.
4 Beat butter and extra sugar in small bowl with electric mixer until light and fluffy. Add eggs one at a time, beating until just combined after each addition. Transfer mixture to large bowl.
5 Stir in combined sifted flour and cornflour, and the reserved orange solids. Pour mixture into prepared pan; bake, uncovered, for about 50 minutes. Stand cake in pan for 5 minutes, then turn, top-side up, onto wire rack set over tray.
6 Meanwhile, simmer reserved syrup over heat in small saucepan until thickened slightly. Pour hot syrup over hot cake; serve warm.

Blueberry cake with orange syrup

preparation time **25 minutes** cooking time **1 hour 10 minutes** serves **10**

125g butter
½ cup (100g) caster sugar
2 eggs
1¾ cups (260g) self-raising flour
½ cup (125ml) yogurt
¼ cup (60ml) orange juice
1 cup (150g) frozen blueberries
1 tablespoon finely grated orange rind

Orange syrup
¾ cup (165g) caster sugar
½ cup (125ml) orange juice
¼ cup (60ml) water
1 tablespoon grated orange rind

1 Preheat oven to moderate (180°C/160°C fan-forced). Grease a deep 20cm round cake pan; line base and side with baking paper.
2 Beat butter and sugar in medium bowl with electric mixer until light and fluffy. Add eggs one at a time, beating until just combined after each addition. Stir in flour and combined yogurt and juice, in two batches. Add frozen blueberries and rind; mix until just combined.
3 Spread mixture into prepared pan; bake for about 1 hour. Stand cake in pan for 5 minutes; turn onto wire rack set over oven tray.
4 Make orange syrup; drizzle hot syrup over hot cake.

Orange syrup Combine sugar, juice and water in small saucepan; stir over heat, without boiling, until sugar dissolves. Stir in rind; simmer, uncovered, without stirring, for 5 minutes. Transfer to a heatproof jug.

Yogurt and lemon syrup cake

preparation time **25 minutes** baking time **50 minutes** serves **12**

250g butter, softened
1 tablespoon finely grated lemon rind
1 cup (220g) caster sugar
3 eggs
½ cup (45g) desiccated coconut
¼ cup (30g) almond meal
2 tablespoons lemon juice
2½ cups (375g) self-raising flour
¾ cup (200g) yogurt
1 medium lemon (140g)
½ cup (125ml) water
¼ cup (90g) honey
4 cardamom pods, bruised

1 Preheat oven to moderate (180°C/160°C fan-forced). Grease a 20cm baba pan.

2 Beat butter, rind and sugar in small bowl with electric mixer until light and fluffy. Add eggs one at a time, beating well after each addition.

3 Transfer mixture to a large bowl; using a wooden spoon, stir in coconut, almond meal and juice, then flour and yogurt. Spoon mixture into prepared pan; spread evenly with plastic spatula.

4 Bake cake for about 50 minutes. Stand cake for 5 minutes then turn onto a wire rack set over an oven tray.

5 Meanwhile, using a vegetable peeler, remove rind from lemon; slice rind finely. Squeeze juice from lemon – you will need ¼ cup (60ml) juice.

6 Combine rind, juice, the water, honey and cardamom in a small saucepan; stir over heat, without boiling, until honey melts. Bring to a boil, reduce heat; simmer, uncovered, for 5 minutes. Using a slotted spoon, carefully remove and discard cardamom pods.

7 Pour hot syrup over hot cake.

tip This cake will keep for up to four days in an airtight container in the refrigerator.

Pumpkin citrus syrup cake

preparation time **25 minutes** cooking time **1 hour 10 minutes** serves **16**

You will need to cook 350g pumpkin for this recipe.

250g butter
2 tablespoons finely grated orange rind
2 tablespoons finely grated lemon rind
1 cup (220g) caster sugar
3 eggs, separated
2 cups (300g) self-raising flour
1 cup mashed pumpkin

Citrus syrup
2 tablespoons lemon juice
2 tablespoons orange juice
¾ cup (165g) sugar

1 Preheat oven to moderate (180°C/160°C fan-forced). Grease a deep 23cm round cake pan; line base with baking paper.
2 Beat butter, rinds and sugar in a small bowl with electric mixer until light and fluffy. Add egg yolks; beat until combined. Transfer to a larger bowl. Stir in half the sifted flour with half the cold pumpkin, then stir in remaining flour and pumpkin.
3 Beat egg whites in a small bowl with electric mixer until soft peaks form; fold through cake mixture. Spread mixture in prepared pan; bake for 1 hour.
4 Meanwhile, make citrus syrup.
5 Pour hot syrup over hot cake. Let stand for 10 minutes before turning onto a wire rack to cool.

Citrus syrup Combine ingredients in a saucepan; stir constantly over heat, without boiling, until sugar is dissolved. Bring to a boil, then reduce heat; simmer, without stirring, for 2 minutes.

tip This cake can be stored in an airtight container for up to four days.

Lime syrup buttermilk cake

preparation time **25 minutes** cooking time **1 hour 10 minutes** serves **8**

250g butter
1 tablespoon finely grated lime rind
1 cup (220g) caster sugar
3 eggs, separated
2 cups (300g) self-raising flour
1 cup (250ml) buttermilk

Lime syrup
⅓ cup (80ml) lime juice
¾ cup (165g) sugar
¼ cup (60ml) water

1 Preheat oven to moderate (180°C/160°C fan-forced). Grease and lightly flour a 20cm baba pan; shake out excess flour.
2 Beat butter, rind and sugar in small bowl with electric mixer until light and fluffy. Add egg yolks one at a time, beating until combined after each addition. Transfer mixture to large bowl. Stir in sifted flour and buttermilk in two batches.
3 Beat egg whites in small bowl with electric mixer until soft peaks form; fold lightly into mixture in two batches.
4 Spread mixture into prepared pan; bake for about 1 hour. Stand cake in pan for 5 minutes before turning onto a wire rack on an oven tray.
5 Make lime suryp; pour hot syrup evenly over hot cake.

Lime syrup Combine ingredients in saucepan; stir over heat until sugar is dissolved. Bring to a boil; remove from heat.

tip The buttermilk can be replaced with skim milk in this recipe, if desired.

Cinnamon and walnut syrup cake

preparation time **20 minutes** cooking time **40 minutes** serves **12**

3 eggs
¾ cup (165g) caster sugar
¾ cup (110g) self-raising flour
3 teaspoons ground cinnamon
185g butter, melted
¾ cup (120g) chopped walnuts

Sugar syrup
1 cup (220) caster sugar
¾ cup (180ml) water

1 Preheat oven to moderate (180°C/160°C fan-forced). Grease a 23cm square slab pan.

2 Beat eggs in small bowl with electric mixer until thick and creamy. Gradually add sugar; beat until dissolved between each addition. Beat in sifted flour and cinnamon in several batches; beat in butter and stir in walnuts.

3 Pour mixture into prepared pan; bake for about 30 minutes. Stand cake in pan for 5 minutes before turning onto wire rack on an oven tray; leave cake upside down.

4 Make sugar syrup; pour hot syrup over hot cake. Serve cake warm or cold.

Sugar syrup Combine ingredients in saucepan; stir constantly over heat without boiling until sugar is dissolved. Bring to a boil, then reduce heat; simmer, uncovered, for 5 minutes.

tip This cake can be stored in an airtight container for up to three days.

Currant cakes with orange glaze

preparation time **20 minutes** (plus standing time) cooking time **20 minutes**
makes **24**

¼ **cup (55g) caster sugar**
¼ **cup (35g) dried currants**
2 teaspoons finely grated orange rind
½ **cup (125ml) orange juice**
125g butter
2 teaspoons finely grated orange rind, extra
½ **cup (110g) caster sugar, extra**
2 eggs
1½ **cups (225g) self-raising flour**
⅓ **cup (80ml) milk**

1 Combine sugar, currants, rind and juice in small saucepan; stir over heat, without boiling, until sugar dissolves. Bring to a boil, then reduce heat; simmer, uncovered, without stirring, for 2 minutes. Remove from heat; let stand for 30 minutes. Strain mixture into a jug; reserve currants and syrup.
2 Preheat oven to moderate (180°C/160°C fan-forced). Grease two deep 12-hole patty pans.
3 Beat butter, extra rind and extra sugar in medium bowl with electric mixer until light and fluffy. Add eggs one at a time, beating until just combined after each addition. Stir in reserved fruit, then flour and milk, in two batches.
4 Divide mixture among holes of prepared pans; bake for about 15 minutes. Turn cakes onto a wire rack on an oven tray; brush the tops of hot cakes with reserved syrup.

Almond orange halva cake

Preparation time **25 minutes** cooking time **50 minutes** serves **10**

125g butter
2 teaspoons finely grated orange rind
½ cup (110g) caster sugar
2 eggs
1 teaspoon baking powder
1 cup (160g) semolina
1 cup (125g) almond meal
¼ cup (60ml) orange juice

Orange and brandy syrup
1 cup (250ml) orange juice
½ cup (110g) caster sugar
1 tablespoon brandy

1 Preheat oven to moderate (180°C/160°C fan-forced). Grease a deep 20cm round cake pan.
2 Cream butter, rind and sugar in small bowl with electric mixer until light and fluffy. Add eggs one at a time, beating until combined after each addition. Transfer mixture to large bowl. Stir in the dry ingredients and orange juice in two batches.
3 Pour mixture into prepared pan; bake for about 40 minutes. Turn cake onto a wire rack on an oven tray.
4 Make orange and brandy syrup; brush half the hot syrup over hot cake. Bake (on wire rack) for a further 5 minutes. Remove from oven and brush with remaining hot syrup. Serve warm or cold.

Orange and brandy syrup Combine orange juice and sugar in a saucepan; stir constantly over heat without boiling until sugar is dissolved. Bring to a boil, then reduce heat; simmer, uncovered, without stirring for 5 minutes; stir in brandy.

tip This cake can be stored in an airtight container for up to three days.

Brandied walnut cake with lemon syrup

preparation time **20 minutes** cooking time **1 hour 5 minutes** serves **12**

2 cups (200g) toasted walnuts
125g butter, softened
3 teaspoons finely grated lemon rind
⅔ cup (150g) caster sugar
1 egg
2 tablespoons brandy
⅓ cup (50g) plain flour
⅓ cup (50g) self-raising flour

Lemon syrup
¼ cup (60ml) lemon juice
¼ cup (55g) caster sugar

1 Preheat oven to moderately slow (170°C/150°C fan-forced). Grease a deep 20cm-round cake pan; line base with baking paper.
2 Blend or process nuts until finely ground.
3 Beat butter, rind, sugar and egg in small bowl with electric mixer until light and fluffy. Transfer mixture to large bowl; using a wooden spoon, stir in brandy, nuts and flours.
4 Spread mixture into prepared pan; bake cake for about 1 hour.
5 Make lemon syrup; pour hot syrup over hot cake in pan. Cover pan tightly with foil; cool to room temperature.

Lemon syrup Combine ingredients in small saucepan; stir over heat, without boiling, until sugar dissolves. Bring to a boil, then remove from heat.

tips This cake can be kept in an airtight container for up to two days. Without the syrup, the cake can also be kept in an airtight container for up to two days, and frozen for up to three months.

Caramel cake with whole-spice syrup

preparation time **25 minutes** cooking time **1 hour 10 minutes** serves **10**

185g butter
¾ cup (150g) firmly packed brown sugar
⅓ cup (80ml) golden syrup
2 eggs
⅓ cup (40g) almond meal
½ cup (125ml) milk
2 cups (300g) self-raising flour
1 teaspoon ground cinnamon
1 teaspoon ground nutmeg
1 teaspoon ground ginger

Whole-spice syrup
1 medium (140g) lemon
¾ cup (165g) caster sugar
¼ cup (60ml) water
4 cardamom pods, crushed
1 cinnamon stick
1 vanilla bean, split

1 Preheat oven to moderate (180°C/160°C fan-forced). Grease a 21cm baba pan.
2 Beat ingredients in medium bowl with electric mixer on low speed until combined. Beat on medium speed for 5 minutes or until mixture is pale and thick.
3 Spread mixture into prepared pan; bake for about 1 hour. Stand cake in pan for 5 minutes; turn onto a wire rack on an oven tray.
4 Make whole-spice syrup; drizzle hot syrup over hot cake, discarding whole spices. Serve cake warm or cold.

Whole-spice syrup Using a vegetable peeler, remove thin slices of lemon rind; cut slices into 1cm strips. Squeeze lemon and reserve ⅓ cup (80ml) juice. Combine rind and juice with remaining ingredients in medium saucepan; stir over heat, without boiling, until sugar dissolves. Simmer, uncovered, without stirring, for 3 minutes; transfer to a heatproof jug.

Blueberry cake with vanilla syrup

preparation time **25 minutes** cooking time **55 minutes** serves **8**

125g butter
½ cup (110g) caster sugar
2 eggs
1¾ cups (260g) self-raising flour
½ cup (125ml) buttermilk
¾ cup (110g) frozen blueberries

Vanilla syrup
½ cup (110g) caster sugar
½ cup (125ml) water
2 teaspoons vanilla extract

1 Preheat oven to moderate (180°C/160°C fan-forced). Grease a deep 20cm ring cake pan; line base and side with baking paper.
2 Beat butter and sugar in medium bowl with electric mixer until light and fluffy. Add eggs one at a time, beating until just combined after each addition. Stir in flour and milk, in two batches.
3 Spread cake mixture into prepared pan; sprinkle with frozen berries, gently pressing them into mixture. Bake for about 45 minutes. Stand cake in pan for 5 minutes; turn onto a wire rack set over an oven tray.
4 Make vanilla syrup; drizzle hot syrup over hot cake.

Vanilla syrup Combine sugar and water in small saucepan; stir over heat, without boiling, until sugar dissolves. Simmer, uncovered, without stirring, for 2 minutes. Stir in extract; transfer to a heatproof jug.

Passionfruit and lemon syrup cake

preparation time **30 minutes** cooking time **1 hour 10 minutes** serves **10**

You will need seven passionfruit for this recipe.

²/₃ cup (160ml) passionfruit pulp
250g butter, chopped
1 tablespoon finely grated lemon rind
1 cup (220g) caster sugar
3 eggs
1 cup (250ml) buttermilk
2 cups (300g) self-raising flour

Lemon syrup
¹/₃ cup (80ml) lemon juice
¹/₄ cup (60ml) water
³/₄ cup (165g) caster sugar

1 Preheat oven to moderate (180°C/160°C fan-forced). Grease a 21cm baba pan.
2 Strain passionfruit over medium jug; reserve both juice and seeds.
3 Beat butter, rind and sugar in small bowl with electric mixer until light and fluffy. Add eggs one at a time, beating until just combined after each addition. Transfer to a large bowl; fold in combined passionfruit juice and buttermilk, then sifted flour, in two batches.
4 Spread mixture into prepared pan; bake about 1 hour. Stand cake in pan for 5 minutes; turn onto a wire rack set over an oven tray.
5 Make lemon syrup; pour hot syrup over hot cake. Serve warm.

Lemon syrup Combine juice, the water, sugar and half of the reserved passionfruit seeds in small saucepan; stir over heat, without boiling, until sugar dissolves. Simmer, uncovered, without stirring, for 5 minutes.

Pistachio butter cake with orange honey syrup

preparation time **30 minutes** cooking **50 minutes** serves **16**

2 cups (280g) shelled pistachios, chopped coarsely
185g butter, softened
1 tablespoon finely grated orange rind
¾ cup (165g) caster sugar
3 eggs
¼ cup (60ml) buttermilk
1½ cups (225g) self-raising flour
¾ cup (110g) plain flour

Orange honey syrup
1 cup (220g) caster sugar
1 cup (250ml) water
1 tablespoon honey
1 cinnamon stick
1 teaspoon cardamom seeds
3 strips orange rind

1 Make orange honey syrup; reserve ⅓ cup of the syrup.
2 Preheat oven to moderate (180°C/160°C fan-forced). Grease a 23cm square slab cake pan; line base and sides with baking paper, extending paper 2cm above the sides. Sprinkle nuts evenly over base of pan.
3 Beat butter, rind and sugar in small bowl with electric mixer until light and fluffy. Add eggs one at a time, beating until just combined after each addition; transfer mixture to large bowl. Stir in combined buttermilk and reserved orange honey syrup, then sifted flours, in two batches.
4 Spread mixture into pan; bake about 40 minutes. Stand cake in pan for 5 minutes; turn, top-side up, onto a baking paper-covered wire rack. Brush surface of hot cake with half of the remaining heated syrup.
5 Cut cake into squares, serve warm, drizzled with remaining heated syrup.

Orange honey syrup Stir ingredients in a small saucepan over low heat, without boiling, until sugar dissolves; bring to a boil. Remove from heat; cool for 15 minutes, then strain.

Lime and poppy seed syrup cake

preparation time **25 minutes** cooking time **1 hour 10 minutes** serves **16**

¼ cup (40g) poppy seeds
½ cup (125ml) milk
250g butter, softened
1 tablespoon finely grated lime rind
1¼ cups (275g) caster sugar
4 eggs
2¼ cups (335g) self-raising flour
¾ cup (110g) plain flour
1 cup (240g) sour cream

Lime syrup
½ cup (125ml) lime juice
1 cup (250ml) water
1 cup (220g) caster sugar

1 Preheat oven to moderate (180°C/160°C fan-forced). Grease a deep 23cm square cake pan.

2 Combine poppy seeds and milk in small jug; soak 10 minutes.

3 Beat butter, rind and sugar together in small bowl with electric mixer until light and fluffy. Add eggs one at a time, beating until just combined after each addition; transfer mixture to large bowl. Stir in sifted flours, sour cream and poppy seed mixture, in two batches.

4 Pour mixture into prepared pan; bake for about 1 hour. Stand cake in pan for 5 minutes, then turn onto wire rack set over an oven tray.

5 Make lime syrup; pour hot syrup over hot cake.

Lime syrup Stir ingredients in small saucepan, over heat, without boiling, until sugar dissolves. Simmer, uncovered, without stirring, for 5 minutes.

Almond honey spice cake

preparation time **20 minutes** (plus refrigeration time)
cooking time **40 minutes** serves **12**

125g butter, softened
⅓ cup (75g) caster sugar
2 tablespoons honey
1 teaspoon ground ginger
1 teaspoon ground allspice
2 eggs
1½ cups (180g) almond meal
½ cup (80g) semolina
1 teaspoon baking powder
¼ cup (60ml) milk

Spiced syrup
1 cup (220g) caster sugar
1 cup (250ml) water
8 cardamom pods, bruised
2 cinnamon sticks

1 Preheat oven to moderate (180°C/160°C fan-forced). Grease a deep 20cm round cake pan; line base with baking paper.
2 Beat butter, sugar, honey and spices in small bowl with electric mixer until light and fluffy. Add eggs one at a time, beating until just combined after each addition; transfer mixture to a medium bowl. Fold in almond meal, semolina, baking powder and milk, in two batches.
3 Spread mixture into prepared pan; bake for about 40 minutes. Stand cake in pan for 5 minutes.
4 Meanwhile, make spiced syrup. Pour strained hot syrup over hot cake in pan (reserve cardamom pods and cinnamon stick to use as decoration, if desired); cool cake in pan to room temperature. Turn cake, in pan, upside-down onto oven tray; refrigerate for 3 hours, or overnight. Remove cake from pan; serve at room temperature.

Spiced syrup Stir ingredients in small saucepan over heat, without boiling, until sugar dissolves, bring to a boil; boil, uncovered, without stirring, for about 5 minutes, or until thickened slightly.

Coffee mudcake with chilli plum syrup

preparation time **25 minutes** cooking time **1 hour 35 minutes** (plus cooling time) serves **12**

250g butter, chopped
200g dark eating chocolate, chopped coarsely
2 cups (440g) caster sugar
1 cup (250ml) milk
2 teaspoons vanilla extract
2 teaspoons instant coffee granules
¼ cup (60ml) boiling water
1½ cups (225g) plain flour
¼ cup (35g) self-raising flour
¼ cup (25g) cocoa powder
2 eggs, beaten lightly

Chilli plums
3 cups (750ml) water
1 cup (220g) caster sugar
1 fresh red thai chilli, halved lengthways
10cm piece orange rind
8 blood plums (800g)

1 Preheat oven to moderately slow (170°C/150°C fan-forced). Grease a deep 22cm-round cake pan; line base with baking paper.
2 Combine butter, chocolate, sugar, milk, extract and combined coffee and the water in medium saucepan; stir over low heat until smooth. Transfer to large bowl; cool 15 minutes. Whisk in combined sifted flours and cocoa, then eggs. Spread mixture into prepared pan.
3 Bake cake for about 1 hour 30 minutes. Stand cake in pan for 5 minutes; turn, top-side up, onto wire rack to cool.
4 Meanwhile, make chilli plums. Serve cake with chilli plums and syrup.

Chilli plums Combine the water, sugar, chilli and rind in medium saucepan. Stir over low heat, without boiling, until sugar dissolves. Bring to a boil; boil 2 minutes. Add plums; simmer 5 minutes or until plums are just tender. Cool plums in poaching liquid. Remove from poaching liquid, halve crossways and discard stones. Bring liquid to a boil; boil for 10 minutes or until liquid thickens slightly; cool. Return plums to poaching liquid.

ALLERGY-FREE CAKES

Flourless chocolate dessert cake

preparation time **25 minutes** cooking time **45 minutes** (plus refrigeration time) serves **8**

100g dark eating chocolate, chopped
100g butter, chopped
2 tablespoons marsala
½ cup (110g) caster sugar
⅔ cup (80g) almond meal
1 tablespoon instant coffee granules
1 tablespoon hot water
3 eggs, separated

1 Preheat oven to moderate (180°C/160°C fan-forced). Grease a deep 20cm round cake pan; line base and side with baking paper.
2 Place chocolate and butter in small saucepan; stir over low heat until both are melted.
3 Combine chocolate mixture, marsala, sugar, almond meal and combined coffee and the water in large bowl. Add egg yolks one at a time, beating well after each addition.
4 Beat egg whites in small bowl with electric mixer until soft peaks form; gently fold into chocolate mixture, in two batches.
5 Pour cake mixture into prepared pan; bake for about 45 minutes. Cool cake in pan; cover, refrigerate for several hours or overnight.
6 Carefully turn cake onto board; cut into slices with a hot knife. Dust with sifted icing sugar, if desired.

Gluten-free chocolate cake

preparation time **25 minutes** cooking time **30 minutes** serves **8**

You will need 1 large overripe banana (230g) for this recipe.

1 cup (125g) soy flour
¾ cup (110g) 100% maize cornflour
1¼ teaspoons bicarbonate of soda
½ cup (50g) cocoa powder
1¼ cups (275g) caster sugar
150g butter, melted
1 tablespoon white vinegar
1 cup (250ml) evaporated milk
2 eggs
½ cup mashed banana
2 tablespoons raspberry jam
300ml whipping cream, whipped

1 Preheat oven to moderate (180°C/160°C fan-forced). Grease two 22cm round sandwich pans; line base with baking paper.
2 Sift flours, soda, cocoa powder and sugar into large bowl. Add butter, vinegar and milk; beat with electric mixer on low speed for 1 minute. Add eggs, banana and jam; beat on medium speed for 2 minutes. Pour cake mixture into prepared pans.
3 Bake for about 30 minutes. Stand cakes in pans for 5 minutes before turning onto wire racks to cool. Sandwich cakes with whipped cream.

Gluten-free orange syrup cake

preparation time **25 minutes** cooking time **1 hour 15 minutes** serves **8**

185g butter, chopped
1 tablespoon finely grated orange rind
1¼ cups (275g) caster sugar
6 eggs
3 cups (375g) almond meal
¾ cup (60g) desiccated coconut
¾ cup (110g) rice flour
1 teaspoon gluten-free baking powder

Orange syrup
1 large orange (300g)
⅓ cup (75g) caster sugar
⅓ cup (80ml) water

1 Preheat oven to moderate (180°C/160°C fan-forced). Grease a 21cm baba cake pan.
2 Beat butter, rind and sugar in medium bowl with electric mixer until light and fluffy. Add eggs one at a time, beating until just combined after each addition (mixture will curdle). Stir in almond meal, coconut and sifted flour and baking powder.
3 Spread cake mixture into prepared pan; bake for about 1 hour. Stand cake in pan for 5 minutes before turning onto wire rack set over an oven tray.
4 Meanwhile, make orange syrup; pour hot syrup over hot cake. Serve warm or cold.

Orange syrup Peel rind thinly from orange; cut rind into thin strips. Squeeze juice from orange (you will need ⅓ cup/80ml) into a small pan; stir in rind, sugar and water. Stir over heat, without boiling, until sugar dissolves. Simmer, uncovered, without stirring, for 10 minutes.

tip This cake can be stored in the refrigerator for up to two days. It is not suitable for freezing.

Egg-free date and nut cake

preparation time **15 minutes** cooking time **45 minutes** (plus cooling time)
serves **9**

1 cup (360g) honey
1 cup (250ml) water
30g butter
2¼ cups (360g) wholemeal self-raising flour
1 teaspoon mixed spice
½ teaspoon ground ginger
1½ cups (250g) seeded chopped dates
¾ cup (90g) chopped walnuts
¼ cup (35g) chopped slivered almonds

1 Preheat oven to moderate (180°C/160°C fan-forced). Grease a deep
19cm square cake pan; line base with baking paper.
2 Combine honey, water and butter in a medium saucepan; stir over low heat
until butter melts.
3 Combine sifted flour and spices, dates and nuts in a medium bowl; stir in
warm honey mixture. Spread cake mixture into prepared pan.
4 Bake for about 40 minutes. Stand cake in pan for 5 minutes before turning
onto wire rack to cool. Glaze with a little extra honey, if desired.

Gluten-free carrot cake with orange frosting

preparation time **25 minutes** cooking time **1 hour** (plus cooling time)
serves **6**

You will need about 3 medium carrots (360g) for this recipe.

1 cup (125g) soy flour
¾ cup (110g) 100% maize cornflour
2 teaspoons gluten-free baking powder
1 teaspoon bicarbonate of soda
2 teaspoons mixed spice
1 cup (220g) firmly packed brown sugar
1½ cups (360g) grated carrot
1 cup (120g) chopped walnuts
½ cup (125ml) extra light olive oil
½ cup (120g) sour cream
3 eggs, beaten lightly

Orange frosting
125g cream cheese, chopped
1 teaspoon finely grated orange rind
1½ cups (240g) pure icing sugar

1 Preheat oven to moderately slow (170°C/150°C fan-forced). Grease deep
20cm round cake pan; line base and side with baking paper.
2 Sift flours, baking powder, soda and spice into a large bowl; stir in sugar,
carrot and nuts. Stir in combined oil, sour cream and egg until smooth. Pour
mixture into prepared pan.
3 Bake for about 1 hour. Stand cake in pan for 5 minutes before turning onto
a wire rack to cool.
4 Make orange frosting; spread on top of cake.

Orange frosting Beat cream cheese and rind in small bowl with electric
mixer until light and fluffy. Gradually beat in sifted icing sugar until smooth.

tips This cake can be stored in the refrigerator for up to two days. Un-iced,
it can be frozen for up to three months. The soy flour can be replaced with
besan, also known as chickpea flour. Cornflour comes in two types, wheaten
and corn. Make sure you use 100% corn (maize) cornflour in this recipe.

Fat-free angel food cake

preparation time **25 minutes** cooking time **30 minutes**
serves **10**

½ cup (75g) plain flour
½ cup (75g) wheaten cornflour
1¼ cups (275g) caster sugar
¼ teaspoon salt
12 egg whites
1 teaspoon cream of tartar
1 teaspoon vanilla extract

1 Preheat oven to moderate (180°C/160°C fan-forced).
2 Sift flours, ¼ cup (55g) of the sugar and the salt together six times.
3 Beat egg whites in large bowl with electric mixer until foamy; beat in cream of tartar. Beat in remaining sugar, 1 tablespoon at a time, beating until dissolved between additions. Add extract; beat until firm peaks form. Transfer to a larger bowl; use a whisk to fold in flour mixture gently.
4 Spread cake mixture into an ungreased 25cm tube pan. Bake 30 minutes or until cake is springy to touch; it will shrink slightly towards the end of cooking time.
5 Invert pan on its "feet" onto bench over a piece of baking paper. Do not move pan until cake is cold. Cake will drop from pan when cold; if necessary, use a metal spatula to release cake from dome and base.

Dairy-free fruit cake

preparation time **20 minutes** (plus cooling time)
cooking time **1 hour 40 minutes** serves **8**

2¾ cups (500g) mixed dried fruit
1 cup (150g) finely chopped dried apricots
440g can crushed pineapple in natural juice
¼ cup (60ml) orange juice
1 teaspoon mixed spice
¼ teaspoon ground cloves
1 teaspoon bicarbonate of soda
2 egg whites
2 cups (320g) wholemeal self-raising flour

1 Preheat oven to moderately slow (170°C/150°C fan-forced). Line base and side of a deep 20cm round cake pan with three layers of baking paper, extending paper 5cm above edge.
2 Cook dried fruits, undrained pineapple, juice and spices in large saucepan, stirring until mixture comes to a boil. Simmer, stirring, for 5 minutes. Transfer to large bowl and cover; cool.
3 Stir sifted soda and egg whites into fruit mixture, then fold in flour. Spread mixture into prepared pan; using a wet hand, pat down the top of cake.
4 Bake cake for about 1½ hours. Cover cake tightly with foil; cool in pan.

Egg-free fruit cake

preparation time **25 minutes** cooking time **2 hours 25 minutes** serves **16**

2¾ cups (500g) dried mixed fruit
1 cup (250ml) water
½ cup (100g) firmly packed brown sugar
60g butter
⅓ cup (55g) seeded chopped dates
1 cup (150g) plain flour
½ cup (75g) self-raising flour
1 teaspoon bicarbonate of soda
1 teaspoon mixed spice
¼ cup (60ml) sweet sherry

1 Preheat oven to slow (150°C/130°C fan-forced). Line base and sides of a deep 19cm square cake pan with three layers of baking paper, extending paper 5cm above edge.
2 Combine dried fruit, water, sugar and butter in a medium pan. Stir over heat, without boiling, until sugar dissolves. Simmer, uncovered, for 3 minutes. Remove from heat, then stir in dates; cool.
3 Stir sifted dry ingredients and sherry into fruit mixture, in two batches. Spread cake mixture into prepared pan.
4 Bake cake for about 2¼ hours. Cover cake tightly with foil; cool in pan.

Egg-free chocolate cake

preparation time **15 minutes** (plus cooling time)
cooking time **1 hour 20 minutes** serves **8**

125g butter
100g dark cooking chocolate, chopped
¾ cup (180ml) milk
¾ cup (165g) caster sugar
1 teaspoon vanilla extract
1 cup (150g) self-raising-flour
½ cup (75g) plain flour
2 tablespoons cocoa

Fudge frosting
50g butter
2 tablespoons water
¼ cup (55g) caster sugar
¾ cup (120g) icing sugar
2 tablespoons cocoa

1 Preheat oven to slow (150°C/130°C fan-forced). Grease a 20cm round cake pan; line base and side with baking paper.
2 Place butter, chocolate, milk and sugar in a medium saucepan; stir over low heat, without boiling, until smooth. Transfer to a large bowl, cool to warm. Whisk in extract, sifted flours and cocoa until smooth.
3 Pour mixture into prepared pan; bake for about 1 hour 10 minutes. Cover loosely with foil if cake is browning too quickly. Stand cake in pan for five minutes before turning onto a wire rack to cool.
4 Make fudge frosting; spread over top of cake.

Fudge frosting Combine butter, the water and caster sugar in small saucepan; stir over heat, without boiling, until sugar is dissolved. Sift icing sugar and cocoa into heatproof bowl; gradually stir in hot butter mixture. Cover and refrigerate until thick. Beat with a wooden spoon until frosting is of a spreadable consistency.

Gluten-free, dairy-free raspberry muffins

preparation time **15 minutes** cooking time **20 minutes** makes **12**

2½ cups (375g) gluten-free plain flour
1 tablespoon gluten-free baking powder
½ teaspoon bicarbonate of soda
⅓ cup (40g) rice bran
⅔ cup (150g) firmly packed brown sugar
1½ cups (375ml) soy milk
1 teaspoon vanilla extract
60g dairy-free spread, melted
2 eggs, beaten lightly
150g frozen raspberries
1 tablespoon coffee sugar crystals

1 Preheat oven to moderately hot (200°C/180°C fan-forced). Grease 12-hole (⅓-cup/80ml) muffin pan, or line with paper patty cases.
2 Sift flour, baking powder and soda into large bowl; stir in bran, sugar and combined milk, extract, spread and egg until almost combined. Add raspberries, stir until just combined.
3 Divide mixture among muffin holes; sprinkle with coffee sugar crystals.
4 Bake muffins for about 20 minutes. Stand muffins in pan for a few minutes before carefully removing from pan to cool on wire rack.

Wheat-free sponge

preparation time **15 minutes** cooking time **20 minutes** serves **8**

3 eggs
½ cup (110g) caster sugar
¾ cup (110g) 100% maize cornflour

1 Preheat oven to moderate (180°C/160°C fan-forced). Grease and line 20cm round cake pan.
2 Beat eggs in small bowl with electric mixer until thick and creamy. Add sugar, 1 tablespoon at a time, beating after each addition until sugar dissolves. Sift cornflour three times, then sift evenly over egg mixture; fold in gently. Spread into pan. Bake for 20 minutes. Turn onto a wire rack to cool.

Allergy-free fruit cake

preparation time **30 minutes** (plus cooling time)
cooking time **1 hour 40 minutes** serves **10**

You will need to cook 500g pumpkin for this recipe.

1 cup (160g) sultanas
¾ cup (135g) currants
¾ cup (120g) chopped raisins
2 cups (500ml) water
1½ cups cold mashed pumpkin
1 tablespoon grated lemon rind
¼ cup (60ml) vegetable oil
1½ cups (185g) soy flour
1½ cups (185g) rice flour
3 teaspoons baking powder
1 teaspoon ground cinnamon
1 teaspoon ground nutmeg
½ teaspoon ground cloves
2 tablespoons sugarless apricot jam

1 Preheat oven to moderately slow (170°C/150°C fan-forced). Line a deep 20cm round cake pan with two sheets of paper.
2 Combine sultanas, currants, raisins and water in saucepan. Bring to a boil, then remove from heat, stir in pumpkin, rind and oil; cool to room temperature. Stir sifted flours, baking powder, cinnamon, nutmeg and cloves into fruit mixture.
3 Spread into prepared pan; bake for about 1½ hours. Cover and cool in pan. Turn cake out when cold; brush top with warmed, sieved jam.

Gluten-free berry cupcakes

preparation time **20 minutes** cooking time **25 minutes** makes **12**

125g butter, softened
2 teaspoons finely grated lemon rind
¾ cup (165g) caster sugar
4 eggs
2 cups (240g) almond meal
½ cup (40g) desiccated coconut
½ cup (100g) rice flour
1 teaspoon bicarbonate of soda
1 cup (150g) frozen mixed berries

1 Preheat oven to moderate (180°C/160°C fan-forced). Grease a 12-hole (⅓-cup/80ml) muffin pan.

2 Beat butter, rind and sugar in small bowl with electric mixer until light and fluffy. Add eggs one at a time, beating until just combined after each addition (mixture might curdle at this stage, but will come together later); transfer to a large bowl. Stir in almond meal, coconut, combined sifted flour and soda, then the berries.

3 Spoon mixture equally among muffin pan holes; bake about 25 minutes. Stand in pan 5 minutes; turn, top-sides up, onto wire rack to cool.

Egg-free ginger jumble cake

preparation time **20 minutes** cooking time **45 minutes** serves **16**

185g butter, chopped
¾ cup (180ml) golden syrup
¾ cup (180ml) water
½ cup (100g) firmly packed brown sugar
2¼ cups (335g) plain flour
1½ teaspoons bicarbonate of soda
1½ tablespoons ground ginger
1½ teaspoons mixed spice
¼ teaspoon ground cloves

1 Preheat oven to moderate (180°C/160°C fan-forced). Grease a 23cm square slab cake pan; line base with baking paper.

2 Place butter, golden syrup, water and sugar in medium saucepan, stir over heat, without boiling, until butter is melted; cool 10 minutes. Stir in flour, soda and spices.

3 Pour cake mixture into prepared pan; bake for about 40 minutes. Stand cake in pan for 5 minutes before turning onto a wire rack to cool.

Flourless hazelnut chocolate cake

preparation time **20 minutes** (plus standing time) cooking time **1 hour**
serves **9**

⅓ **cup (35g) cocoa powder**
⅓ **cup (80ml) hot water**
150g dark cooking chocolate, melted
150g butter, melted
1 ⅓ cups (275g) firmly packed brown sugar
1 cup (125g) hazelnut meal
4 eggs, separated
1 tablespoon cocoa powder, extra

1 Preheat oven to moderate (180°C/160°C fan-forced). Grease a deep 19cm square cake pan; line base and sides with baking paper.

2 Blend cocoa with the hot water in large bowl until smooth. Stir in chocolate, butter, sugar, hazelnut meal and egg yolks.

3 Beat egg whites in small bowl with electric mixer until soft peaks form; fold into chocolate mixture in two batches.

4 Pour cake mixture into prepared pan; bake for about 1 hour, or until firm. Stand cake in pan for 15 minutes before turning onto a wire rack, top-side up, to cool. Dust with sifted extra cocoa to serve.

tip This cake can be made up to four days ahead; store, covered in the refrigerator. It can also be frozen for up to three months.

ONE-BOWL CAKES

Cinnamon teacake

preparation time **15 minutes** cooking time **30 minutes** serves **10**

60g butter, softened
1 teaspoon vanilla extract
²⁄₃ cup (150g) caster sugar
1 egg
1 cup (150g) self-raising flour
¹⁄₃ cup (80ml) milk
10g butter, extra, melted
1 teaspoon ground cinnamon
1 tablespoon caster sugar, extra

1 Preheat oven to moderate (180°C/160°C fan-forced). Grease a deep 20cm round cake pan; line base with baking paper.
2 Beat softened butter, extract, sugar and egg in small bowl with electric mixer until very light and fluffy; this process will take 5-10 minutes, depending on type of mixer used.
3 Using wooden spoon, gently stir in sifted flour and milk. Spread mixture into pan. Bake about 30 minutes. Stand cake in pan for 5 minutes before turning top-side up onto wire rack. Brush top with melted butter, then sprinkle with combined cinnamon and extra sugar. Serve warm with butter, if desired.

Melt 'n' mix coconut cake

preparation time **10 minutes** cooking time **45 minutes** serves **8**

1½ cups (225g) self-raising flour
1¼ cups (275g) caster sugar
1¼ cups (110g) desiccated coconut
125g butter, melted
3 eggs, beaten lightly
¾ cup (180ml) milk

1 Preheat oven to moderate (180°C/160°C fan-forced). Grease and flour a 21cm baba pan.

2 Combine ingredients in medium bowl; mix well with a wooden spoon, pour into prepared pan. Bake for about 45 minutes. Stand cake in pan for 5 minutes; turn onto wire rack to cool.

Cream cheese and chocolate brownie

preparation time **20 minutes**   cooking time **30 minutes**   serves **16**

80g butter, melted
1 teaspoon vanilla extract
1 cup (220g) firmly packed brown sugar
½ cup (50g) cocoa powder
⅔ cup (100g) plain flour
¼ cup (35g) self-raising flour
3 egg whites, beaten lightly
¼ cup (60ml) low-fat milk
¼ cup (25g) pecans, halved lengthways

Cream cheese topping
125g light cream cheese, softened
¼ cup (55g) caster sugar
1 egg

1 Preheat oven to moderately slow (170°C/150°C fan-forced). Grease a deep 19cm square cake pan; line base and sides with baking paper.

2 Combine butter, extract and sugar in large bowl; stir in combined sifted cocoa and flours until smooth. Add egg whites and milk; mix until combined.

3 Spread mixture into prepared pan; bake for 15 minutes.

4 Meanwhile, make cream cheese topping.

5 Remove brownie from oven; carefully pour topping on top, sprinkle with nuts. Bake for a further 12 minutes, or until topping is firm to touch. Cool in pan.

Cream cheese topping Beat cheese and sugar together in a small bowl with an electric mixer until smooth; add the egg and beat until combined.

Chocolate butterscotch cake

preparation time **20 minutes** (plus refrigeration time) cooking time **1 hour** serves **10**

¼ cup (25g) cocoa powder
250g butter, softened
1 cup (220g) firmly packed dark brown sugar
2 eggs
1 tablespoon golden syrup
1¼ cups (185g) self-raising flour
½ cup (125ml) milk

Mascarpone cream
250g mascarpone cheese
300ml double cream

Caramel icing
60g butter
½ cup (110g) firmly packed dark brown sugar
¼ cup (60ml) milk
1½ cups (240g) icing sugar

1 Preheat oven to moderate (180°C/160°C fan-forced). Grease a deep 20cm round cake pan; line base and side with baking paper.
2 Sift cocoa into large bowl; add remaining ingredients. Beat with electric mixer on low speed until combined. Increase speed to medium; beat until mixture just changes colour. Pour mixture into prepared pan; bake 1 hour. Stand cake in pan for 10 minutes; turn, top-side up, onto wire rack to cool.
3 Whisk ingredients for mascarpone cream in small bowl until soft peaks form. Make caramel icing.
4 Using a large serrated knife, split cake into three layers. Centre one layer on serving plate; spread with a third of the mascarpone cream and a third of the caramel icing. Repeat with second layer and half of the remaining mascarpone cream and half of the remaining caramel icing; top with remaining cake layer. Cover top cake layer with remaining mascarpone cream, then drizzle with remaining caramel icing. Swirl to create a marbled effect; refrigerate for about 30 minutes or until icing is firm.

Caramel icing Heat butter, brown sugar and milk in small saucepan, stirring constantly, without boiling, until sugar dissolves; remove from heat. Add icing sugar; stir until smooth.

Choc-carrot cake

preparation time **15 minutes** cooking time **1 hour 15 minutes** serves **10**

You will need about 3 medium carrots (360g) for this recipe.

2 cups (300g) self-raising flour
1 teaspoon ground cinnamon
1 teaspoon ground nutmeg
1 cup (220g) caster sugar
1½ cups firmly packed coarsely grated carrot
½ cup (60g) chopped walnuts or pecans
½ cup (80g) sultanas
2 tablespoons chopped mixed peel
1 tablespoon finely chopped glacé ginger
100g dark eating chocolate, chopped finely
3 eggs, beaten lightly
1 cup (250ml) vegetable oil

1 Preheat oven to moderate (180°C/160°C fan-forced). Grease a 21cm baba cake pan.
2 Sift flour and spices into a large bowl, stir in remaining ingredients.
3 Spread mixture into prepared pan; bake about 1¼ hours. Stand in pan for 5 minutes; turn onto wire rack to cool.

Quick-mix chocolate cake

preparation time **20 minutes** cooking time **1 hour 15 minutes** serves **10**

1½ tablespoons white vinegar
1½ cups (375ml) milk
250g butter, softened
2 teaspoons vanilla extract
1¾ cups (385g) caster sugar
2¼ cups (335g) plain flour
¾ cup (75g) cocoa powder
2 teaspoons bicarbonate of soda
4 eggs

1 Preheat oven to moderately slow (170°C/150°C fan-forced). Grease a deep 22cm square cake pan; line base and sides with two layers of baking paper.

2 Combine vinegar and milk in a small jug.

3 Beat butter, extract, sugar, sifted dry ingredients, eggs and milk mixture in large bowl with electric mixer on low speed until combined. Increase speed to medium; beat for 2 minutes or until smooth. Do not over-beat.

4 Spread mixture into prepared pan; bake for about 1 hour 10 minutes, or until cooked when tested. Cool cake in pan for 5 minutes before turning onto a wire rack to cool.

tip This cake is suitable to freeze.

Sherried sultana cake

preparation time **15 minutes** cooking time **2 hours 15 minutes** serves **10**

3 cups (500g) sultanas
½ cup (75g) chopped dried apricots
⅓ cup (55g) mixed peel
1 small (130g) peeled apple, grated coarsely
2 tablespoons sweet sherry
¾ cup (165g) caster sugar
3 teaspoons golden syrup
3 eggs, beaten lightly
185g butter, melted
1½ cups (225g) plain flour
⅓ cup (50g) self-raising flour
1½ teaspoons ground ginger
¾ teaspoon mixed spice

1 Preheat oven to slow (150°C/130°C fan-forced). Grease a 14cm x 21cm loaf pan; line base with three layers of baking paper.

2 Combine ingredients in large bowl; mix well.

3 Spread mixture into prepared pan; bake for about 2 hours 15 minutes. Cover tightly with foil; cool in pan.

Fudgy choc nut brownies

preparation time **15 minutes** cooking time **35 minutes** makes about **12**

125g butter, chopped
90g dark eating chocolate, chopped coarsely
90g milk eating chocolate, chopped coarsely
½ cup (110g) firmly packed brown sugar
2 tablespoons honey
2 eggs, beaten lightly
1 cup (150g) plain flour
⅔ cup (100g) macadamia nuts, chopped coarsely

1 Preheat oven to moderate (180°C/160°C fan-forced). Grease deep 19cm square cake pan; line base with baking paper.
2 Combine butter and chocolate in medium saucepan; stir over low heat until melted. Remove from heat; stir in sugar and honey. Stir in egg, then sifted flour and nuts; pour mixture into prepared pan.
3 Bake about 30 minutes or until firm. Cool in pan; cut into squares when cold.

Pineapple and macadamia loaf

preparation time **10 minutes** cooking time **45 minutes** serves **8**

450g can pineapple pieces in syrup
1 cup (150g) self-raising flour
½ cup (110g) caster sugar
1 cup (90g) desiccated coconut
1 cup (150g) macadamias, toasted, coarsely chopped
1 egg, beaten lightly
½ cup (125ml) milk

1 Preheat oven to moderate (180°C/160°C fan-forced). Grease a 14cm x 21cm loaf pan.
2 Drain pineapple well, chop finely; discard syrup. Combine pineapple with remaining ingredients in large bowl, mix well; spread into prepared pan.
3 Bake about 45 minutes. Stand loaf in pan 10 minutes before turning onto wire rack to cool.

Quick honey gingerbread cake

preparation time **10 minutes** cooking time **35 minutes** serves **12**

1 cup (150g) plain flour
½ cup (75g) self-raising flour
½ teaspoon bicarbonate of soda
3 teaspoons ground ginger
½ teaspoon ground nutmeg
½ cup (110g) firmly packed brown sugar
½ cup (180g) honey
½ cup (125ml) hot water
125g butter, melted

1 Preheat oven to moderate (180°C/160°C fan-forced). Grease a 19cm x 29cm slice pan; line base with baking paper.

2 Combine flours, soda, spices and sugar in processor; process a few seconds until combined. Add combined honey, water and butter; process until mixture is smooth.

3 Pour mixture into prepared pan; bake for about 35 minutes. Stand cake in pan for 2 minutes before turning onto wire rack to cool. Dust with sifted icing sugar, if desired.

Carrot and prune cake

preparation time **20 minutes** cooking time **1 hour 15 minutes** serves **14**

You will need to grate about 3 carrots for this recipe.

¾ cup (110g) self-raising flour
¾ cup (110g) plain flour
1 tablespoon mixed spice
½ teaspoon bicarbonate of soda
¾ cup (120g) seeded prunes
½ cup (60g) pecan nuts
½ cup (80g) sultanas
3 eggs
1 cup (220g) firmly packed brown sugar
300g sour cream
¼ cup (60m) vegetable oil
2 cups grated carrots

1 Preheat oven to moderately slow (170°C/150°C fan-forced). Grease a 19cm square cake pan; line base with baking paper.
2 Combine flours, spice and soda in processor; process a few seconds to combine. Transfer mixture to large bowl, leaving a tablespoonful of mixture in the processor. Add prunes and pecans to processor; process until coarsely chopped. Stir into flour mixture with sultanas.
3 Combine eggs, sugar, sour cream and oil in processor; process until combined. Stir into flour mixture with carrots. Pour into prepared pan.
4 Bake cake for about 1 hour 15 minutes. Stand cake in pan for 10 minutes before turning onto wire rack to cool.

tip This cake will keep in an airtight container in the refrigerator for up to five days.

Apple chocolate cake

preparation time **15 minutes** cooking time **1 hour 5 minutes** serves **9**

We used granny smith apples for this recipe.

185g butter
1 ¼ cups (275g) caster sugar
3 eggs
2 apples, peeled, quartered
2 cups (300g) self-raising flour
⅓ cup (35g) cocoa
¼ teaspoon bicarbonate of soda
⅓ cup (80ml) water

Chocolate icing
1 cup (160g) icing sugar
1 tablespoon cocoa
1 teaspoon soft butter
1 tablespoon milk, approximately

1 Preheat oven to moderate (180°C/160°C fan-forced). Grease a 23cm square slab pan; line base with baking paper.
2 Combine butter, sugar, eggs, apple, flour and combined cocoa, soda and water in processor; process until mixture is smooth.
3 Pour mixture into prepared pan; bake for about 1 hour. Stand cake in pan for 5 minutes before turning onto wire rack to cool.
4 Make chocolate icing; spread over cold cake.

Chocolate icing Sift icing sugar and cocoa into small heatproof bowl; stir in butter and enough milk to make a stiff paste. Stir over hot water until icing is of a spreadable consistency.

tip This cake can be kept in the refrigerator for up to three days.

Moist orange cake

preparation time **15 minutes** cooking time **45 minutes** serves **8**

150g butter
2 teaspoons finely grated orange rind
²/₃ cup (150g) caster sugar
3 eggs
1 ¼ cups (185g) self-raising flour
¼ cup (60ml) milk

Orange icing
1 cup (160g) icing sugar
1 teaspoon soft butter
1 tablespoon orange juice, approximately
1 tablespoon coconut

1 Preheat oven to moderate (180°C/160°C fan-forced). Grease a deep
20cm round cake pan; line base with baking paper.
2 Beat ingredients in large bowl with electric mixer on low speed until
combined. Increase speed to medium; beat for about 3 minutes, or until
mixture is changed in colour and smooth.
3 Spread mixture into prepared pan; bake for about 45 minutes. Stand cake
in pan for 2 minutes before turning onto wire rack to cool.
4 Make orange icing; spread icing over cold cake, sprinkle with coconut.

Orange icing Sift icing sugar into small heatproof bowl; stir in butter
and enough juice to make a stiff paste. Stir over hot water until icing is of
a spreadable consistency.

tip This cake can be kept in an airtight container for up to two days.

Honey-iced coffee cake

preparation time **20 minutes** (plus cooling time) cooking time **40 minutes**
serves **8**

3 teaspoons instant coffee granules
1 tablespoon hot water
125g butter
2 teaspoons vanilla extract
¾ cup (165g) firmly packed brown sugar
2 eggs
1 cup (150g) self-raising flour
¼ cup (30g) custard powder
⅓ cup (80ml) milk

Honey icing
30g butter, melted
1 teaspoon instant coffee granules
1 tablespoon hot water
1 teaspoon honey
1 teaspoon vanilla extract
1 cup (160g) icing sugar, approximately

1 Preheat oven to moderate (180°C/160°C fan-forced). Grease a 20cm ring pan; line base with baking paper.
2 Dissolve coffee in the water.
3 Beat butter, extract, sugar, eggs, sifted flour and custard powder, milk and coffee mixture in large bowl with electric mixer on low speed until combined. Increase speed to medium; beat for about 3 minutes, or until mixture is smooth and changed in colour.
4 Spread mixture into prepared pan; bake for about 40 minutes. Stand cake in pan for 5 minutes, before turning on to wire rack to cool.
5 Make honey icing; spread over cold cake.

Honey icing Combine coffee and the water, honey, vanilla and half the sifted icing sugar in medium bowl. Gradually stir in enough remaining icing sugar until it is of a spreadable consistency.

tip This cake can be kept in an airtight container for up to three days.

Chocolate fudge cake

preparation time **10 minutes** (plus standing time) cooking time **30 minutes**
serves **12**

250g dark eating chocolate, melted
125g butter, melted
²/₃ cup (150g) caster sugar
²/₃ cup (100g) self-raising-flour
4 eggs, beaten lightly

1 Preheat oven to moderate (180°C/160°C fan-forced). Grease a 19cm x
29cm lamington pan; line base with baking paper.
2 Beat ingredients in medium bowl with electric mixer low speed until
combined. Increase speed to medium; beat for about 3 minutes, or until
mixture is changed in colour and smooth.
3 Pour mixture into prepared pan; bake for about 30 minutes. Stand cake in
pan for 5 minutes before turning onto a wire rack to cool.

tip Store cake in an airtight container in the refrigerator for up to three days.

Vanilla butter cake

preparation time **20 minutes** cooking time **50 minutes** serves **9**

3 eggs
1 tablespoon vanilla extract
1 cup (220g) caster sugar
1½ cups (225g) self-raising flour
125g butter, melted
¾ cup (180ml) milk

1 Preheat oven to moderate (180°C/160°C fan-forced). Grease a deep
19cm square cake pan; line base with baking paper.
2 Beat eggs and extract in large bowl with electric mixer until thick and
creamy; gradually add sugar, then beat until dissolved after each addition.
3 Stir in sifted flour and combined butter and milk. Pour into prepared pan.
Bake for about 45 minutes. Stand cake in pan for 2 minutes before turning
onto a wire rack to cool. When cold, dust with sifted icing sugar.

tip This cake can be kept in an airtight container for up to a week.

One-bowl sultana loaf

preparation time **15 minutes** cooking time **1 hour 30 minutes** serves **8**

125g butter, melted
750g sultanas
½ cup (110g) firmly packed brown sugar
2 tablespoons marmalade
2 eggs, lightly beaten
¼ cup (60ml) sweet sherry
¾ cup (110g) plain flour
¼ cup (35g) self-raising flour

1 Preheat oven to slow (150°C/130°C fan-forced). Grease a 15cm x 25cm loaf pan; line base with baking paper.
2 Beat ingredients in large bowl using a wooden spoon until combined.
3 Spread mixture into prepared pan; decorate top with blanched almonds, if desired.
4 Bake loaf for about 1 hour 30 minutes. Cover with foil; cool in pan.

tip This loaf can be kept in an airtight container for up to two weeks.

Rich chocolate cake

preparation time **20 minutes**   cooking time **1 hour 40 minutes**   serves **14**

185g butter
2 teaspoons vanilla extract
1 ¾ cups (385g) caster sugar
3 eggs
2 cups (300g) self-raising flour
⅔ cup (70g) cocoa
1 cup (250ml) water

Chocolate icing
90g dark eating chocolate, chopped
30g butter
1 cup (160g) icing sugar
2 tablespoons hot water, approximately

1 Preheat oven to moderate (180°C/160°C fan-forced). Grease a deep 23cm round cake pan; line base with baking paper.
2 Beat butter, extract, sugar, eggs, sifted flour and cocoa and the water in a large bowl with electric mixer on low speed until combined. Increase speed to medium; beat for 3 minutes or until mixture is smooth and changed in colour.
3 Spread mixture into prepared pan; bake cake for about 1 hour 30 minutes. Stand cake in pan for 5 minutes before turning on to wire rack to cool.
4 Make chocolate icing; spread over cold cake.

Chocolate icing Melt chocolate and butter in bowl over hot water; gradually stir in sifted icing sugar, then stir in enough hot water to mix icing to a spreadable consistency.

tip This cake can be kept in an airtight container in the refrigerator for up to three days.

Golden caramel cake

preparation time **20 minutes** cooking time **45 minutes** serves **10**

185g butter
¾ cup (150g) firmly packed brown sugar
2 eggs
⅓ cup (80ml) golden syrup
1½ cups (225g) self-raising flour
½ cup (75g) plain flour
¾ cup (180ml) milk

1 Preheat oven to moderate (180°C/160°C fan-forced). Grease a 21cm baba cake pan.
2 Beat ingredients in medium bowl with electric mixer on low speed until combined. Increase speed to medium; beat until mixture is smooth and changed in colour.
3 Spread mixture into prepared pan; bake for about 45 minutes. Stand cake in pan for a few minutes before turning onto wire rack to cool.
4 Serve cold cake with chocolate glacé icing (see page 288) and chopped almonds, if desired.

Buttery butterscotch cake

preparation time **15 minutes** cooking time **50 minutes** serves **8**

250g butter, chopped
1 cup (220g) firmly packed brown sugar
2 eggs
1 tablespoon golden syrup
1½ cups (225g) self-raising flour
½ cup (125ml) milk

1 Preheat oven to moderate (180°C/160°C fan-forced). Grease a deep 20cm round cake pan; line base with baking paper.
2 Beat ingredients in medium bowl with electric mixer on low speed until combined. Increase speed to medium; beat until mixture is smooth and changed in colour. Spread mixture into prepared pan.
3 Bake about 50 minutes. Stand cake in pan for 10 minutes before turning onto wire rack to cool. Dust cold cake with sifted icing sugar, if desired.

Orange date cake

preparation time **15 minutes** cooking time **40 minutes** serves **10**

125g butter
2 teaspoons finely grated orange rind
¾ cup (165g) caster sugar
2 eggs
1 cup (150g) self-raising flour
½ cup (75g) plain flour
⅓ cup (80ml) orange juice
1 cup (140g) coarsely chopped dates

1 Preheat oven to moderate (180°C/160°C fan-forced). Grease a 20cm ring pan; line base with baking paper.
2 Beat butter, rind, sugar, eggs, sifted flours and orange juice in small bowl with electric mixer on low speed until combined. Increase speed to medium; beat 2 minutes or until mixture changes in colour and is smooth. Stir in dates.
3 Spread mixture into prepared pan; bake for about 40 minutes. Stand cake in pan for 2 minutes, before turning on to wire rack to cool.

tip This cake can be stored in an airtight container in the refrigerator for up to two days.

Apple walnut cake

preparation time **20 minutes** cooking time **55 minutes** serves **12**

125g butter, chopped
2 teaspoons finely grated orange rind
1 cup (220g) caster sugar
½ cup (110g) firmly packed brown sugar
2 eggs
1½ cups (225g) self-raising flour
½ cup (75g) plain flour
½ teaspoon bicarbonate of soda
1 cup (250ml) evaporated milk
1 large (200g) apple, peeled, chopped
½ cup (60g) chopped walnuts

1 Preheat oven to moderate (180°C/160°C fan-forced). Grease 23cm square slab cake pan; cover base with baking paper.
2 Beat butter, rind, sugars, eggs, flours, soda and milk in medium bowl with electric mixer on low speed until combined. Increase speed to medium; beat until mixture is smooth and changed in colour. Stir in apple and nuts.
3 Spread mixture into prepared pan; bake for about 55 minutes. Stand cake in pan for 5 minutes before turning onto a wire rack to cool.
4 Spread cold cake with citrus frosting (see page 292) and sprinkle with extra walnuts, if desired.

Cherry almond cake

preparation time **15 minutes** cooking time **1 hour** serves **8**

185g butter, chopped
¾ cup (165g) caster sugar
3 eggs
2 cups (300g) self-raising flour
2 tablespoons almond meal
¼ cup (60ml) milk
1 cup (210g) glacé cherries

1 Preheat oven to moderate (180°C/160°C fan-forced). Grease deep 20cm round cake pan; line base with baking paper.
2 Beat butter, sugar, eggs, flour, almond meal and milk in medium bowl with

electric mixer on low speed until combined. Increase speed to medium; beat until mixture is smooth and changed in colour. Stir in cherries.

3 Spread mixture into prepared pan; bake for about 1 hour. Stand cake in pan for 10 minutes before turning onto wire rack to cool.

4 Serve cold cake dusted with sifted icing sugar, if desired.

Hazelnut butter cake

preparation time **20 minutes** cooking time **50 minutes** serves **8**

125g butter, chopped
1 teaspoon vanilla extract
1 cup (220g) caster sugar
2 eggs
1½ cups (225g) self-raising flour
¾ cup (180ml) milk
⅔ cup (70g) hazelnut meal

1 Preheat oven to moderate (180°C/160°C fan-forced). Grease deep 20cm round cake pan; cover base with baking paper.

2 Beat butter, extract, sugar, eggs, flour and milk in medium bowl with electric mixer on low speed until combined. Increase speed to medium; beat until mixture is smooth and changed in colour. Stir in hazelnut meal.

3 Pour mixture into prepared pan; bake for about 50 minutes. Turn onto a wire rack to cool.

4 Split cold cake into three layers and sandwich layers with chocolate liqueur cream (page 293), if desired.

Wholemeal banana coconut cake

preparation time **20 minutes** cooking time **45 minutes** serves **10**

You will need about 2 overripe medium bananas for this cake.

125g butter, chopped
2 teaspoons finely grated lemon rind
⅔ cup (130g) firmly packed brown sugar
3 eggs
¾ cup mashed banana
⅓ cup (30g) coconut
¾ cup (110g) white self-raising flour
¾ cup (120g) wholemeal self-raising flour
1 teaspoon bicarbonate of soda

1 Preheat oven to moderate (180°C/160°C fan-forced). Grease a 21cm baba cake pan.
2 Beat ingredients in medium bowl with electric mixer on low speed until combined. Increase speed to medium speed; beat until mixture is smooth and changed in colour.
3 Spread mixture into prepared pan; bake for about 45 minutes. Turn onto wire rack to cool.
4 Top cold cake with lemon glacé icing (see page 288), if desired.

Rum and raisin coffee cake

preparation time **20 minutes** cooking time **55 minutes** serves **8**

185g butter, chopped
½ cup (110g) caster sugar
3 eggs
1½ cups (225g) self-raising flour
2 tablespoons milk
1 tablespoon dark rum
2 teaspoons instant coffee granules
1 cup (170g) coarsely chopped raisins

1 Preheat oven to moderate (180°C/160°C fan-forced). Grease a deep 20cm round cake pan; line base with baking paper.
2 Beat butter, sugar, eggs, flour, milk, rum and coffee in medium bowl with

electric mixer on low speed until combined. Increase speed to medium; beat until mixture is smooth and changed in colour. Stir in raisins.

3 Spread mixture into prepared pan; bake for about 55 minutes. Stand cake in pan for 5 minutes before turning onto wire rack to cool.

4 Top cold cake with coffee vienna cream frosting (see page 290), if desired.

Chocolate mayonnaise cake

preparation time **15 minutes** cooking time **1 hour 10 minutes** serves **10**

2 cups (300g) self-raising flour
1 cup (220g) caster sugar
⅓ cup (35g) cocoa
1 cup (250ml) water
⅔ cup (160ml) whole egg mayonnaise

1 Preheat oven to slow (150°C/130°C fan-forced). Grease deep 20cm round cake pan; line base with baking paper.

2 Beat ingredients in medium bowl with electric mixer on low speed until combined. Increase speed to medium; beat until mixture is smooth and changed in colour.

3 Pour mixture into prepared pan; bake for about 1 hour 10 minutes. Stand cake in pan for a few minutes before turning onto a wire rack to cool.

4 If desired, make 1½ quantities chocolate butter cream (see page 288). Spread side of cold cake with some of the butter cream; roll in crushed nuts. Spread top with more butter cream and decorate with white chocolate curls.

Marmalade cake

preparation time **15 minutes** cooking time **35 minutes** serves **8**

125g butter, chopped
1 teaspoon finely grated orange rind
¾ cup (150g) firmly packed brown sugar
2 eggs
¼ cup (60ml) marmalade
1½ cups (225g) self-raising flour
¼ cup (60ml) milk

1 Preheat oven to moderate (180°C/160°C fan-forced). Grease a 20cm ring cake pan.
2 Beat ingredients in medium bowl with electric mixer on low speed until combined. Increase speed to medium; beat until mixture is smooth and changed in colour.
3 Spread into prepared pan; bake 35 minutes. Turn onto a wire rack to cool.
4 Top cold cake with citrus frosting (see page 292) and mixed peel, if desired.

Cream cheese lemon cake

preparation time **20 minutes** cooking time **55 minutes** serves **10**

125g butter, chopped
125g cream cheese, chopped
3 teaspoons finely grated lemon rind
1 cup (220g) caster sugar
2 eggs
¾ cup (110g) self-raising flour
½ cup (75g) plain flour

1 Preheat oven to moderately slow (170°C/150°C fan-forced). Grease a 21cm baba cake pan.
2 Beat ingredients in medium bowl with electric mixer on low speed until combined. Increase speed to medium; beat until mixture is smooth and changed in colour.
3 Spread mixture into prepared pan; bake for about 55 minutes. Stand cake in pan for a few minutes before turning onto wire rack to cool.
4 Dust cold cake with sifted icing sugar, if desired.

Lemon delicious cake

preparation time **15 minutes** cooking time **50 minutes** serves **8**

125g butter, chopped
2 teaspoons finely grated lemon rind
1¼ cups (275g) caster sugar
3 eggs
½ cup (125ml) milk
1½ cups (225g) self-raising flour
¼ cup (60ml) lemon juice

1 Preheat oven to moderate (180°C/160°C fan-forced). Grease a 21cm baba cake pan.
2 Beat ingredients in medium bowl with electric mixer on low speed until combined. Increase speed to medium; beat until mixture is smooth and changed in colour.
3 Spread mixture into prepared pan; bake for about 50 minutes. Turn onto wire rack to cool. Dust cold cake with sifted icing sugar, if desired.

Maple syrup cake

preparation time **15 minutes** cooking time **45 minutes** serves **8**

185g butter, chopped
¾ cup (150g) firmly packed brown sugar
⅓ cup (80ml) maple syrup
2 eggs
1½ cups (225g) self-raising flour
½ cup (75g) plain flour
½ cup (125ml) milk

1 Preheat oven to moderate (180°C/160°C fan-forced). Grease a 21cm baba cake pan.
2 Beat ingredients in medium bowl with electric mixer on low speed until combined. Increase speed to medium; beat until mixture is smooth and changed in colour.
3 Spread mixture into prepared pan; bake for about 45 minutes. Turn onto wire rack to cool. Stand cake in pan 5 minutes; turn onto wire rack to cool.
4 Top cold cake with maple syrup glacé icing (see page 288), if desired.

Mocha yogurt cake

preparation time **20 minutes** cooking time **50 minutes** serves **10**

60g butter, chopped
1 cup (220g) caster sugar
2 eggs
1 ½ cups (225g) self-raising flour
⅓ cup (35g) cocoa
2 teaspoons instant coffee granules
1 teaspoon bicarbonate of soda
1 cup (250ml) plain yogurt

1 Preheat oven to moderate (180°C/160°C fan-forced). Grease a 21cm baba cake pan.
2 Beat ingredients in medium bowl with electric mixer on low speed until combined. Increase speed to medium; beat until mixture is smooth and changed in colour.
3 Spoon mixture into prepared pan; bake for about 50 minutes. Stand cake in pan for a few minutes before turning onto a wire rack to cool.
4 Drizzle cold cake with coffee glacé icing (see page 288) and decorate with walnuts, if desired.

Double lemon loaf

preparation time **15 minutes** cooking time **1 hour** serves **8**

90g butter, chopped
1 tablespoon finely grated lemon rind
½ cup (110g) caster sugar
2 eggs
1 ¾ cups (260g) self-raising flour
¾ cup (180ml) milk
¼ cup (40g) mixed peel
¼ cup (60ml) lemon-flavoured spread

1 Preheat oven to moderate (180°C/160°C fan-forced). Grease a 14cm x 21cm loaf pan; line base with baking paper.
2 Beat butter, rind, sugar, eggs, flour and milk in medium bowl with electric mixer on low speed until combined. Increase speed to medium; beat until

mixture is just smooth and changed in colour; do not over-beat. Stir in peel.
3 Spread mixture into prepared pan; drop teaspoons of lemon spread over mixture and swirl with a knife. Bake for about 1 hour. Turn onto a wire rack to cool.

Fruity white chocolate bars

preparation time **15 minutes** cooking time **45 minutes** makes about **16**

²/₃ **cup (90g) slivered almonds**
1 ¼ **cups (210g) brazil nuts, coarsely chopped**
1 ½ **cups (135g) desiccated coconut**
1 **cup (150g) chopped dried apricots**
1 **cup (150g) dried currants**
¼ **cup (35g) plain flour**
250g **white cooking chocolate, melted**
½ **cup (160g) apricot jam**
½ **cup (180g) honey**
1 **tablespoon icing sugar**

1 Preheat oven to moderately slow (170°C/150°C fan-forced). Lightly grease 19cm x 29cm rectangular pan; line base with baking paper.
2 Combine nuts, coconut, fruit and flour in large bowl. Stir in combined hot chocolate, sieved jam and honey.
3 Spread mixture evenly into prepared pan; bake for 45 minutes. Cool in pan before cutting into pieces.

tip This recipe can be made a week ahead and the bars kept, covered, in the refrigerator. They can also be frozen for up to two months.

Prune loaf

preparation time **20 minutes** cooking time **1 hour** serves **8**

60g butter, chopped
2 teaspoons finely grated lemon rind
¾ cup (150g) firmly packed brown sugar
2 eggs
1½ cups (240g) wholemeal self-raising flour
¾ cup (200g) cottage cheese
½ cup (105g) coarsely chopped seeded prunes

1 Preheat oven to moderate (180°C/160°C fan-forced). Grease a 14cm x 21cm loaf pan, cover base with baking paper.
2 Combine butter, rind, sugar, eggs and flour in medium bowl of electric mixer; beat on low speed until ingredients are combined. Beat on medium speed until mixture is smooth and changed in colour. Stir in cheese and prunes. Spread mixture into prepared pan. Bake for about 1 hour. Turn onto wire rack to cool.

Mixed spice cake

preparation time **20 minutes** cooking time **45 minutes** serves **8**

3 eggs
¾ cup (165g) caster sugar
1½ cups (225g) self-raising flour
1 teaspoon ground cinnamon
1 teaspoon ground ginger
1 teaspoon ground cloves
1 teaspoon ground cardamom
125g butter, melted
⅓ cup (80ml) milk

1 Preheat oven to moderate (180°C/160°C fan-forced). Grease deep 20cm round cake pan; line base with baking paper.
2 Beat eggs and sugar in small bowl with electric mixer on high speed until thick and creamy. Gently fold in remaining ingredients. Pour mixture into prepared pan; bake for about 45 minutes. Turn cake onto wire rack to cool.
3 If desired, split cold cake, fill and top with honey-flavoured whipped cream; sprinkle lightly with combined ground cinnamon and nutmeg.

Wholemeal honey beer fruit cake

preparation time **25 minutes** cooking time **2 hours 45 minutes** serves **24**

205g butter, chopped
1 ¼ cups (310ml) honey
3 eggs
1 ½ cups (240g) wholemeal self-raising flour
1 ½ cups (240g) wholemeal plain flour
1 teaspoon mixed spice
1 ½ cups (250g) chopped raisins
1 ½ cups (240g) chopped pitted dates
1 ½ cups (240g) sultanas
¾ cup (125g) mixed peel
¾ cup (110g) chopped dried apricots
⅓ cup (65g) chopped glacé ginger
¼ cup (60g) glacé cherries, quartered
375ml can beer

1 Preheat oven to slow (150°C/130°C fan-forced). Grease deep 23cm square cake pan; line base and sides with three layers of baking paper, extending paper 5cm above edges.
2 Beat butter, honey, eggs, flours and spice in large bowl with electric mixer on low speed until combined. Increase speed to medium; beat until mixture is smooth and changed in colour. Stir in fruit and beer.
3 Spread mixture into prepared pan; bake for about 2¾ hours. Cover hot cake tightly with foil; cool in pan.

PACKET MIX CAKES

Black forest torte

preparation time **35 minutes** (plus refrigeration time)
cooking time **55 minutes** serves **12**

You do not need to use the ingredients listed on the packet.

370g packet rich chocolate cake mix
60g butter, softened
2 eggs
⅓ cup (80ml) buttermilk
½ cup (125ml) sour cream
60g dark cooking chocolate, melted
¼ cup (60ml) kirsch
900ml whipping cream, whipped

Cherry filling
2 x 425g cans pitted black cherries
1½ tablespoons cornflour

1 Preheat oven to moderate (180°C/160°C fan-forced). Grease a deep 22cm round cake pan; line base with baking paper.
2 Beat cake mix, butter, eggs, buttermilk, sour cream and cooled chocolate in small bowl with electric mixer on low speed until combined. Increase speed to medium; beat for 2 minutes or until lighter in colour. Pour into prepared pan; bake 50 minutes. Stand cake in pan 5 minutes; turn onto a wire rack to cool.
3 Make cherry filling.
4 Split cold cake horizontally into three layers; brush one layer with a little liqueur, then spread with half the cold cherry filling and a quarter of the whipped cream. Top with second layer. Repeat layering with remaining liqueur, filling and another quarter of whipped cream, finishing with the third cake layer. Decorate with remaining whipped cream; refrigerate 3 hours.

Cherry filling Drain cherries over jug, reserve ⅔ cup (160ml) syrup. Chop cherries roughly. Combine blended cornflour and syrup with cherries in small pan; stir over heat until mixture boils and thickens; cover, cool.

Irresistible choc-on-choc cake

preparation time **30 minutes** (plus cooling time)
cooking time **1 hour 15 minutes** serves **16**

You do not need to use the ingredients listed on the packet.

370g packet rich chocolate cake mix
1 cup (250ml) vegetable oil
2½ cups (625ml) water
300g dark eating chocolate, melted
1 cup (200g) firmly packed brown sugar
2 eggs
2 cups (300g) plain flour
½ cup (50g) cocoa powder
1 teaspoon bicarbonate of soda

Choc-cream filling
250g dark eating chocolate
185g unsalted butter
½ cup (125ml) sour cream

1 Preheat oven to moderate (180°C/160°C fan-forced). Grease a deep 25cm round cake pan; line base and side with baking paper, extending paper 5cm above edge.
2 Combine cake mix with oil, water, cooled chocolate, sugar, eggs and sifted dry ingredients in large bowl; beat on low speed with electric mixer until combined. Increase speed to medium; beat for 2 minutes, or until mixture has changed to a lighter colour.
3 Pour mixture into prepared pan; bake about 1¼ hours. Stand cake in pan for 10 minutes; turn onto a wire rack to cool.
4 Make choc-cream filling.
5 Level top of cold cake; split cake into three layers horizontally. Place one cake layer on serving plate, spread with a quarter of the choc-cream filling; top with a second cake layer. Repeat layering with another quarter of the choc-cream filling, finishing with the third cake layer. Spread top and side of cake with remaining choc-cream filling.

Choc-cream filling Melt chocolate and butter in a medium bowl; stir in sour cream. Allow to cool, stirring occasionally, until the filling thickens and is spreadable.

Minted tropical cake

preparation time **35 minutes** (plus cooling time) cooking time **50 minutes**
serves **12**

*You do not need to use the ingredients listed on the packet. You will need
about 15 passionfruit for this recipe.*

1 cup (250ml) milk
1 cup (20g) loosely packed fresh mint leaves, chopped
½ cup (125ml) passionfruit pulp
340g packet golden buttercake mix
2 eggs
60g butter
⅓ cup (30g) desiccated coconut
2 tablespoons sour cream
600ml cream
¼ cup (60ml) passionfruit pulp, extra

Passionfruit butter
¼ cup (55g) caster sugar
¼ cup (60ml) water
½ cup (125ml) passionfruit pulp
1 tablespoon cornflour
1 tablespoon water, extra
60g butter

1 Stir milk and mint in small pan with wooden spoon over heat until milk
boils. Remove from heat. Cover, cool and strain; you will need ¾ cup (180ml)
milk. Discard mint.
2 Strain passionfruit pulp – you will need ⅓ cup (80ml) juice; discard seeds.
3 Preheat oven to moderate (180°C/160°C fan-forced). Grease a deep
22cm round cake pan; line base with baking paper.
4 Beat cake mix, eggs, butter and cold minted milk in a medium bowl with
electric mixer on low speed for 1 minute. Increase speed to medium; beat
for 4 minutes or until thick. Stir in coconut, sour cream and passionfruit juice
with a wooden spoon.
5 Pour mixture into prepared pan; bake about 45 minutes. Stand cake in pan
5 minutes; turn onto a wire rack to cool.
6 Meanwhile, make passionfruit butter.
7 Beat half the cream in small bowl until soft peaks form; fold in half the
passionfruit butter.

8 Split cold cake into three layers horizontally; sandwich cake layers together with passionfruit cream.

9 Beat remaining cream in small bowl until firm peaks form. Spread over top and side of cake; spoon extra passionfruit pulp on top.

Passionfruit butter Stir sugar and water in medium pan over heat, without boiling, until sugar dissolves. Bring to a boil, then reduce heat and simmer, uncovered, for 5 minutes. Add pulp and blended cornflour and extra water; stir over heat until mixture boils and thickens. Remove from heat, whisk in butter; cover, cool.

Rich fudge cake

preparation time **20 minutes** cooking time **1 hour** serves **8**

You need the ingredients listed on the packet of cake mix for this recipe.

370g packet rich chocolate cake mix
150g dark cooking chocolate, melted
½ cup (125ml) sour cream
½ cup (125ml) chocolate hazelnut spread
½ cup (40g) flaked almonds, toasted

1 Preheat oven to moderate (180°C/160°C fan-forced). Grease deep 22cm round cake pan; line base with baking paper.
2 Beat cake mix with packet ingredients, cooled chocolate and cream in medium bowl with electric mixer on low speed. Increase speed to medium; beat for 2 minutes, or until lighter in colour.
3 Pour mixture into prepared pan; bake for about 1 hour. Stand cake in pan 10 minutes; turn onto wire rack to cool.
4 Level top of cake; spread with hazelnut spread and sprinkle with nuts.

Apricot coconut rolls

preparation time **15 minutes** cooking time **1 hour** serves **8**

You do not need to use the ingredients listed on the packet.

1 cup (150g) finely chopped dried apricots
¾ cup (180ml) boiling water
½ teaspoon bicarbonate of soda
½ cup (45g) desiccated coconut
340g packet muffin mix
¾ cup (120g) wholemeal self-raising flour
½ cup (125ml) milk
1 egg

1 Preheat oven to moderate (180°C/160°C fan-forced). Grease two 8cm x 17cm nut roll tins and lids; place one lid on each tin.
2 Combine apricots and boiling water in medium heatproof bowl, stand for 5 minutes; stir in soda, then remaining ingredients.
3 Spoon mixture into prepared tins; place remaining lids on tins, stand tins upright on oven tray. Bake about 1 hour. Stand rolls in tins 10 minutes; turn onto a wire rack, serve rolls warm or cold.

Berry jelly cake

preparation time **30 minutes** cooking time **50 minutes** serves **8**

You do not need to use the ingredients listed on the packet.

340g packet golden buttercake mix
85g packet raspberry jelly crystals
⅔ cup (160ml) milk
2 eggs
60g butter, chopped

1 Preheat oven to moderate (180°C/160°C fan-forced). Grease a 15cm x 25cm loaf pan; line base with baking paper.
2 Place cake mix and jelly crystals in small bowl, add milk, eggs and butter. Follow method on the packet for making cake.
3 Pour mixture into prepared pan; bake for about 50 minutes. Stand cake for a few minutes before turning onto a wire rack to cool.

Banana cinnamon cake

preparation time **20 minutes** cooking time **40 minutes** serves **16**

You will need to use the ingredients listed on the packet. You will need about 2 medium over-ripe bananas and 1 firm medium banana for this cake.

340g packet golden buttercake mix
1 teaspoon ground cinnamon
⅔ cup mashed over-ripe banana
1 firm banana, finely chopped

1 Preheat oven to moderate (180°C/160°C fan-forced). Grease a 23cm square slab cake pan; line base with baking paper.
2 Place cake mix in a small bowl, add cinnamon, mashed banana and ingredients listed on the packet. Follow method on packet for making cake. Fold in chopped banana.
3 Pour mixture into prepared pan; bake about 40 minutes. Turn onto wire rack to cool.

Chocolate pudding cake

preparation time **20 minutes** cooking time **50 minutes** serves **10**

You do not need to use the ingredients listed on the packet.

370g packet chocolate cake mix
85g packet chocolate instant pudding dessert mix
¼ cup (60ml) vegetable oil
60g unsalted butter, chopped
3 eggs
¾ cup (180ml) water

1 Preheat oven to moderate (180°C/160°C fan-forced). Grease a 21cm baba cake pan.
2 Place cake mix and pudding mix in small bowl with oil, butter, eggs and water. Follow method for mixing on cake mix packet.
3 Pour mixture into prepared pan; bake for about 50 minutes. Stand cake in pan for a few minutes before turning onto wire rack to cool.

Coffee hazelnut supreme

Preparation time **35 minutes** cooking time **1 hour 15 minutes** serves **10**

You will need the ingredients listed on the packets of cake mix for this recipe.

1 tablespoon instant coffee powder
1 tablespoon hot water
2 x 340g packets golden buttercake mix
1¾ cups (200g) hazelnut meal
2 tablespoons caster sugar
¼ cup (60ml) water, extra
2 tablespoons coffee-flavoured liqueur

Coffee cream
1 tablespoon instant coffee powder
1 tablespoon hot water
1 tablespoon coffee-flavoured liqueur
600ml cream
⅓ cup (55g) icing sugar

Chocolate topping
100g dark eating chocolate
50g unsalted butter

1 Preheat oven to moderate (180°C/160°C fan-forced). Grease a deep 22cm round cake pan; line base and side with baking paper, extending paper 5cm above edge.
2 Stir coffee and hot water in small bowl until coffee dissolves.
3 Beat cake mixes with ingredients listed on packets with cold coffee mixture and 1 cup of the hazelnut meal in large bowl with electric mixer on low speed until ingredients are combined. Increase speed to medium; beat 2 minutes or until lighter in colour.
4 Pour mixture into prepared pan; bake about 1¼ hours. Stand cake in pan for 5 minutes; turn onto a wire rack to cool.
5 Stir sugar, extra water and liqueur in small saucepan over heat, without boiling, until sugar dissolves; cool.
6 Make coffee cream; reserve ½ cup (125ml) coffee cream.
7 Make chocolate topping.
8 Level top of cold cake; split into five layers horizontally. Place one cake layer on serving plate, brush with some of the liqueur syrup; spread thinly with some of the remaining coffee cream. Repeat layering with remaining

cake layers, liqueur syrup and coffee cream. Spread chocolate topping over top of cake. Spread reserved coffee cream around side of cake; press on remaining hazelnut meal.

Coffee cream Stir coffee and hot water in small bowl until coffee dissolves; stir in liqueur. Beat cream, icing sugar and cold coffee mixture in a small bowl with electric mixer until soft peaks form.

Chocolate topping Melt chocolate and butter in a small bowl; cool. Stir until mixture is thick and of a spreadable consistency.

Honey roll

preparation time **20 minutes** cooking time **20 minutes** serves **8**

You do not need to use the ingredients listed on the packet.

280g packet golden sponge cake mix
2 eggs
1 teaspoon ground ginger
1 teaspoon ground cinnamon
½ teaspoon ground cloves
⅓ cup (80ml) water
2 tablespoons golden syrup
⅓ cup (30g) coconut
300ml whipping cream, whipped

1 Preheat oven to moderate (180°C/160°C fan-forced). Grease a 25cm x 35cm swiss roll pan; line base with baking paper.
2 Place cake mix in a small bowl, add eggs, spices, water and golden syrup in large bowl. Follow method on packet for making cake.
3 Spread mixture into prepared pan; bake for about 20 minutes.
4 Sprinkle sheet of baking paper with coconut. Turn sponge onto paper, peel off lining paper; trim edges of sponge with a sharp knife. Gently roll hot sponge from the long side, rolling the baking paper inside as you go; cool.
5 When sponge is cold, carefully unroll, spread with whipped cream; roll up to enclose cream.

Chocolate cream cake

Preparation time **35 minutes** cooking time **1 hour** serves **16**

You do not need to use the ingredients listed on the packet.

370g packet chocolate cake mix
60g butter, chopped
2 eggs
⅓ cup (80ml) water
½ cup (125ml) sour cream
60g dark eating chocolate, melted
100g dark eating chocolate, grated, extra
1 teaspoon icing sugar
1 teaspoon cocoa

Syrup
2 tablespoons caster sugar
2 tablespoons water
2 tablespoons coffee-flavoured liqueur

Filling
185g unsalted butter, chopped
185g dark eating chocolate, melted

1 Preheat oven to moderate (180°C/160°C fan-forced). Grease a deep 23cm round cake pan; line base with baking paper.
2 Place cake mix in small bowl with butter, eggs, water, sour cream and cooled melted chocolate. Follow method on packet for making cake.
3 Pour mixture into prepared pan; bake for about 50 minutes. Turn onto a wire rack to cool.
4 Make syrup. Make filling.
5 Split cold cake horizontally into three layers, brush each layer with syrup. Sandwich layers together with one-third of filling. Cover top and side of cake with remaining filling. Decorate side with grated extra chocolate. Sprinkle cake with sifted icing sugar, if desired.

Syrup Combine sugar and water in small saucepan, stir over heat, without boiling, until sugar is dissolved; cool, stir in liqueur.

Filling Beat butter in small bowl with electric mixer until light and fluffy. Gradually add cooled chocolate, beating well.

Chocolate orange liqueur cake

preparation time **30 minutes** cooking time **50 minutes** serves **12**

You will need the ingredients listed on the cake mix packet for this recipe.

340g packet orange cake mix
60g butter, chopped
¼ cup (30g) chopped roasted hazelnuts
90g dark cooking chocolate, melted
2 tablespoons grand marnier
1 cup (125g) chopped roasted hazelnuts, extra

Filling
600ml whipping cream
2 tablespoons icing sugar

1 Preheat oven to moderate (180°C/160°C fan-forced). Grease deep 23cm round cake pan; line base with baking paper.
2 Place cake mix in small bowl; add butter and ingredients listed on packet. Follow method on packet for making cake. Fold in nuts and swirl in chocolate.
3 Spread mixture into prepared pan; bake about 50 minutes. Turn onto wire rack to cool.
4 Beat ingredients for filling in small bowl with electric mixer until firm.
5 Split cold cake in half horizontally. Sprinkle half the cake with half the liqueur, top with about quarter of the filing; top with remaining cake layer, then sprinkle with remaining liqueur. Spread remaining filling on top and side of cake. Decorate with extra whole nuts.

DESSERT CAKES

Pistachio and polenta cake with blood orange syrup

preparation time **10 minutes** cooking time **1 hour 15 minutes** serves **12**

300g sour cream
125g butter, softened
1 cup (220g) caster sugar
2 cups (300g) self-raising flour
½ teaspoon bicarbonate of soda
⅔ cup (110g) polenta
1 teaspoon finely grated blood orange rind
¾ cup (180ml) water
⅔ cup (100g) toasted shelled pistachios

Blood orange syrup
1 cup (250ml) blood orange juice
1 cup (220g) caster sugar
1 cinnamon stick

1 Preheat oven to moderately slow (170°C/150°C fan-forced). Grease deep 20cm round cake pan; line base and side with baking paper.
2 Make blood orange syrup.
3 Beat sour cream, butter, sugar, sifted flour and soda, polenta, rind and the water in large bowl with electric mixer on low speed until just combined. Increase speed to medium; beat until mixture changes to a slightly lighter colour. Stir in nuts.
4 Spread mixture into prepared pan; bake, uncovered, for about 1 hour. Stand cake in pan 10 minutes; turn cake, top-side up, onto wire rack to cool.
5 Serve cake warm or cold with strained blood orange syrup.

Blood orange syrup Combine ingredients in small saucepan, bring to a boil, stirring, then reduce heat; simmer, uncovered, about 15 minutes or until syrup thickens. Cool to room temperature.

Sticky date roll with butterscotch sauce

preparation time **15 minutes** cooking time **30 minutes** serves **12**

2 tablespoons white sugar
1 cup (160g) seeded dates
¾ cup (180ml) boiling water
1 teaspoon bicarbonate of soda
50g butter, chopped
⅔ cup (150g) firmly packed brown sugar
2 eggs
¾ cup (110g) self-raising flour
300ml double cream

Butterscotch sauce
½ cup (100g) firmly packed brown sugar
⅔ cup (160ml) double cream
100g butter, chopped

1 Preheat oven to moderate (180°C/160°C fan-forced). Grease 25cm x 30cm swiss roll pan; line base and short sides of pan with baking paper, extending paper 5cm above edge. Place a piece of baking paper cut the same size as swiss roll pan on board or bench; sprinkle evenly with white sugar.
2 Place dates, the water and soda in food processor; let stand, covered, for 5 minutes. Add butter and brown sugar; process until almost smooth. Add eggs and flour; process until just combined.
3 Pour mixture into prepared pan; bake for about 15 minutes.
4 Turn cake onto sugared paper, peel lining paper away; working quickly, trim crisp edges from all sides. Using hands and sugared paper as a guide, gently roll cake loosely from a long side; hold for 30 seconds, then unroll. Cover with tea towel; cool.
5 Make butterscotch sauce.
6 Beat cream in small bowl with electric mixer until firm peaks form. Fold ¼ cup of the butterscotch sauce into cream; spread evenly over cake. Roll cake, from same long side, by lifting paper and using it to guide into shape.
7 Serve sticky date roll drizzled with remaining warmed butterscotch sauce.

Butterscotch sauce Combine ingredients in small saucepan; stir over heat until sugar dissolves and butter melts.

Blackberry and orange mascarpone cake

preparation time **30 minutes** (plus refrigeration time)
cooking time **50 minutes** serves **10**

185g butter
1 tablespoon finely grated orange rind
1 cup (220g) caster sugar
3 eggs, beaten lightly
1 cup (150g) self-raising flour
⅓ cup (40g) almond meal
½ cup (125ml) orange juice
350g blackberries
⅓ cup (110g) blackberry jam, warmed
1 tablespoon orange-flavoured liqueur
1 tablespoon icing sugar

Mascarpone cream
⅔ cup (160ml) double cream
1 cup (250g) mascarpone cheese
⅓ cup (55g) icing sugar
1 teaspoon finely grated orange rind
1 tablespoon orange-flavoured liqueur

1 Preheat oven to moderately slow (170°C/150°C fan-forced). Grease deep 22cm round cake pan; line base and side with baking paper.
2 Beat butter, rind and caster sugar in medium bowl with electric mixer until light and fluffy. Add eggs one at a time, beating until combined after each addition. Fold in flour, almond meal and juice, in two batches.
3 Pour mixture into prepared pan; bake, uncovered, about 50 minutes. Stand cake 5 minutes, then turn onto wire rack; turn cake top-side up to cool.
4 Meanwhile, make mascarpone cream.
5 Reserve 10 blackberries. Using large serrated knife, split cake into three layers. Place one layer of cake on serving plate; spread with half of the combined jam and liqueur. Spread with half of the mascarpone cream, then top with half of the blackberries. Repeat layering process, finishing with layer of cake. Cover; refrigerate 1 hour. Serve cake sprinkled with sifted icing sugar and reserved blackberries.

Mascarpone cream Beat cream, cheese and sugar in small bowl with electric mixer until soft peaks form; stir in rind and liqueur.

Peach and almond cake

preparation time **30 minutes** (plus cooling time)
cooking time **1 hours 35 minutes** serves **8**

125g butter, chopped
¾ cup (165g) caster sugar
3 eggs
⅔ cup (160g) sour cream
⅔ cup (100g) plain flour
⅔ cup (100g) self-raising flour
¼ cup (40g) blanched almonds, toasted, chopped coarsely
40g dark eating chocolate, chopped coarsely
½ cup (60g) almond meal
3 peaches, sliced thinly
¼ cup (80g) apricot jam, warmed

1 Preheat oven to moderately slow (170°C/150°C fan-forced). Insert base of 23cm springform tin upside down in pan to give a flat base; grease pan.
2 Beat butter and sugar in medium bowl with electric mixer until light and fluffy. Add eggs one at a time, beating until just combined after each addition. Add sour cream; beat until just combined. (Mixture may curdle at this stage but will come together later.) Stir in flours, nuts, chocolate and almond meal.
3 Spread cake mixture into prepared tin; arrange peach slices over mixture.
4 Bake for about 1 hour 35 minutes. Stand cake in pan 10 minutes; remove from pan. Serve warm, brushed with jam.

Chocolate, nut and coffee ice-cream cake

preparation time **35 minutes** (plus freezing time) serves **10**

2 litres vanilla ice-cream
1 tablespoon instant coffee granules
1 tablespoon hot water
½ cup (70g) almonds, chopped coarsely
100g dark eating chocolate, melted
1 tablespoon crème de cacao
100g white eating chocolate, melted
½ cup (75g) roasted shelled pistachios, chopped coarsely

1 Grease a 21cm springform tin; line base and side with baking paper.
2 Divide ice-cream into three portions; return two portions to freezer. Soften remaining ice-cream in a medium bowl.
3 Dissolve coffee in the water in a small jug; stir into softened ice-cream with two-thirds of the almonds. Spoon into prepared tin, cover; freeze for about 2 hours, or until firm.
4 Meanwhile, soften second portion of the ice-cream in a medium bowl; stir in dark chocolate. Microwave, uncovered, on MEDIUM-HIGH (80%) for about 2 minutes, or until chocolate melts; whisk until smooth. Stir in liqueur, cover; freeze for about 1 hour, or until almost firm. Spoon dark chocolate ice-cream over coffee layer, cover; freeze for about 2 hours or until firm.
5 Soften remaining ice-cream in a medium bowl; fold in white chocolate. Microwave, uncovered, on MEDIUM-HIGH (80%) for about 2 minutes, or until chocolate melts; whisk until smooth. Stir in two-thirds of the pistachios, cover; freeze for about 1 hour, or until almost firm, stirring ice-cream occasionally to suspend pistachios evenly. Spoon white chocolate ice-cream over dark chocolate layer; cover and freeze for about 2 hours or until firm.
6 Remove ice-cream cake from pan just before serving; sprinkle with remaining almonds and pistachios.

Little peach jam puddings with vanilla custard

preparation time **30 minutes** cooking time **25 minutes** serves **6**

¾ cup (255g) peach jam
2 tablespoons finely chopped glacé peaches
125g softened butter
½ cup (110g) caster sugar
2 eggs
1 cup (150g) self-raising flour
1 teaspoon baking powder
½ cup (125ml) milk
2 tablespoons finely chopped glacé peaches, extra

Vanilla custard
4 eggs
¼ cup (55g) caster sugar
1½ cups (375ml) milk
¾ cup (180ml) cream
1 vanilla bean, split lengthways

1 Preheat oven to moderate (180°C/160°C fan-forced). Grease six 1-cup (250ml) dariole moulds or ovenproof dishes; line base with baking paper.
2 Warm jam in a small saucepan (or microwave on HIGH for 20 seconds); stir in glacé peaches. Divide mixture among prepared moulds.
3 Beat butter and sugar in small bowl with an electric mixer until light and fluffy. Add eggs one at a time, beat well after each addition. Stir in sifted flour and baking powder with milk in two batches. Stir in extra glacé peaches.
4 Spoon mixture over jam in moulds; place moulds in a large baking dish. Pour enough boiling water into baking dish to come 1cm up sides of moulds.
5 Bake puddings, uncovered, about 25 minutes or until cooked through. Stand puddings for 5 minutes before turning out.
6 Meanwhile, make vanilla cutard; serve with puddings.

Vanilla custard Beat eggs in small bowl with electric mixer until thick and creamy; combine sugar, milk and cream in medium saucepan. Using a blunt knife, scrape seeds from vanilla bean into milk mixture. Stir milk mixture over heat until sugar dissolves and mixture is hot but not boiling. Gradually add milk mixture to egg, stirring constantly. Return this mixture to saucepan, stir over a low heat until custard thickens and coats the back of a spoon.

Choc-strawberry meringue gâteau

preparation time **40 minutes** cooking time **45 minutes** serves **12**

125g butter
4 eggs, separated
¾ cup (165g) caster sugar
1 cup (150g) self-raising flour
⅓ cup (35g) cocoa powder
½ teaspoon bicarbonate of soda
1 cup (250ml) buttermilk
⅔ cup (150g) caster sugar, extra
¼ cup (30g) coarsely chopped roasted hazelnuts
⅔ cup (160ml) double cream
1 tablespoon icing sugar
250g strawberries, halved

1 Preheat oven to moderately slow (170°C/150°C fan-forced). Grease two 20cm sandwich pans; line base and side with baking paper.
2 Beat butter, egg yolks and caster sugar in medium bowl with electric mixer until light and fluffy. Stir in combined sifted flour, cocoa and soda, then buttermilk. Divide mixture between prepared pans.
3 Beat egg whites in small bowl with electric mixer until soft peaks form; gradually add extra caster sugar, a tablespoon at a time, beating until sugar dissolves between additions.
4 Divide meringue mixture over cake mixture in pans, spreading to cover cake mixture. Sprinkle nuts over meringue mixture on one of the cakes.
5 Bake cakes, uncovered, for 25 minutes. Cover pans loosely with foil; bake a further 20 minutes. Stand cakes 5 minutes; turn onto wire racks, turning top-side up to cool.
6 Beat cream and icing sugar in small bowl with electric mixer until soft peaks form. Place cake without nuts on serving plate; spread with cream mixture. Sprinkle with strawberries; top with remaining cake.

Brandied apricot cake

preparation time **25 minutes** cooking time **1 hour 5 minutes** serves **10**

125g dark eating chocolate, chopped
½ cup (125ml) water
125g butter
1 cup (220g) firmly packed brown sugar
2 eggs
½ cup (120g) sour cream
1 ⅓ cups (200g) plain flour
⅓ cup (50g) self-raising flour
½ cup apricot jam
2 tablespoons brandy
300ml whipping cream

Chocolate icing
90g dark eating chocolate, chopped
15g butter, extra

1 Preheat oven to moderately slow (170°C/150°C fan-forced). Grease a deep 20cm round cake pan; line base with baking paper.
2 Melt chocolate and the water over hot water; cool.
3 Cream butter and sugar in small bowl with electric mixer until light and fluffy. Add eggs one at a time, beating until combined after each addition. Transfer mixture to large bowl; stir in chocolate mixture, sour cream and sifted flours in two batches.
4 Spread mixture into prepared pan; bake for about 1 hour. Stand cake in pan for 5 minutes before turning on to wire rack to cool.
5 Meanwhile, melt ingredients for chocolate icing over hot water; cool.
6 Combine jam and brandy. Beat cream in small bowl until soft peaks form.
7 Split cold cake into four layers. Join layers together with jam mixture and cream. Spread cake with chocolate icing; refrigerate until set.

tip This cake can be kept in an airtight container in the refrigerator for up to two days.

Frosted chocolate yogurt cake

preparation time **35 minutes** (plus standing)
cooking time **45 minutes** serves **10**

100g dark chocolate, chopped
½ cup (125ml) water
185g butter
1 teaspoon vanilla extract
1½ cups (330g) firmly packed brown sugar
3 eggs
½ cup (140g) plain yogurt
2¼ cups (335g) self-raising flour

Frosting
250g dark chocolate
½ cup (120g) sour cream
1 cup (160g) icing sugar

1 Preheat oven to moderate (180°C/160°C fan-forced). Grease two deep 20cm round cake pans; line base with baking paper.
2 Melt chocolate and the water over hot water; cool.
3 Cream butter, extract and sugar in small bowl with electric mixer until light and fluffy. Add eggs one at a time, beating until combined after each addition. Transfer mixture to large bowl; stir in chocolate mixture and yogurt, then sifted flour in two batches.
4 Spread mixture into prepared pans; bake for about 40 minutes. Turn onto wire rack to cool.
5 Meanwhile, make frosting.
6 Split cold cakes in half; join with three-quarters of the frosting. Spread top with remaining frosting. Spread side with whipped cream, if desired.

Frosting Melt chocolate in heatproof bowl over hot water. Stir in sour cream; gradually stir in sifted icing sugar. Refrigerate until frosting is thick.

tip This cake can be kept in an airtight container in the refrigerator for up to two days.

Decadent chocolate roulade

preparation time **15 minutes** (plus refrigeration time)
cooking time **15 minutes** serves **8**

200g dark eating chocolate, chopped coarsely
¼ cup (60ml) hot water
1 teaspoon instant coffee granules
4 eggs, separated
¾ cup (165g) caster sugar
300ml whipping cream
150g raspberries

1 Preheat oven to moderate (180°C/160°C fan-forced). Grease a 25cm x
30cm swiss roll pan; line base and long sides with baking paper, extending
paper 5cm above edge.
2 Place chocolate, the water and coffee granules in large heatproof bowl; stir
over large saucepan of simmering water until smooth. Remove from heat.
3 Beat egg yolks and ½ cup of the sugar in small bowl with electric mixer
for about 5 minutes or until thick and creamy. Fold egg mixture into warm
chocolate mixture.
4 Beat egg whites in small bowl with electric mixer until soft peaks form; fold
into chocolate mixture, in two batches.
5 Spread mixture into prepared pan; bake, uncovered, for about 10 minutes.
6 Meanwhile, place a piece of baking paper cut the same size as swiss roll
pan on a board; sprinkle evenly with remaining sugar. Turn cooked cake onto
sugared paper; peel lining paper away. Cool.
7 Beat cream in small bowl of electric mixer until firm peaks form. Spread
cream over cake; sprinkle with raspberries. Roll cake, from long side, by lifting
paper and using it to guide the roll into shape. Cover roll; refrigerate for
30 minutes before serving.

tip The roulade can be made a day in advance, then filled and rolled six
hours before serving.

Pecan and chocolate brownies

preparation time **15 minutes** cooking time **22 minutes** makes **8**

80g butter, chopped
150g dark eating chocolate, chopped
¾ cup (150g) firmly packed brown sugar
2 eggs, beaten lightly
1 teaspoon vanilla extract
⅔ cup (100g) plain flour
1 tablespoon cocoa powder
50g dark eating chocolate, chopped, extra
¼ cup (30g) chopped pecans

1 Preheat oven to moderately hot (200°C/180°C fan-forced). Grease eight holes of a 12-hole (⅓-cup/80ml) muffin pan; line bases with rounds of baking paper.
2 Combine butter, chocolate and sugar in medium heavy-based saucepan; stir over a low heat until smooth.
3 Transfer mixture to large bowl; stir in egg, extract, sifted flour and cocoa, then extra chocolate.
4 Divide mixture among prepared muffin-pan holes; sprinkle with nuts. Bake for about 20 minutes.

tip These brownies can be made up to three days ahead and stored in an airtight container. They are suitable for freezing.

Chocolate espresso mousse cake

preparation time **40 minutes** (plus refrigeration time)
cooking time **15 minutes** serves **12**

6 eggs, separated
½ cup (80g) icing sugar
¼ cup (25g) cocoa powder
2 tablespoons cornflour
150g dark eating chocolate, melted
1 tablespoon water
1 tablespoon instant coffee granules
1 tablespoon hot water
3 cups (750ml) whipping cream
450g dark eating chocolate, melted, extra
2 teaspoons cocoa powder, extra

1 Preheat oven to moderate (180°C/160°C fan-forced). Grease 25cm x 30cm swiss roll pan; line base and two long sides with baking paper, extending paper 5cm above edge.

2 Beat egg yolks and sugar in small bowl with electric mixer until thick and creamy; transfer mixture to large bowl. Fold in combined sifted cocoa and cornflour, then chocolate and the water.

3 Beat egg whites in small bowl with electric mixer until soft peaks form. Fold egg whites, in two batches, into chocolate mixture.

4 Spread mixture into prepared pan; bake, uncovered, for about 15 minutes. Turn cake onto baking-paper-lined wire rack to cool.

5 Grease 23cm springform tin; line side with baking paper, extending paper 5cm above edge. Cut a 23cm-diameter circle from cooled cake; place in prepared pan. Discard remaining cake.

6 Dissolve coffee in the hot water in a small jug; cool. Beat cream and coffee mixture in medium bowl with electric mixer until soft peaks form. Fold in cooled extra chocolate. Pour coffee mixture over cake in tin. Cover; refrigerate about 3 hours or until set.

7 Transfer cake from tin to serving plate; dust with sifted extra cocoa.

Irish cream and dark chocolate mousse cake

preparation time **30 minutes** (plus refrigeration time)
cooking time **15 minutes** serves **12**

6 eggs, separated
½ cup (80g) icing sugar
¼ cup (25g) cocoa powder
2 tablespoons cornflour
150g dark eating chocolate, melted
1 tablespoon water
600ml cream
450g dark eating chocolate, chopped coarsely, extra
¾ cup (180ml) irish cream liqueur
1 tablespoon cocoa powder, extra

1 Preheat oven to moderate (180°C/160°C fan-forced). Grease 25cm x 30cm swiss roll pan; line base and sides with baking paper.

2 Beat egg yolks and sugar in small bowl with electric mixer until thick and creamy; transfer to large bowl. Fold in combined sifted cocoa and cornflour, then chocolate; fold in the water.

3 Beat egg whites in medium bowl with electric mixer until soft peaks form. Fold in egg whites, in two batches.

4 Spread mixture into prepared pan; bake about 15 minutes. Turn cake onto baking paper-lined wire rack. Cover cake with baking paper; cool to room temperature.

5 Grease a 22cm springform tin; line side with baking paper, extending paper 5cm above edge. Cut a 22cm-diameter circle from cooled cake; place in prepared pan. Discard remaining cake.

6 Combine cream and extra chocolate in medium saucepan; stir over low heat until smooth. Transfer to large bowl; refrigerate until just cold.

7 Add liqueur to chocolate mixture; beat with electric mixer until mixture changes to a paler colour. Pour into prepared tin; refrigerate about 3 hours or until set.

8 Transfer cake to serving plate; dust with sifted extra cocoa.

Rich truffle and raspberry mudcake

Preparation time **10 minutes** (plus refrigeration time) cooking time **1 hour** serves **12**

6 eggs
½ cup (110g) firmly packed brown sugar
400g dark eating chocolate, melted
1 cup (250ml) double cream
⅓ cup (80ml) tia maria
150g frozen raspberries

1 Preheat oven to moderate (180°C/160°C fan-forced). Grease deep 22cm round cake pan; line base and side with baking paper.

2 Beat eggs and sugar in large bowl with electric mixer about 5 minutes or until thick and creamy. With motor operating, gradually beat in barely warm chocolate; beat until combined.

3 Using a metal spoon, gently fold in cream, liqueur and raspberries to chocolate mixture.

4 Pour mixture into prepared pan. Place pan in baking dish; pour enough boiling water into dish to come halfway up side of pan. Bake, uncovered, for about 30 minutes. Cover loosely with foil; bake another 30 minutes. Discard foil; cool cake in pan.

5 Turn cake onto serving plate and cover; refrigerate overnight. Serve dusted with a little sifted cocoa powder, if desired.

tips This cake is best made the day before serving. It will keep for up to four days in an airtight container in the refrigerator.

Warm chocolate polenta cakes with chocolate sauce

preparation time **20 minutes** cooking time **30 minutes** makes **8**

125g softened butter
⅔ cup (150g) caster sugar
1¼ cups (150g) almond meal
¼ cup (25g) cocoa powder
50g dark eating chocolate, grated
2 eggs
½ cup (85g) instant polenta
⅓ cup (80ml) milk

Chocolate sauce
125g dark eating chocolate, chopped
½ cup (125ml) cream

1 Preheat oven to moderately slow (170°C/150°C fan-forced). Grease eight almond cake tins; line base with baking paper.
2 Beat butter and sugar in a small bowl with an electric mixer until light and fluffy. Add almond meal, sifted cocoa and chocolate; beat until just combined. Add eggs one at a time, beating well after each addition. Stir in combined polenta and milk.
3 Divide mixture among prepared tins; bake for about 30 minutes or until cooled slightly.
4 Make chocolate sauce; serve with cakes.

Chocolate sauce Combine chocolate and cream in a heatproof bowl; stir over a pan of simmering water until melted.

tip These cakes are suitable to freeze.

Vanilla bean cheesecake with hazelnut crust

preparation time **35 minutes** (plus refrigeration and cooling time)
cooking time **55 minutes** serves **12**

80g butter, melted
½ teaspoon vanilla extract
¾ cup (110g) plain flour
¼ teaspoon ground cinnamon
Pinch ground nutmeg
⅓ cup (75g) caster sugar
⅓ cup (50g) hazelnuts, roasted, chopped coarsely
¼ cup (80g) apricot jam, warmed

Vanilla bean filling
1 vanilla bean
250g cream cheese, softened
500g ricotta cheese
⅔ cup (150g) caster sugar
2 tablespoons lemon juice
2 eggs

1 Preheat oven to moderate (180°C/160°C fan-forced). Lightly grease a
24cm springform tin.
2 Combine butter, extract, flour, spices, sugar and hazelnuts in medium bowl.
Press mixture over base of prepared tin; place tin on an oven tray. Refrigerate
for 20 minutes.
3 Bake base for about 20 minutes or until browned. Remove from oven and
spread with jam. Reduce oven temperature to slow (150°C/130°C fan-forced).
4 Meanwhile, make vanilla bean filling.
5 Pour filling over prepared base. Bake in slow oven 35 minutes or until firm
to touch. Cool cheesecake in oven with door ajar; refrigerate overnight.

Vanilla bean filling Split vanilla bean in half lengthways; scrape out seeds.
Beat cream cheese, ricotta, vanilla seeds, half the sugar and juice in a small
bowl with an electric mixer until just combined; do not over-beat. Transfer
to a large bowl. Beat remaining sugar and eggs in a bowl with electric mixer
for 5 minutes on high speed or until thick and creamy. Fold egg mixture into
cheese mixture.

Irish cream cheesecake with chocolate sauce

preparation time **20 minutes** (plus refrigeration time)
cooking time **5 minutes** serves **10**

250g choc-chip biscuits
75g butter, melted
3 teaspoons gelatine
¼ cup (60ml) water
500g cream cheese
¾ cup (165g) caster sugar
300ml double cream
⅓ cup (80ml) irish cream liqueur
2 egg whites

Chocolate sauce
200g dark eating chocolate, chopped
1 cup (250ml) cream
2 tablespoons irish cream liqueur

1 Blend or process biscuits until they resemble fine breadcrumbs. Transfer to a large bowl; add butter, stir to combine. Press biscuit mixture evenly over the base of a 24cm springform tin; refrigerate for 30 minutes or until firm.
2 Sprinkle gelatine over the water in a small heatproof jug; stand jug in small saucepan of simmering water, stirring until gelatine dissolves. Cool 5 minutes.
3 Beat cream cheese and sugar in a medium bowl with an electric mixer until smooth. Add cream; beat until thick. Stir in gelatine mixture and liqueur.
4 Beat egg whites in a clean small bowl with an electric mixer until soft peaks form; fold into cheese mixture.
5 Pour mixture over base. Cover; refrigerate for about 4 hours or until set.
6 Make chocolate sauce; serve with cheesecake.

Chocolate sauce Combine chocolate and cream in a small heavy-based saucepan; stir over low heat until smooth. Stir in liqueur.

Rich chocolate meringue cake

preparation time **15 minutes** cooking time **1 hour 30 minutes**
serves **8**

8 egg whites
1 cup (220g) caster sugar
60g dark eating chocolate, chopped finely
¼ cup (60g) finely chopped glacé figs
¼ cup (50g) finely chopped seeded prunes
¾ cup (45g) stale breadcrumbs
¼ cup (25g) cocoa powder
1 tablespoon icing sugar
1 tablespoon cocoa powder, extra
⅓ cup (80ml) whipping cream, whipped

1 Preheat oven to very slow (120°C/100°C fan-forced). Grease a 22cm
springform tin; line base and side with baking paper.
2 Beat egg whites in medium bowl with electric mixer until soft peaks form.
Add sugar, 1 tablespoon at time, beating until sugar dissolves between each
addition. Fold in chocolate, fruit, breadcrumbs and sifted cocoa.
3 Spoon mixture into prepared tin; bake for 1½ hours. Cool in oven with
door ajar.
4 Dust cake with combined sifted icing sugar and extra cocoa; serve with
whipped cream.

Choc-brownies with caramel sauce

preparation time **10 minutes** cooking time **20 minutes** serves **6**

80g butter
150g dark eating chocolate, chopped coarsely
¾ cup (150g) firmly packed brown sugar
2 eggs, beaten lightly
1 teaspoon vanilla extract
¾ cup (110g) plain flour
300ml vanilla ice-cream
⅓ cup (45g) candied (vienna) almonds, chopped coarsely

Caramel sauce
⅔ cup (160ml) cream
60g butter
¾ cup (150g) firmly packed brown sugar

1 Preheat oven to hot (220°C/200°C fan forced). Grease a 6-hole texas (¾-cup/180ml) muffin pan.
2 Combine butter, chocolate and sugar in medium saucepan; stir over medium heat until smooth. Stir in egg, extract and flour.
3 Divide mixture among muffin pan holes; cover pan tightly with foil. Bake for about 20 minutes. Remove foil; let brownies stand for 5 minutes in pan.
4 Make caramel sauce.
5 Place brownies on serving plates; top with ice-cream, caramel sauce and candied almonds.

Caramel sauce Combine ingredients in small saucepan; stir over medium heat until smooth. Simmer for 2 minutes.

Cookies and cream cheesecake

preparation time **20 minutes** (plus refrigeration time)
cooking time **5 minutes** serves **12**

250g plain chocolate biscuits
150g butter, melted
2 teaspoons gelatine
¼ cup (60ml) water
1½ cups (360g) cream cheese, softened
300ml cream
1 teaspoon vanilla extract
½ cup (110g) caster sugar
180g white eating chocolate, melted
150g cream-filled chocolate biscuits, quartered
50g dark eating chocolate, melted

1 Line base of 23cm springform tin with baking paper.

2 Blend or process plain chocolate biscuits until mixture resembles fine breadcrumbs. Add butter; process until just combined. Using your hand, press biscuit mixture evenly over base and 3cm up side of prepared tin. Cover and refrigerate for 20 minutes.

3 Sprinkle gelatine over the water in a small heatproof jug; stand jug in a small saucepan of simmering water, stirring until gelatine dissolves. Cool for 5 minutes.

4 Beat cheese, cream, extract and sugar in a medium bowl with electric mixer until smooth. Stir in gelatine mixture and white chocolate; fold in biscuit pieces.

5 Pour cheesecake mixture over biscuit base in tin; cover and refrigerate for about 3 hours or until set. Drizzle with melted dark chocolate to serve.

Soft-centred chocolate cakes with warm sour cherry sauce

preparation time **15 minutes** cooking time **25 minutes** serves **6**

185g dark eating chocolate, chopped coarsely
185g butter, chopped
3 egg yolks
⅓ cup (50g) plain flour
4 eggs
⅓ cup (75g) caster sugar
350g sour cherry jam

1 Preheat oven to moderate (180°C/160°C fan-forced). Grease a texas-style 6-hole (¾-cup/180ml) muffin pan. Sprinkle with a little plain flour, then tilt to coat side of holes; shake off excess.
2 Place chocolate and butter in small saucepan; stir over low heat until mixture is smooth. Transfer to large bowl; stir in yolks and flour.
3 Beat eggs and sugar in small bowl with electric mixer about 5 minutes or until light and fluffy. Fold egg mixture into chocolate mixture.
4 Spoon mixture into holes of prepared pan. Bake for about 10 minutes; cakes should be soft in the centre. Stand cakes in pan for 5 minutes, then remove carefully.
5 Melt jam in small saucepan over low heat, then blend or process until smooth; strain. Return jam to pan, add a little water to give pouring consistency; bring to a boil. Skim surface; let stand for 5 minutes.
6 Serve cakes warm, drizzled with warm sour cherry sauce.

White chocolate and strawberry cheesecake

preparation time **25 minutes** (plus refrigeration time)
cooking time **5 minutes** serves **10**

185g plain biscuits
80g butter, melted
3 teaspoons gelatine
2 tablespoons water
500g cream cheese, softened
400g can sweetened condensed milk
300ml whipping cream
150g white eating chocolate, melted
500g large strawberries, halved
¼ cup (80g) strawberry jam, warmed, strained
1 tablespoon lemon juice

1 Grease a 23cm springform tin.

2 Blend or process biscuits until mixture resembles fine breadcrumbs. Add butter; process until combined. Using your hand, press the biscuit mixture evenly over base of prepared tin. Cover and refrigerate about 30 minutes or until firm.

3 Meanwhile, sprinkle gelatine over the water in small heatproof jug; stand jug in small saucepan of simmering water, stirring until gelatine dissolves. Cool 5 minutes.

4 Beat cheese and condensed milk in a medium bowl with electric mixer until smooth.

5 Beat cream in small bowl with electric mixer until soft peaks form.

6 Stir warm gelatine mixture into cheese mixture; fold in cream and chocolate.

7 Pour cheesecake mixture into prepared tin, spreading evenly over biscuit base. Cover; refrigerate overnight.

8 To serve, place strawberries on top of cheesecake and brush with combined jam and juice.

Black forest roulade

preparation time **20 minutes** (plus refrigeration time)
cooking time **20 minutes** serves **6**

200g dark eating chocolate, chopped coarsely
¼ cup (60ml) hot water
1 teaspoon instant coffee granules
4 eggs, separated
½ cup (110g) caster sugar
1 tablespoon caster sugar, extra
½ cup (125ml) whipping cream
1 tablespoon kirsch

Cherry filling
425g can seedless black cherries
3 teaspoons cornflour
1 tablespoon kirsch

1 Preheat oven to moderate (180°C/160°C fan-forced). Grease 25cm x 30cm swiss roll pan; line base with baking paper.
2 Combine chocolate, the water and coffee in large heatproof bowl; place over saucepan of simmering water. Using wooden spoon, stir until chocolate melts then immediately remove bowl from pan.
3 Beat egg yolks and sugar in small bowl with electric mixer 5 minutes or until thick and creamy. Using a large metal spoon, fold egg mixture into warm chocolate mixture.
4 Beat egg whites in a small bowl with electric mixer until soft peaks form. Using a metal spoon, gently fold egg whites into chocolate mixture, in two batches. Spread mixture into prepared pan; bake for about 10 minutes.
5 Meanwhile, place a large sheet of baking paper on board; sprinkle with extra sugar. Turn cake onto sugared baking paper; carefully remove lining paper, cover cake loosely with tea towel. Cool cake to room temperature.
6 Make cherry filling.
7 Beat cream and kirsch in small bowl with electric mixer until firm peaks form.
8 Spread cake evenly with cooled cherry filling, then spread kirsch cream over cherry mixture. Roll cake from a long side, using paper to lift and guide the roll; place on serving plate. Cover roll and refrigerate for 30 minutes before serving.

Cherry filling Drain cherries, reserving ¼ cup (60ml) of syrup. Using knife, chop cherries coarsely. Using a wooden spoon, blend cornflour and reserved syrup in small saucepan. Add cherries; stir over heat until mixture boils and thickens. Remove from heat and stir in kirsch; cover surface of mixture with plastic wrap; cool to room temperature.

tip This recipe is best made on the day of serving.

Dark chocolate dessert cake

preparation time **15 minutes** cooking time **1 hour 15 minutes** serves **10**

125g butter, chopped
1 ½ cups (330g) caster sugar
3 eggs
1 cup (150g) plain flour
1 cup (150g) self-raising flour
¾ cup (75g) cocoa
½ cup (125ml) water
1 cup (250ml) milk

1 Preheat oven to moderately slow (170°C/150°C fan-forced). Grease deep 23cm round cake pan; line base with baking paper.
2 Beat ingredients in medium bowl with electric mixer on low speed until combined. Increase speed to medium; beat until mixture is smooth and changed in colour.
3 Pour mixture into prepared pan; bake about 1 ¼ hours. Stand cake in pan for 5 minutes before turning onto wire rack to cool.
4 Top cold cake with chocolate glaze (see page 290), if desired.

Cumquat layer cake

preparation time **30 minutes**   cooking time **35 minutes**   serves **10**

3 eggs
½ cup (110g) caster sugar
¼ cup (35g) plain flour
¼ cup (35g) self-raising flour
¼ cup (35g) cornflour
2 tablespoons cointreau
300ml whipping cream

Cumquat filling
250g cumquats
½ cup (125ml) water
½ cup (110g) caster sugar
1 tablespoon cointreau
3 egg yolks
⅓ cup (75g) caster sugar, extra
1 tablespoon plain flour
1 tablespoon cornflour
1½ cups (375ml) milk
½ cup (125ml) whipping cream

1 Preheat oven to moderate (180°C/160°C fan-forced). Grease a deep 20cm round cake pan; line base with baking paper.
2 Beat eggs in small bowl with electric mixer until thick and creamy. Gradually add sugar; beat until dissolved between additions. Transfer to large bowl; carefully fold in sifted flours. Spread mixture into prepared pan; bake for about 30 minutes, or until just firm. Turn cake onto wire rack to cool.
3 Meanwhile, make cumquat filling.
4 Cut cold cake into three layers. Brush each layer with liqueur. Sandwich layers with cumquat filling. Beat cream until soft peaks form. Cover and decorate cake with cream and reserved cooked cumquats. Sprinkle with a little ground nutmeg, if desired.

Cumquat filling Slice unpeeled cumquats finely; discard seeds. Combine cumquats, water and sugar in medium saucepan; stir over heat, without boiling, until sugar is dissolved. Bring to boil, then reduce heat and simmer, uncovered and without stirring, for 5 minutes. Remove from heat and stir in liqueur; cool to room temperature. Combine egg yolks, extra sugar and flours in medium saucepan; gradually stir in milk. Stir over high heat until mixture boils and thickens; remove from heat, cover, then cool to room temperature. Beat cream in small bowl until soft peaks form; fold into custard. Stir in three-quarters of the cumquat mixture; reserve remaining mixture for decoration.

Layered ricotta chocolate cake

preparation time **25 minutes** cooking time **1 hour** serves **14**

100g unsalted butter
½ cup (110g) caster sugar
2 eggs
150g dark eating chocolate, melted
1½ cups (225g) self-raising flour
½ cup (125ml) water
300ml double cream
¼ cup (40g) icing sugar

Ricotta fruit filling
250g ricotta cheese
¼ cup (55g) caster sugar
1 tablespoons cointreau
½ cup (125g) finely chopped glacé apricots
½ cup (115g) finely chopped glacé pineapple
50g dark eating chocolate, grated

1 Preheat oven to moderately slow (170°C/150°C fan-forced). Grease deep 25cm round cake pan; line base with baking paper.
2 Beat butter and sugar in small bowl with electric mixer until light and fluffy. Add eggs one at a time, beating after each addition. Stir in cooled chocolate. Transfer to large bowl; fold in sifted flour and the water in two batches.
3 Spread mixture into prepared pan; bake for about 1 hour or until firm. Stand cake in pan for 5 minutes before turning onto a wire rack to cool.
4 Make ricotta fruit filling.
5 Cut cold cake into three layers; sandwich layers with ricotta fruit filling. Beat cream and sifted icing sugar in small bowl until soft peaks form; spread over top and side of cake. Decorate with extra glacé pineapple and grated chocolate, if desired.

Ricotta fruit filling Beat cheese, sugar and liqueur in small bowl with electric mixer until smooth; stir in fruit and chocolate.

Chocolate ganache meringue

preparation time **40 minutes** (plus cooling time) cooking time **45 minutes**
serves **8**

3 egg whites
¾ cup (165g) caster sugar
1 tablespoon cocoa powder
2 cups whipped cream
Extra cocoa powder, for dusting

Ganache
100g dark eating chocolate, chopped
½ cup (125ml) cream

1 Preheat oven to very slow (120°C/100°C fan-forced). Line three oven trays
with baking paper. Draw a 8cm x 25cm rectangle on each piece of paper;
turn it over.

2 Beat egg whites in small bowl with electric mixer until soft peaks form.
Gradually add sugar, beating until dissolved between additions. Fold in
sifted cocoa.

3 Spread mixture evenly over rectangles; bake for about 45 mintues, or until
firm. Cool in oven with the door ajar.

4 Meanwhile, make ganache.

5 Place one meringue layer on a serving plate; spread with half the ganache,
then top with half the whipped cream. Place another meringue layer on top
of the cream; repeat layers with remaining ganache and cream. Top with the
remaining meringue layer. Dust with extra sifted cocoa.

Ganache Combine chocolate and cream in small saucepan; stir over low
heat until smooth. Refrigerate until almost firm.

tip Meringue layers can be made four days ahead and stored in an airtight
container. This cake should only be assembled six hours before serving.

Coffee cream meringue cake

preparation time **20 minutes** cooking time **1 hour 45 minutes** serves **10**

2 tablespoons instant coffee granules
⅓ cup (80ml) boiling water
6 egg whites
1½ cups (330g) caster sugar
1 teaspoon white vinegar
½ cup (80g) blanched almonds, toasted, chopped coarsely
300ml whipping cream
1 tablespoon icing sugar
1 tablespoon irish cream liqueur
½ cup (120g) candied (vienna) almonds, chopped

1 Combine coffee and the water in a small jug, stir well; stand for 10 minutes. Line a sieve with a piece of absorbent paper; place over a jug. Strain the coffee mixture through paper. You will need 1½ tablespoons for this recipe.
2 Preheat oven to very slow (120°C/100°C fan-forced). Line two oven trays with baking paper; draw a 20cm circle on each paper.
3 Beat egg whites in large bowl with electric mixer until soft peaks form. Gradually add caster sugar, beating until dissolved between additions. Quickly and gently fold in vinegar and almonds.
4 Divide meringue mixture between circles; level tops. Bake for about 1 hour 45 minutes or until firm. Cool in the oven with door ajar.
5 Beat cream, icing sugar, cooled coffee and liqueur in small bowl with an electric mixer until firm peaks form. Place one meringue disc on a serving plate, top with two-thirds of the cream mixture and remaining meringue disc. Top with remaining cream mixture; sprinkle with candied almonds.

tip The meringue layers can be made two days ahead; store in an airtight container in a cool, dry place. Assemble close to serving.

Chocolate date dessert cake

preparation time **15 minutes** (plus standing time) cooking time **45 minutes**
serves **10**

1 cup (160g) coarsely chopped seeded dates
250g butter, chopped
1¾ cups (430ml) water
1 cup (220g) sugar
⅓ cup (35g) cocoa
1⅔ cups (250g) plain flour
1 teaspoon bicarbonate of soda

1 Preheat oven to moderate (180°C/160°C fan-forced). Grease 19cm x
29cm rectangular slice pan, cover base with baking paper.
2 Combine dates, butter, the water, sugar and cocoa in medium saucepan.
Bring to a boil; cook, stirring, uncovered, for 5 minutes. Cover, cool to
room temperature.
3 Stir flour and soda into mixture; pour mixture into prepared pan. Bake
about 40 minutes. Stand 5 minutes in pan; turn onto wire rack to cool.
4 Serve cake warm or cold with whipped cream and chocolate shavings,
if desired.

Italian ricotta cheesecake

preparation time **30 minutes** (plus refrigeration time)
cooking time **1 hour 10 minutes** serves **16**

90g butter, softened
1 egg
¼ cup (55g) caster sugar
1 ¼ cups (185g) plain flour
¼ cup (35g) self-raising flour

Ricotta filling
1kg ricotta
5 eggs, beaten lightly
1 tablespoon finely grated lemon rind
¼ cup (60ml) lemon juice
½ teaspoon vanilla extract
1 cup (220g) caster sugar
¼ cup (40g) sultanas
½ cup (125g) finely chopped mixed glacé fruit

1 Beat butter in small bowl with electric mixer until smooth; add egg and sugar, beating until just combined. Stir in half of the combined sifted flours; work remaining flour in by hand. Knead gently on floured surface until smooth. Cover with plastic wrap; refrigerate 30 minutes. Grease 25cm springform tin.
2 Roll pastry between sheets of baking paper until large enough to cover base of prepared tin. Lift pastry into tin; press into base. Lightly prick pastry with fork; cover and refrigerate for 30 minutes.
3 Preheat oven to moderately hot (200°C/180°C fan-forced).
4 Bake pastry base, uncovered, for 20 minutes. Reduce oven temperature to moderately slow (170°C/150°C fan-forced).
5 Meanwhile, make ricotta filling; pour over pastry base.
6 Bake cheesecake for about 50 minutes, or until filling sets. Cool at room temperature; refrigerate until cold.

Ricotta filling Blend or process ricotta, eggs, rind, juice, extract and sugar until smooth. Stir in sultanas and glacé fruit.

tip This recipe is best made a day ahead. Cover; refrigerate overnight.

Passionfruit and mango charlotte

preparation time **40 minutes** (plus refrigeration time) serves **8**

You will need about three passionfruit for this recipe.

1½ teaspoons gelatine
¼ cup (60ml) boiling water
1½ cups (375ml) mango nectar
2 tablespoons orange juice
1 cup (200g) ricotta
½ cup (110g) caster sugar
1 cup (250ml) whipping cream
1 large (600g) mango, sliced thinly
¼ cup (60ml) passionfruit pulp
14 (140g) small sponge finger biscuits

1 Line base and two long sides of 11cm x 18cm loaf pan with baking paper, extending paper 5cm over edge.
2 Sprinkle gelatine over the water; whisk until the gelatine dissolves. Cool for 5 minutes.
3 Combine mango nectar and juice in large, shallow bowl. Blend ricotta and sugar until smooth. Transfer to a large bowl. Beat cream in a small bowl until soft peaks form. Stir a little cream into the gelatine mixture. Fold the cream through ricotta mixture, then spread into the prepared pan. Top with half the mango and 2 teaspoons of the passionfruit pulp.
4 Dip half the sponge fingers into the mango mixture, then place lengthways over ricotta layer in pan. Brush biscuits with a little more of the mango mixture. Repeat with ricotta mixture, fruit and sponge fingers, ending with ricotta mixture. Cover and refrigerate overnight to soften biscuits. Turn out, drizzle with rest of passionfruit pulp and serve sliced.

Almond rum dessert cake

preparation time **20 minutes** (plus refrigeration time)
cooking time **30 minutes** Serves **10**

¼ cup (55g) caster sugar
2 tablespoons water
¼ cup (30g) almond meal
250g milk eating chocolate, melted
250g dark eating chocolate, melted
60g unsalted butter, melted
2 tablespoons white rum
1 tablespoon plain flour
2 teaspoons caster sugar, extra
2 eggs, separated

Almond cream
300ml whipping cream
⅓ cup (55g) icing sugar
¼ teaspoon almond essence

1 Preheat oven to moderately hot (200°C/180°C fan-forced). Grease 20cm springform tin; line base with baking paper.
2 Combine sugar and water in small saucepan; stir constantly over heat, without boiling, until sugar is dissolved. Bring to boil, then boil, without stirring, until syrup turns golden brown. Add almonds, then pour onto lightly greased oven tray; cool. When toffee is set, process until fine.
3 Combine both chocolates, butter, rum, flour and extra sugar in large bowl; stir until smooth. Stir in egg yolks.
4 Beat egg whites in a small bowl with electric mixer until soft peaks form; fold into chocolate mixture. Spread into prepared tin; bake for 10 minutes.
5 Sprinkle cake with ¼ cup of the almond toffee mixture, then bake for another 10 minutes. Allow to cool in oven with door ajar. Refrigerate cake until ready to serve.
6 Just before serving, make almond cream.

Almond cream Beat cream with sifted icing sugar in small bowl until soft peaks form; fold in remaining toffee and essence.

tip This dessert is best prepared a day ahead; keep, covered, in refrigerator.

Walnut cake with roasted caramel pears

preparation time **40 minutes** cooking time **1 hour 30 minutes** serves **8**

125g butter, chopped
¾ cup (165g) caster sugar
3 eggs
⅔ cup (160g) sour cream
⅔ cup (100g) plain flour
⅔ cup (100g) self-raising flour
½ cup (60g) almond meal
1 teaspoons ground cinnamon
½ cup (80g) walnuts, toasted, chopped coarsely

Roasted caramel pears
4 medium pears (800g), cut into 8 wedges
½ cup (100g) firmly packed brown sugar
½ cup (125ml) white wine
100g butter, chopped
½ cup (100g) firmly packed brown sugar, extra
⅔ cup (160ml) cream

1 Preheat oven to hot (220°C/200°C fan-forced). Make roasted caramel pears.
2 Reduce oven to moderately slow (170°C/150°C fan-forced). Grease a deep 22cm round cake pan; line base and side with baking paper.
3 Beat butter and sugar in small bowl with an electric mixer until smooth. Add eggs one at a time, beating until just combined after each addition. Add sour cream, then beat until just combined. Transfer to a large bowl. Stir in sifted combined flours, almond meal, cinnamon, then walnuts. Spread into prepared pan.
4 Bake cake about 50 minutes or until cooked when tested. Stand cake in pan for 10 minutes before turning onto a rack to cool.
5 Serve cake warm with pears and drizzled with caramel sauce.

Roasted caramel pears Place pears in a medium flameproof baking dish. Top with sugar, wine and butter pieces. Bake in hot oven about 30 minutes or until pears are soft and browned lightly (cooking time will depend on the ripeness of pears). Stir halfway through cooking time. Remove from baking dish; place dish on stove top. Stir in extra sugar and boil, stirring, until a dark caramel colour. Stir in cream; return to the boil.

Lime meringue slice

preparation time **30 minutes** cooking time **35 minutes** serves **15**

1½ **cups (225g) plain flour**
½ **cup (80g) icing sugar**
150g cold butter, chopped
1 teaspoon iced water
395g can sweetened condensed milk
2 eggs, separated
2 teaspoons grated lime rind
½ **cup (125ml) lime juice**
⅓ **cup (75g) caster sugar**
½ **cup (25g) flaked coconut**

1 Preheat oven to moderate (180°C/160°C fan-forced). Grease a 20cm x 30cm lamington pan; line base and sides with baking paper.
2 Blend or process flour, icing sugar, butter and water until ingredients just cling together. Bring mixture together with hands, then press evenly over base of prepared pan. Bake for about 18 minutes, or until browned.
3 Meanwhile, combine condensed milk, egg yolks, rind and juice in a bowl; pour over base. Bake a further 10 minutes.
4 Beat egg whites in small bowl with electric mixer until soft peaks form; gradually add caster sugar, beat until sugar is dissolved.
5 Spread meringue over lime filling; sprinkle with coconut. Bake a further 7 minutes or until browned. Cool in pan.
6 Serve cut into rectangles or squares.

tip This slice can be stored in an airtight container in the refrigerator for up to three days.

White chocolate cheesecake brownies

preparation time **30 minutes** (plus refrigeration time)
cooking time **30 minutes** serves **9**

125g butter, chopped
150g white cooking chocolate, chopped
1 egg
²/₃ cup (150g) caster sugar
¾ cup (110g) plain flour
¼ cup (35g) self-raising flour

Cheesecake topping
250g cream cheese, softened
1 teaspoon vanilla extract
⅓ cup (75g) caster sugar
½ cup (125ml) cream
1 egg

1 Preheat oven to moderate (180°C/160°C fan-forced). Grease a deep 19cm square cake pan; line base and sides with baking paper.
2 Place butter and chocolate in heatproof bowl over saucepan of simmering water; stir until melted.
3 Beat egg and sugar in small bowl with electric mixer until thick and creamy. Gradually stir in chocolate mixture and sifted flours.
4 Spread mixture into prepared pan;bake for about 10 minutes, or until just firm to touch.
5 Make cheesecake topping; pour over brownie base. Bake a further 15 minutes, or until cheesecake is just set; cool. Refrigerate 2 hours or until completely cold. Cut into squares.

Cheesecake topping Meanwhile, beat cheese, extract and sugar in small bowl with electric mixer until smooth; add cream, beat until thick. Add egg and beat until just combined.

tip These brownies are suitable to freeze.

Chocolate and raspberry mousse cake

preparation time **30 minutes** (plus refrigeration time)
cooking time **15 minutes** serves **8**

100g butter, chopped
100g dark eating chocolate, chopped
2 eggs, separated
½ cup (110g) caster sugar
¼ cup (25g) cocoa powder
300g dark eating chocolate, chopped, extra
1½ cups (375ml) cream
360g fresh raspberries or halved strawberries
Cocoa powder and icing sugar, extra, to serve

1 Preheat the oven to moderate (180°C/160°C fan-forced). Grease a 25cm x 30cm swiss roll pan; line base and sides with baking paper.

2 Combine butter and chocolate in small saucepan; stir over low heat until smooth, cool.

3 Beat egg yolks and sugar in small bowl with electric mixer about 3-5 minutes or until thick and creamy. Transfer to a large bowl; fold in sifted cocoa, then chocolate mixture.

4 Beat egg whites in small bowl with electric mixer until soft peaks form; fold into chocolate mixture in two batches.

5 Spread mixture into prepared pan; bake for about 20 minutes. Turn cake onto a baking paper-lined wire rack. Cover cake with a sheet of baking paper; cool to room temperature.

6 Meanwhile, combine extra chocolate and half the cream in heatproof bowl over a pan of simmering water; stir until smooth. Transfer to small bowl; refrigerate until just cold.

7 Add remaining cream to chocolate mixture, beat with an electric mixer until a paler colour and soft peaks form (do not over-beat as the mixture will separate).

8 Cut cake in half lengthways. Place one piece of cake on a serving platter. Spread half the chocolate mixture over cake; top with half of the raspberries. Repeat with another layer of the cake, the remaining chocolate mixture and remaining raspberries. Cover cake; refrigerate about 3 hours or until firm.

9 Dust with sifted extra cocoa and/or icing sugar, if desired.

tip This cake is suitable to freeze.

FESTIVE CAKES

Grand marnier fruit cake

preparation time **2 hours** (plus standing time)
cooking time **3 hours 40 minutes** (plus cooling time) serves **14**

3 cups (500g) sultanas
1½ cups (250g) mixed peel
¾ cup (120g) coarsely chopped raisins
¾ cup (120g) coarsely chopped seeded dried dates
⅔ cup (140g) coarsely chopped seeded prunes
½ cup (125g) coarsely chopped glacé apricots
⅔ cup (150g) coarsely chopped glacé pineapple
½ cup (70g) slivered almonds
½ cup (60g) coarsely chopped walnuts
1 tablespoon finely grated orange rind
½ cup (110g) caster sugar
¼ cup (60ml) orange juice
½ cup (125ml) grand marnier
250g butter, softened
½ cup (110g) firmly packed brown sugar
5 eggs
2 cups (300g) plain flour
2 tablespoons grand marnier, extra
1kg ready-made fondant
1 egg white, beaten lightly
½ cup (80g) icing sugar, sifted
25cm-round covered cake board
Decorative ribbon
13g packet silver cachous

1 Combine fruit, nuts and rind in large bowl. Cook caster sugar in large frying pan over low heat, without stirring, until it begins to melt, then stir until melted and browned lightly. Remove from heat; slowly stir in juice. Return to low heat; stir until dissolved (do not boil). Add liqueur. Pour over fruit mixture; cover with plastic wrap. Store in a cool, dark place for 10 days, stirring every day.

2 Preheat oven to slow (150°C/130°C fan-forced). Line base and sides of deep 22cm round or deep 19cm square cake pan with one thickness of brown paper and two thicknesses of baking paper, extending papers 5cm above edge.

3 Beat butter and brown sugar in small bowl with electric mixer until just combined. Add eggs one at a time, beating until just combined after each addition. Stir butter mixture into fruit mixture; mix in flour; spread into prepared pan. Tap pan firmly on bench to settle mixture; level the mixture with a wet spatula.

4 Bake cake for 3½ hours. Remove cake from oven; brush with extra liqueur. Cover hot cake with foil then turn upside down to cool overnight.

5 Trim top of cake with a sharp knife to ensure it sits flat when turned upside down. Mix a little fondant and cold, boiled water to a sticky paste. Spread about 2 tablespoons of fondant mixture into the centre of a sheet of baking paper about 5cm larger than the cake; position cake upside down on paper.

6 Using a spatula and small pieces of fondant, patch any holes on cake.

7 Brush egg white evenly over cake. Knead fondant on a surface dusted with icing sugar until smooth; roll to 7mm thickness. Lift fondant onto cake with a rolling pin, smoothing the fondant all over cake with hands dusted with icing sugar. Using a sharp knife, cut excess fondant away from base of cake.

8 Mix scraps of fondant and cold, boiled water to a sticky paste. Spread about 2 tablespoons of the paste in centre of board; centre cake on prepared board. Move cake to correct position on board; using a sharp craft knife or scalpel, carefully cut away excess baking paper extending around the base of cake.

9 Secure ribbon around cake using pins (remove to a safe place before cutting cake). Push cachous gently into fondant to form the design of your choice.

Super-moist rich fruit cake

preparation time **30 minutes** (plus standing time) cooking time **4 hours**
(plus cooling time) serves **36**

2¼ cups (380g) raisins, chopped coarsely
3 cups (480g) sultanas
¾ cup (110g) currants
1 cup (250g) quartered red glacé cherries
1½ cups (250g) coarsely chopped seeded prunes
⅓ cup (120g) honey
½ cup (125ml) brandy
250g butter, softened
1 cup (220g) firmly packed black sugar
5 eggs
1¼ cups (185g) plain flour
2 tablespoons brandy, extra

1 Combine fruit, honey and brandy in large bowl; cover, then stand overnight.
2 Preheat oven to slow (150°C/130°C fan-forced). Line base and sides
of deep 19cm square cake pan with three thicknesses of baking paper,
extending paper 5cm above sides.
3 Beat butter and sugar in small bowl with electric mixer until just combined.
Add eggs one at a time, beating until just combined after each addition
(mixture may curdle at this point but will come together later).
4 Add butter mixture to fruit mixture with flour; mix thoroughly with one
hand. Drop dollops of mixture into corners of pan to hold baking paper in
position; spread remaining mixture into pan.
5 Drop cake pan from a height of about 15cm onto bench to settle mixture
and break any large air bubbles; level surface with a wet metal spatula.
6 Bake cake, uncovered, for about 4 hours, giving the cake quarter turns
several times during baking to prevent it browning unevenly – cover loosely
with foil during baking if it starts to over-brown. Remove cake from oven;
brush with extra brandy. Cover tightly with foil; cool in pan.

tips You can use dark brown or brown sugar rather than black, if you prefer.
This cake is quite soft and is best cut after refrigeration. To store, wrap cold
cake tightly in plastic, then in foil. Wrapped cake can be kept in a cool, dark
place for three months; in a humid climate, it is best stored, wrapped, in the
refrigerator. It can be frozen for up to 12 months.

Celebration fruit cake

preparation time **20 minutes** (plus standing time)
cooking time **3 hours 30 minutes** (plus cooling time) serves **16**

3 cups (500g) sultanas
1¾ cups (300g) raisins, halved
1¾ cups (300g) dried dates, chopped finely
1 cup (150g) dried currants
⅔ cup (110g) mixed peel
⅔ cup (150g) glacé cherries, halved
¼ cup (55g) coarsely chopped glacé pineapple
¼ cup (60g) coarsely chopped glacé apricots
½ cup (125ml) dark rum
250g butter, softened
1 cup (220g) firmly packed brown sugar
5 eggs
1½ cups (225g) plain flour
⅓ cup (50g) self-raising flour
1 teaspoon mixed spice
2 tablespoons dark rum, extra

1 Combine fruit and rum in a large bowl; mix well. Cover tightly with plastic wrap. Store in a cool, dark place overnight or up to a week, stirring every day.
2 Preheat oven to slow (150°C/130°C fan-forced). Line a deep 22cm round cake pan with three thicknesses of baking paper, extending paper 5cm above edge.
3 Beat butter and sugar in small bowl with electric mixer until just combined. Add eggs one at a time, beating until just combined after each addition.
4 Add butter mixture to fruit mixture; mix well. Mix in sifted dry ingredients; spread mixture evenly into prepared pan. Bake, uncovered, about 3½ hours.
5 Remove cake from oven; brush with extra rum. Cover tightly with foil; cool in pan, overnight.

Festive fruit and nut cake

preparation time **20 minutes** cooking time **1 hour 45 minutes** (plus standing time) serves **24**

Store this cake in an airtight container for up to a month; not suitable to freeze.

½ cup (115g) coarsely chopped glacé pineapple
½ cup (125g) coarsely chopped glacé apricots
1½ cups (250g) seeded dried dates
½ cup (110g) red glacé cherries
½ cup (110g) green glacé cherries
1 cup (170g) brazil nuts
½ cup (75g) macadamia nuts
2 eggs
½ cup (110g) firmly packed brown sugar
1 tablespoon dark rum
100g butter, melted
⅓ cup (50g) plain flour
¼ cup (35g) self-raising flour

Fruit and nut topping
⅓ cup (75g) coarsely chopped glacé pineapple
¼ cup (55g) red glacé cherries, halved
¼ cup (55g) green glacé cherries, halved
¼ cup (40g) brazil nuts
¼ cup (35g) macadamia nuts

Toffee topping
½ cup (110g) caster sugar
¼ cup (60ml) water

1 Preheat oven to slow (150°C/130°C fan-forced). Grease 20cm ring pan; line base and side with baking paper, extending paper 5cm above edge.
2 Combine fruit and nuts in large bowl. Beat eggs and sugar in small bowl with electric mixer until thick. Add rum, butter and sifted flours; beat until just combined. Stir egg mixture into fruit mixture. Press firmly into pan.
3 Combine ingredients for fruit and nut topping in medium bowl. Gently press topping evenly over cake mixture; bake, covered with foil, for 1 hour. Uncover; bake for a further 45 minutes. Stand cake in pan 10 minutes.
4 Meanwhile, make toffee topping.
5 Turn cooled cake, top-side up, onto wire rack over oven tray; drizzle with toffee topping.

Toffee topping Combine ingredients in small saucepan, stirring over heat, without boiling, until sugar dissolves. Bring to a boil, then reduce heat and simmer, uncovered, without stirring, for about 10 minutes or until mixture is golden. Remove from heat; stand mixture until bubbles subside before using.

Last-minute fruit cake

preparation time **20 minutes** cooking time **2 hours** (plus cooling time) serves **12**

1½ cups (240g) sultanas
1 cup (170g) raisins, chopped coarsely
1 cup (150g) dried currants
½ cup (85g) mixed peel
⅓ cup (70g) glacé cherries, halved
2 tablespoons coarsely chopped glacé pineapple
2 tablespoons coarsely chopped glacé apricots
185g butter, chopped
¾ cup (165g) firmly packed brown sugar
⅓ cup (80ml) brandy
⅓ cup (80ml) water
2 teaspoons finely grated orange rind
1 teaspoon finely grated lemon rind
1 tablespoon treacle
3 eggs, beaten lightly
1¼ cups (185g) plain flour
¼ cup (35g) self-raising flour
½ teaspoon bicarbonate of soda
½ cup (80g) blanched almonds

1 Combine fruit, butter, sugar, brandy and the water in medium saucepan, stir over medium heat until butter is melted and sugar is dissolved; bring to a boil. Transfer mixture to large bowl; cool to room temperature.
2 Preheat oven to slow (150°C/130°C fan-forced). Line deep 20cm round cake pan with three thicknesses of baking paper, extending paper 5cm above side.
3 Stir rinds, treacle and eggs into fruit mixture; add sifted dry ingredients. Spread mixture into prepared pan; decorate with nuts. Bake, uncovered, for about 2 hours. Cover hot cake with foil; cool in pan overnight.

Fruit mince slice

preparation time **55 minutes** (plus standing time) cooking time **25 minutes** serves **12**

You only need one-quarter of the basic fruit mixture for this recipe; store remaining mixture in refrigerator, or use for other fruit cakes such as Moist Christmas cake p265.

2 sheets ready-rolled puff pastry
1 egg white, beaten lightly
1 tablespoon caster sugar

Basic fruit mixture
6 cups (1kg) sultanas
2½ cups (375g) dried currants
2¼ cups (425g) raisins, chopped
1½ cups (250g) seeded dried dates, chopped
1½ cups (250g) seeded prunes, chopped
1¼ cups (250g) glacé cherries, quartered
½ cup (125g) glacé apricots, chopped
½ cup (115g) glacé pineapple, chopped
½ cup (115g) glacé ginger, chopped
¾ cup (120g) mixed peel
3 medium apples (450g), peeled, grated
⅔ cup (240g) fig jam
2 tablespoons finely grated orange rind
¼ cup (60ml) lemon juice
2 cups (440g) firmly packed brown sugar
1 tablespoon mixed spice
1⅓ cups (330ml) grand marnier

1 Mix ingredients for basic fruit mixture in large bowl; cover tightly with plastic wrap. Store in cool, dark place for a month (or longer, if desired) before using; stir mixture every two or three days.
2 Preheat oven to hot (220°C/200°C fan-forced). Grease 20cm x 30cm lamington pan.
3 Cut one pastry sheet large enough to cover base of prepared pan. Using a fork, prick pastry all over several times. Place a 19cm x 29cm slice pan on top to prevent pastry rising during cooking. Bake for about 10 minutes, or until browned lightly and crisp. Remove slice pan; spread one-quarter of the fruit mixture evenly over pastry.

4 Cut remaining pastry sheet large enough to cover fruit mixture; brush with egg white; sprinkle with sugar. Carefully score pastry in a crisscross pattern.
5 Bake slice, uncovered, for further 15 minutes, or until pastry is browned.

Moist christmas cake

preparation time **15 minutes** cooking time **3 hours** (plus cooling time)
serves **36**

½ **quantity basic fruit mixture (see page 264)**
250g butter, melted, cooled
5 eggs, beaten lightly
2½ **cups (375g) plain flour**
2 tablespoons grand marnier

1 Preheat oven to slow (150°C/130°C fan-forced). Line base and sides of deep 22cm square cake pan with one thickness of brown paper and two thicknesses baking paper, extending papers 5cm above edges.
2 Place basic fruit mixture in large bowl. Mix in butter and eggs, then sifted flour in two batches.
3 Spread mixture into prepared pan; level top with spatula. Bake, uncovered, for about 3 hours. Brush with liqueur; cover hot cake in pan with foil and leave to cool overnight.

tip This cake can be made three months ahead and stored in an airtight container in the refrigerator.

Super-rich chocolate drambuie fruit cake

preparation time **1 hour 15 minutes** (plus overnight standing time)
cooking time **3 hours** serves **variable**

2 ⅓ cups (375g) sultanas
2 ¼ cups (375g) raisins, chopped
1 ⅔ cups (250g) currants
1 ½ cups (250g) pitted prunes, chopped
1 ½ cups (250g) pitted dates, chopped
¾ cup (125g) mixed peel
⅔ cup (140g) red glacé cherries, halved
1 ⅓ cup (340ml) drambuie or whisky
⅓ cup (115g) honey
1 tablespoon finely grated lemon rind
250g butter, chopped
1 ½ cups (300g) firmly packed dark brown sugar
6 eggs
1 tablespoon parisian essence
90g dark chocolate, grated
1 ¼ cups (125g) pecans, toasted, chopped
2 cups (300g) plain flour
1 cup (150g) self-raising flour
¼ cup (25g) cocoa powder
Extra pecans and glacé cherries, optional

1 Combine fruit, 1 cup of the drambuie, honey and rind in a bowl; mix well.
Cover and stand overnight, or for several days.
2 Preheat oven to very slow (120°C/100°C fan-forced). Grease six ¾-cup
(180ml) paper cake moulds (or a 6-hole texas muffin pan). Line base and side
of a deep 22cm round cake pan (or deep 19cm square cake pan) with two
layers of baking paper, extending paper 5cm above edge.
3 Beat butter and sugar in large bowl with electric mixer until just combined.
Add eggs one at a time, beating until just combined after each addition. Beat
in essence. Add butter mixture to fruit mixture; mix well. Stir in chocolate.
Add nuts, then sifted dry ingredients in two batches; mix well.
4 Fill paper cake moulds to within 1cm of top (fill muffin pans level with top
of pan). Spread remaining cake mixture into prepared round or square cake
pan. Decorate tops with extra pecans and glacé cherries, if desired.

5 Bake individual cakes for about 1½ hours, or until cooked when tested. Brush hot cakes with a little remaining drambuie, cover tightly with foil; cool in pans. Increase oven temperature to slow (150°C/130°C fan-forced).
6 Bake large cake in slow oven for about 3 hours, or until cooked when tested. Brush hot cake with drambuie. Cover tightly with foil; cool in pan.

tip We made this quantity of mixture in one 22cm round cake and six individual cakes ideal for gift-giving. If you prefer, you can make one large cake from this mixture. Use a deep 22cm square or deep 25cm round cake pan and bake for about 4-4½ hours. This cake can be made three months ahead and stored in the refrigerator. It is suitable to freeze.

Little chocolate Christmas puddings

preparation time **30 minutes**   cooking time **2 minutes**   makes **about 44**

700g purchased plum pudding
250g dark eating chocolate, melted
½ cup (125ml) brandy
½ cup (80g) icing sugar
200g white eating chocolate, chopped
½ cup (125ml) double cream
Citron
Glacé cherries

1 Crumble plum pudding into a bowl. Stir in dark chocolate, brandy and sifted icing sugar; mix well.
2 Roll level tablespoons of mixture into balls; place on oven tray, cover and refrigerate until firm.
3 Melt white chocolate in heatproof bowl over a pan of simmering water. Cool chocolate for 10 minutes. Stir in cream; allow to stand until mixture has thickened slightly.
4 Drizzle white chocolate mixture over puddings to form 'custard'; decorate with citron and cherries.

tip These puddings are not suitable to freeze.

Gluten-free fruit and almond loaves

preparation time **35 minutes** (plus standing time) cooking time **2 hours**
serves **24**

Be sure to check all labels to ensure ingredients do not contain gluten.

1kg mixed dried fruit
1 tablespoon grated range rind
⅔ cup (160ml) sweet sherry
150g butter, softened
⅔ cup (150g) firmly packed dark brown sugar
4 eggs
100g marzipan, chopped coarsely
1 small (130g) apple, grated coarsely
¾ cup (100g) almond meal
1¼ cups (185g) gluten-free plain flour
1 cup (160g) whole blanched almonds
¼ cup (60ml) sweet sherry, extra

1 Combine fruit, rind and sherry in a large bowl; mix well. Cover and stand
overnight or for several days.
2 Preheat oven to slow (150°C/130°C fan-forced). Line base and sides of
two 9cm x 21cm loaf pans with two layers of brown paper and two layers of
baking paper, extending paper 5cm above edges.
3 Beat butter and sugar in a small bowl with an electric mixer until just
combined. Add butter mixture to fruit mixture; mix well. Stir in marzipan,
apple, almond meal and sifted flour; mix well together.
4 Spread mixture evenly into prepared pans; decorate with blanched
almonds. Bake about 2 hours or until loaves are cooked when tested. Brush
hot loaves with extra sweet sherry and wrap tightly with foil; cool in pans.

tip This cake is suitable to freeze.

Irish pudding cake

preparation time **25 minutes** (plus standing time) cooking time **3 hours** (plus cooling time) serves **12**

1½ cups (250g) seeded dried dates, chopped coarsely
1¼ cups (200g) seeded prunes, chopped coarsely
1½ cups (250g) raisins, chopped coarsely
1 cup (150g) dried currants
¾ cup (125g) sultanas
1 large apple (200g), grated coarsely
1½ cups (375ml) irish whiskey
1¼ cups (275g) firmly packed dark brown sugar
185g butter, softened
3 eggs, beaten lightly
½ cup (50g) hazelnut meal
1½ cups (225g) plain flour
1 teaspoon ground nutmeg
½ teaspoon ground ginger
½ teaspoon ground cloves
½ teaspoon bicarbonate of soda

1 Combine fruit and 1 cup of the whiskey in a large bowl; cover tightly with plastic wrap. Let stand at room temperature overnight.
2 Preheat oven to very slow (120°C/100°C fan-forced). Line deep 20cm round cake pan with two thicknesses of baking paper, extending paper 5cm above edge.
3 Combine remaining whiskey and ½ cup of the sugar in small saucepan. Stir over heat until sugar dissolves; bring to a boil. Remove from heat; cool for 20 minutes.
4 Meanwhile, beat butter and remaining sugar in small bowl with electric mixer until just combined (do not overbeat). Add eggs one at a time, beating until just combined after each addition. Add butter mixture to fruit mixture; stir in hazelnut meal, sifted combined dry ingredients and ½ cup of the cooled syrup. Spread mixture into prepared pan.
5 Bake pudding, uncovered, about 3 hours. Brush cake with reheated remaining syrup; cover cake with foil and cool in pan.

Glacé fruit slice with limoncello cream

preparation time **30 minutes** cooking time **45 minutes** (plus refrigeration time) serves **12**

90g butter, softened
1 tablespoon finely grated lemon rind
¾ cup (165g) caster sugar
2 eggs
¾ cup (110g) plain flour
½ cup (75g) self-raising flour
⅓ cup (80ml) milk
⅔ cup (150g) coarsely chopped glacé pineapple
⅔ cup (170g) coarsely chopped glacé apricots
⅔ cup (170g) coarsely chopped glacé peaches
¾ cup (110g) coarsely chopped dried pears
¾ cup (110g) toasted shelled pistachios

Lemon syrup
½ cup (125ml) lemon juice
1 cup (220g) caster sugar

Limoncello cream
300ml whipping cream
2 tablespoons limoncello (or any other lemon-flavoured liqueur)

1 Preheat oven to moderately slow (170°C/150°C fan-forced). Line 20cm x 30cm lamington pan with baking paper, extending paper 3cm over long sides.
2 Beat butter, rind and sugar in small bowl with electric mixer until light and fluffy. Add eggs one at a time, beating well after each addition. (Mixture may curdle at this stage, but will come together later.) Transfer to large bowl; stir in sifted flours, milk, fruit and nuts.
3 Spread mixture into prepared pan; bake, uncovered, about 45 minutes.
4 Meanwhile, make lemon syrup. Remove slice from oven; pour hot syrup over hot slice in pan. Cover; refrigerate overnight.
5 Beat ingredients for limoncello cream in small bowl with electric mixer until soft peaks form. Cut slice into small squares; serve with limoncello cream.

Lemon syrup Stir ingredients in small saucepan over heat, without boiling, until sugar dissolves. Bring to a boil, reduce heat; simmer, uncovered, without stirring, for about 10 minutes or until thickened slightly.

Multi-purpose fruit cake

preparation time **30 minutes** (plus standing time) cooking time **3 hours**
serves **16**

1½ cups (250g) sultanas
1½ cups (250g) chopped raisins
⅔ cup (140g) chopped seeded prunes
¾ cup (110g) dried currants
½ cup (125g) chopped glacé apricots
⅔ cup (110g) chopped seeded dates
¼ cup (60g) chopped glacé cherries
½ cup (125ml) brandy
250g butter
2 teaspoons finely grated lemon rind
1 cup (200g) firmly packed brown sugar
2 tablespoons honey
4 eggs
1½ cups (225g) plain flour
½ cup (75g) self-raising flour
1 teaspoon mixed spice
¼ cup (60ml) brandy, extra

1 Combine fruit and brandy in a large bowl. Cover and stand overnight or for up to a week.
2 Preheat oven to slow (150°C/130°C fan-forced). Line base and side of 19cm square cake pan with three thicknesses of baking paper, extending paper 5cm above edge.
3 Beat butter, rind and sugar in small bowl with electric mixer until changed to a lighter colour; add honey, beat until just combined. Add eggs, one at a time, beating until just combined between additions (mixture may curdle). Stir into fruit mixture, then stir in sifted flours and spice in two batches.
4 Spread mixture into prepared pan; bake for about 3 hours.
5 Brush hot cake with extra brandy; cover tightly with foil. Cool in pan.

Pan variations
1 quantity mixture: Use a deep 22cm round; bake for 3 hours. OR Use two deep 17cm round or two deep 15cm square cake pans; bake for 2 hours.
2 quantities mixture: Use a deep 28cm round or deep 23cm square cake pan bake for 4 hours.
¾ quantity mixture: Use a deep 20cm round cake pan; bake for 2¼ hours.

Steamed christmas pudding

preparation time **25 minutes** cooking time **4 hours 15 minutes** (plus cooling time) serves **14**

3 cups (450g) chopped mixed dried fruit
¾ cup (120g) finely chopped dried seedless dates
¾ cup (120g) finely chopped raisins
¾ cup (180ml) water
1 cup (220g) firmly packed brown sugar
100g butter, chopped
1 teaspoon bicarbonate of soda
2 eggs, beaten lightly
¾ cup (110g) plain flour
¾ cup (110g) self-raising flour
1 teaspoon mixed spice
½ teaspoon ground cinnamon
2 tablespoons dark rum

1 Combine fruit, the water, sugar and butter in medium saucepan. Stir over medium heat until butter melts and sugar dissolves. Bring to a boil, then reduce heat; simmer, uncovered, for 6 minutes. Stir in soda. Transfer mixture to large bowl; cool to room temperature. Stir in eggs, sifted dry ingredients and rum.
2 Grease a 2-litre (8-cup) pudding steamer; spoon mixture into steamer. Top with one layer of baking paper and one layer of foil, pleated down the centre to allow pudding to expand as it cooks; secure with kitchen string or lid.
3 Place pudding in a large boiler with enough boiling water to come halfway up side of steamer. Cover boiler with a tight-fitting lid; boil for 4 hours, replenishing with water as necessary to maintain water level.
4 Stand pudding for 10 minutes before turning onto a serving plate. Serve with cream, if desired.

tips To store pudding: allow to come to room temperature, then wrap in plastic wrap. Refrigerate in cleaned steamer, or seal tightly in freezer bag or airtight container. Pudding can be stored in refrigerator up to two months or frozen up to 12 months. To reheat: thaw frozen pudding for three days in refrigerator; remove 12 hours before reheating. Remove from plastic wrap and return to steamer. Steam for 2 hours following instructions in step 4. To reheat in microwave oven: reheat up to four single serves at once. Cover with plastic wrap; microwave on HIGH (100%) for up to 1 minute per serve. To reheat whole pudding, cover with plastic wrap and microwave on MEDIUM (55%) for about 15 minutes or until hot.

Fruit cake 'n' eggnog cheesecake

preparation time **25 minutes** (plus cooling and refrigeration time)
cooking time **55 minutes** serves **10**

350g fruit cake, cut into 1cm slices
750g cream cheese, softened
300g sour cream
1 teaspoon vanilla extract
¼ cup (60ml) brandy
½ teaspoon ground nutmeg
2 cups (440g) caster sugar
3 eggs
1 cup (250ml) water
1 medium pink grapefruit (425g), segmented
1 large orange (300g), segmented
150g strawberries, halved
100g red seedless grapes
1 large kiwifruit (100g), cut into eight wedges

1 Preheat oven to moderate (180°C/160°C fan-forced). Line base of 22cm springform tin with baking paper.

2 Cover base of prepared tin with cake slices. Bake for 10 minutes or until browned lightly. Reduce oven temperature to slow (150°C/130°C fan-forced).

3 Meanwhile, beat cream cheese, sour cream, extract, brandy, nutmeg and half the sugar in a medium bowl with electric mixer until smooth. Add eggs one at a time, beating until just combined after each addition.

4 Pour mixture into prepared tin. Bake for about 45 minutes or until just set. Cool cheesecake in oven with door ajar. Cover; then refrigerate overnight.

5 Stir remaining sugar and the water in a medium heavy-based frying pan over high heat until sugar dissolves. Bring to a boil, then reduce heat; simmer, without stirring, uncovered, about 10 minutes or until toffee mixture is golden brown in colour. Remove from heat; allow to stand until bubbles subside.

6 Meanwhile, remove cheesecake from tin, place on serving plate; top with fruit. Working quickly, drizzle toffee over fruit.

Little fruit mince tarts

preparation time **1 hour** (plus refrigeration time) cooking **30 minutes**
makes **48**

3⅓ cups (500g) plain flour
½ cup (80g) icing sugar
300g butter, chopped
3 egg yolks
2½ tablespoons water, approximately
sifted icing sugar, extra
¾ cup (60g) flaked almonds

Fruit mince
¾ cup (120g) finely chopped dates
¾ cup (105g) dried currants
1 cup (160g) chopped raisins
1 cup (160g) sultanas
¼ cup (50g) finely chopped glacé cherries
3 teaspoons finely grated lemon rind
⅓ cup (80ml) rum
¼ cup (60ml) orange juice
½ cup (70g) pecans, toasted, chopped finely
⅓ cup (75g) firmly packed brown sugar
¼ cup (80g) plum jam

Frangipane
100g unsalted butter
⅓ cup (75g) caster sugar
2 eggs
1 egg yolk
¾ cup (90g) almond meal

1 Process flour, icing sugar and butter in food processor until well combined. Add egg yolks and enough water to process to a soft dough. Wrap dough in plastic wrap and refrigerate for 30 minutes.
2 Meanwhile, make fruit mince.
3 Lightly grease four mini muffin pans (1½ tablespoon). Divide pastry into 48 pieces, roll into balls and gently press into prepared pans. Refrigerate for 20 minutes.
4 Make frangipane.
5 Preheat oven to moderate (180°C/160°C fan-forced).

6 Fill each pastry case with 2 level teaspoons of fruit mince. Top with rounded teaspoons of frangipane, spreading to the edge; sprinkle with flaked almonds.

7 Bake tarts for about 25 minutes or until browned. Stand tarts in pan for 5 minutes before removing to cool on a wire rack. Dust with extra sifted icing sugar, if desired.

Fruit mince Place all ingredients in a large saucepan, stir over low heat until sugar is dissolved and jam melted; cool.

Frangipane Beat butter and sugar in a small bowl with an electric mixer until combined. Add the eggs and the egg yolk, one at a time, beating until just combined between additions. Stir in almond meal.

tips This recipe can be made a week ahead or frozen for up to three months. Refresh tarts by heating in a moderately slow oven (170°C/150°C fan-forced) for about 5 minutes, or until warm. Bottled fruit mince can be also used in this recipe.

NO-FUSS BIRTHDAY CAKES

A cake board often becomes part of a cake's decoration. Place cake, as directed, on a board covered with greaseproof decorative paper, contact or any type of patterned foil-like gift wrapping. We've given an approximate board size, allowing for some space around the cake. Using masonite or similarly strong board, cut your selected paper 5-10cm larger than the shape of the board. A variety of board sizes can be bought, already covered, from cake-decorating suppliers and some craft shops.

Howdy sheriff

preparation time **45 minutes** (plus standing time)
cooking time **1 hour 15 minutes** serves **36**

3 x 340g packets buttercake mix
35cm-square prepared board (see note page 276)
2 quantities butter cream (page 294)
Yellow and red colouring

Decorations
6 chocolate freckles
42 silver cachous

1 Preheat oven to moderate (180°C/160°C fan-forced). Grease a deep 30cm square cake pan and line with paper. Make cake according to directions on packets. Pour mixture into prepared pan; bake for about 1¼ hours. Stand cake in pan for 10 minutes before turning onto a wire rack to cool. Using a serrated knife, level cake top.

2 Turn cake cut-side down. Cut a star-shape from cake; place on prepared board, cut-side down. Discard remaining cake.

3 Tint two-thirds of the butter cream with yellow colouring; spread over cake.

4 Tint the remaining butter cream with red colouring. Spoon into a piping bag fitted with a 4mm plain tube. Pipe half the red butter cream around edges of badge.

5 Position freckles on badge. Using tweezers, decorate cake with cachous.

6 Pipe name onto cake with remaining red butter cream.

Sleeping moon

preparation time **45 minutes** (plus standing time) cooking time **1 hour**
serves **18**

2 x 340g packets buttercake mix
33cm-round prepared board (see note page 276)
1 quantity butter cream (page 294)
Yellow colouring

Decorations
½ cup (110g) white sugar
Yellow colouring
1 black licorice strap

1 Preheat oven to moderate (180°C/160°C fan-forced). Grease a deep
22cm round cake pan and line with paper. Make cake according to directions
on packets. Pour mixture into prepared pan; bake for about 1 hour. Stand
cake in pan for 5 minutes before turning onto a wire rack to cool. Using a
serrated knife, level cake top.
2 Turn cake cut-side down. Cut a moon-shape from cake; place on prepared
board, cut-side down. Discard remaining cake.
3 Tint butter cream with yellow colouring; spread all over cake.
4 Place sugar and yellow colouring in a small plastic bag; rub until sugar is
evenly coloured. Sprinkle sugar evenly over moon.
5 Cut licorice strap into thin strips; position on top of cake to form eye,
mouth and moon outline.

Balloon banana cakes

preparation time **1½ hours** cooking time **20 minutes** makes **24**

You will need about 3 over-ripe bananas for this recipe.

24 multi-coloured paper muffin cases
185g butter, softened
1 cup (220g) firmly packed brown sugar
3 eggs
2½ cups (375g) self-raising flour
1½ cups mashed banana
½ cup (125ml) milk
4 food colourings to match ribbons
4 colours x 4 metres each satin ribbon
40cm x 60cm prepared rectangular board (see note page 276)
2 quantities butter cream (see page 294)
Coloured sprinkles

1 Preheat oven to moderately hot (200°C/180°C fan-forced). Line two 12-hole (⅓-cup/80ml capacity) muffin pans with muffin cases.
2 Beat butter and sugar in a small bowl with electric mixer until light and fluffy. Add eggs one at a time, beating until just combined after each addition. Transfer to a large bowl; stir in the sifted flour, banana and milk. Divide among prepared pans.
3 Bake in a moderately hot oven for about 20 minutes, or until cooked when tested. Transfer to a wire rack to cool.
4 Divide butter cream into four equal portions; tint each portion with a different colouring. Spread each colour icing over six cakes. Tie a small loop and knot in the end of each piece of ribbon and attach a ribbon to each cake. Place cakes on board in the shape of a large balloon, cutting ribbons to correct length so they line up at the bottom. Gather ribbons and tie.
5 Tint some of the remaining icing in a stronger or different colour. Place in a piping bag and pipe a message on cakes. Sprinkle remaining cakes with coloured sprinkles, if desired.

Girlie ghost

preparation time **45 minutes** cooking time **1 hour** serves **16**

2 x 340g packets buttercake mix
40cm-round prepared board (see note page 276)
1 quantity butter cream (see page 294)
Blue colouring

Decorations
1.2kg ready-made soft icing
Icing sugar
Purple bow

1 Preheat oven to moderate (180°C/160°C fan-forced). Grease a 2.5-litre (10-cup) Dolly Varden pan.
2 Make buttercake cake according to directions on packets. Spread mixture into prepared pan; bake about 1 hour. Stand cake in pan 5 minutes; turn onto wire rack to cool. Using serrated knife, level cake top.
3 Place cake on board, cut-side down. Tint butter cream with blue colouring; spread all over cake.
4 Knead soft icing on surface dusted with icing sugar until smooth; roll icing into 5mm-thick circle large enough to generously cover cake. Using metal cutters or small sharp-pointed knife, cut eyes and mouth near centre of icing circle. Using rolling pin, lift icing over cake, draping so the cut-out eyes and mouth are positioned in the right place. (Icing will stretch slightly when lifted over the cake.) Trim draped icing on board to neaten shape of ghost.
5 Using a little butter cream, secure bow to cake.

Funny face cupcakes

preparation time **45 minutes** cooking time **20 minutes** makes **18**

The buttercake mix and butter cream are enough to make 12 patty cakes.
Decorate the remaining six patty cakes with your own favourite funny faces.

340g packet buttercake mix
1 quantity butter cream (see page 294)
Yellow, red, green and blue colouring

Decorations
(Enough for six patty cakes.)
1 tablespoon apricot jam, warmed, sieved
250g ready-made soft icing
Icing sugar
Flesh colouring
Cake decorating stars
Cake decorating hearts
Cake decorating moons
12 candy-covered chocolate buttons, assorted colours
Red glossy decorating gel
Black glossy decorating gel

1 Preheat oven to moderate (180°C/160°C fan-forced). Line a 12-hole
(⅓-cup/80ml) muffin pan with paper patty cases.
2 Make cake according to the directions on the packet. Pour ¼ cup of the
mixture into each muffin pan hole; bake for about 20 minutes. Stand cakes
in pan for 5 minutes before turning onto a wire rack to cool.
3 Divide butter cream among four small bowls. Tint each quantity with one
of the suggested colours: yellow, red, green or blue.
4 Brush the tops of the cakes with jam.
5 Knead soft icing on surface dusted with icing sugar until smooth. Knead
flesh colouring into the icing, then roll out until 3mm thick. Using a 7.5cm
cutter, cut six rounds from icing. Cover each patty cake with one round.
6 Place yellow butter cream a into piping bag fitted with a fluted tube. Pipe
different hairstyles onto one or two patty cakes. Repeat with the red, green
and blue butter creams, making sure to clean or replace the piping bag
between colours.
7 Decorate the hairstyles with stars, hearts and moons. Position the coloured
chocolate buttons on the top of each cake to form eyes, securing with tiny
dabs of butter cream.

8 Using red and black decorating gels, pipe pupils, eyebrows, noses, freckles, mouths, eyelashes, ears and glasses onto the cakes.

Picture perfect

preparation time **35 minutes** (plus standing time) cooking time **1 hour**
serves **24**

2 x 340g packets buttercake mix
35cm-square prepared board (see note page 276)
2 quantities butter cream (see page 294)

Decorations
11cm-square photograph, laminated
1kg mixed lollies

1 Preheat oven to moderate (180°C/160°C fan-forced). Grease a deep 23cm-square cake pan and and line with paper. Make cake according to directions on packets. Pour mixture into prepared pan; bake for about 1 hour. Stand cake in pan for 5 minutes before turning onto a wire rack to cool. Using serrated knife, level cake top.
2 Place cake on prepared board, cut-side down.
3 Spread butter cream all over cake.
4 Place photograph, centred, on cake.
5 Scatter mixed lollies all over cake, pressing them gently into butter cream.

tips You can use any photographic print you like, but remember to laminate it if you want it to remain after the cake is gone.
Use a selection of your favourite lollies to decorate this cake.

Heart of hearts ice-cream cake

preparation time **45 minutes** (plus freezing and refrigeration time)
cooking time **5 minutes** serves **24**

4 litres vanilla ice-cream, softened
300ml cream
300g white eating chocolate, chopped coarsely
Pink colouring
24cm-square piece thick cardboard
35cm-square prepared board (see note page 276)

Decorations
500g white eating chocolate, melted
Pink colouring
2 teaspoons coloured cachous

1 Line a 24cm heart-shaped cake pan with plastic wrap. Spoon ice-cream into pan and press down evenly. Cover with foil; freeze overnight.
2 Meanwhile, combine cream and chocolate in a medium saucepan. Stir over low heat until smooth. Tint with pink colouring. Transfer mixture to a medium jug. Cover, then refrigerate for 3 hours or overnight.
3 Tint one-third of the extra chocolate light pink and one-third of the extra chocolate dark pink.
4 Place light pink, dark pink and remaining white chocolate in separate piping bags. Pipe different-sized free-form hearts onto sheets of baking paper using chocolate of each colour. Refrigerate until set.
5 Using the cake pan as a guide, cut cardboard into a heart shape; wrap cardboard in foil, place cardboard on top of ice-cream cake (this makes it easier to handle). Working quickly, invert the cake onto a wire rack over an oven tray. Discard plastic wrap.
6 Pour the pink chocolate over the ice-cream cake to cover completely. Freeze for 3 hours.
7 Transfer cake from the rack to the prepared board.
8 Working quickly, position chocolate hearts all over the cake and sprinkle with coloured cachous. Freeze until ready to serve.

tip This cake can be made two days ahead of time.

Colin caterpillar

preparation time **45 minutes** cooking time **30 minutes** serves **12**

2 x 340g packets buttercake mix
2 quantities butter cream (see page 294)
Orange, red, green and blue colouring
4 cups (280g) shredded coconut
45cm x 80cm prepared rectangular board (see note page 276)

Decorations
44 yellow jelly beans
2 brown Smarties
2 large round mints
1 black licorice strap
1 pink Fruit Stick or Musk Stick
1 yellow Fruit Stick
1 green Fruit Stick
2 yellow pipe cleaners
59 mini M&Ms

1 Preheat oven to moderate (180°C/160°C fan-forced). Grease two 6-hole texas (¾-cup/180ml) muffin pans. Make cakes according to directions on packets. Divide evenly among holes. Bake about 30 minutes. Stand cakes in pans 5 minutes; turn onto wire racks to cool.
2 Using small knife, trim four of the cakes for the end of the caterpillar's body, making each one slightly smaller than the previous one.
3 Divide butter cream among four bowls; tint each quantity with one of the suggested colours: orange, red, green or blue. Spread butter cream of each colour over tops and sides of three cakes.
4 Place 1 cup coconut and orange colouring in a small plastic bag; rub until coconut is evenly coloured, gently press onto same coloured cake. Repeat with remaining coconut, colouring and cakes.
5 Assemble on board to form caterpillar. Place jelly beans as feet. Using a little butter cream, attach Smarties to mints for eyes; position on cake. Cut a thin strip from licorice strap and place on cake for mouth. Thinly slice Fruit Sticks lengthways; place on cake for hair. Curl ends of pipe cleaners and place on head for antennae. Scatter M&Ms over top remaining cakes.

Daisy bunch

preparation time **45 minutes** (plus standing and refrigeration time)
cooking time **20 minutes** serves **12**

340g packet buttercake mix
1½ quantities butter cream (see page 294)
Yellow and pink colouring
40cm x 50cm prepared rectangular board (see note page 276)

Decorations
2 x 250g packets coloured marshmallows
5 purple Smarties
7 pink Smarties
350g ready-made soft icing
Icing sugar
Green colouring
Pink bow
16 spearmint leaves

1 Preheat oven to moderate (180°C/160°C fan-forced). Line a 12-hole
(⅓ cup/80ml) muffin pan with paper patty cases.
2 Make cake according to directions on packet. Pour ¼ cup of mixture into
each hole; bake 20 minutes. Stand cakes in pan for 5 minutes before turning
onto a wire rack to cool.
3 Tint one-third of the butter cream with yellow colouring and spread over
five cakes. Tint the remaining butter cream with pink colouring and spread
over remaining cakes.
4 Using scissors, cut 18 pink marshmallows and 24 yellow marshmallows in
half horizontally. Squeeze the ends of each marshmallow together to form
petals. Decorate pink cakes with six or seven yellow marshmallow petals and
yellow cakes with six or seven pink marshmallow petals.
5 Place purple Smarties in centre of pink flowers; place pink Smarties
in centre of yellow flowers. Place flowers on prepared board.
6 Knead soft icing on surface dusted with icing sugar until smooth. Knead
green colouring into icing, then divide icing into quarters. Roll one-quarter of
the icing into a 5mm thick cord. Enclose the remaining icing in plastic wrap
and set aside. Cut the icing cord into three uneven lengths; position on board.
Repeat with reserved icing to make 12 stems in total.
7 Pinch stems together near the ends and secure bow with a little butter
cream. Position spearmint leaves along stems; secure with butter cream.

Construction site

preparation time **45 minutes** (plus standing time)
cooking time **1 hour** serves **18**

2 x 340g packets buttercake mix
30cm-round prepared board (see note page 276)
2 quantities butter cream (see page 294)
Yellow colouring

Decorations
2 x 50g Crunchie bars, crushed
300g packet chocolate-covered fruit and nut mix
1 road works sign
1 toy dump truck
2 toy construction workers
2 toy witches' hats

1 Preheat oven to moderate (180°C/160°C fan-forced). Grease a deep
22cm round cake pan and line with paper.
2 Make cake according to directions on packets. Pour into prepared pan;
bake for about 1 hour. Stand cake in pan for 5 minutes before turning onto a
wire rack to cool.
3 Place the cake on prepared board top-side up. Using a serrated knife,
shape cake to make a pit and hill.
4 Tint butter cream with yellow colouring; spread all over cake.
5 Sprinkle cake with Crunchie.
6 Place chocolate fruit and nuts around base of cake.
7 Position toys on top of cake.

Sandcastle ice-cream cake

preparation time **35 minutes** (plus freezing time) serves **18**

3 litres vanilla ice-cream, softened
2 litre plastic sandcastle bucket
30cm-round prepared board (see note page 276)

Decorations
1 cup (90g) desiccated coconut
Brown and yellow colouring
12 chocolate seashells
Small flag

1 Spoon ice-cream into a clean, dry bucket; press flat and cover with foil. Freeze overnight.

2 Dip the base of the bucket into hot water for a few seconds, then invert ice-cream onto a foil-covered tray. Freeze for 3 hours.

3 Meanwhile, place coconut, brown and yellow colouring in small plastic bag; rub colouring into coconut until evenly coloured.

4 Transfer ice-cream to prepared board. Working quickly, press coconut all over ice-cream cake. Sprinkle remaining coconut around the base of cake. Freeze until ready to serve.

5 Just before serving, place chocolate seashells around the cake and position the flag on top.

tip This cake can be make two days in advance.

Lucy ladybird

preparation time **45 minutes** (plus standing time) cooking time **35 minutes**
serves **24**

340g packet buttercake mix
25cm x 30cm prepared rectangular board (see note page 276)
1 quantity butter cream (see page 294)
Black and red colouring

Decorations
1 black licorice strap
14 chocolate freckles
2 x 15cm (3mm) black pipe cleaners
2 yellow Smarties

1 Preheat oven to moderate (180°C/160°C fan-forced). Grease one hole of
a 12-hole (⅓ cup/80ml) muffin pan and 1.25-litre (5-cup) pudding steamer.
2 Make cakes according to directions on packet, pour ¼ cup of mixture into
prepared muffin hole and remaining mixture into prepared pudding steamer.
Bake muffins for about 20 minutes and the large cake for about 35 minutes.
Stand cakes in their pans for 5 minutes before turning onto a wire rack to
cool. Using a serrated knife, level large cake top.
3 Using a serrated knife, cut off tops from muffin. Turn the large cake cut-side
down. Trim dome to make more rounded. Place cake on prepared board,
flat-side down.
4 Tint ¼ cup of butter cream with black colouring and the remaining butter
cream with red colouring. Spread red butter cream all over body of ladybird.
5 Position muffin top against body for head; spread all over with black butter
cream. Cut an outside strip of licorice from licorice strap; position along
centre of body. Position freckles on body.
6 Curl one end of each pipe cleaner and position on cake for antennae. Place
Smarties on cake for eyes.

ICINGS AND TOPPINGS

All of these icings and toppings make enough to top one 22cm round or one 19cm square cake.

Glacé icing

preparation time **5 minutes** cooking time **5 minutes**

1½ **cups (240g) icing sugar**
1 **teaspoon soft butter**
2 **tablespoons milk, approximately**

Sift icing sugar into small heatproof bowl Stir in butter and enough milk to form a firm paste. Stir over hot water until icing reaches a spreadable consistency; do not overheat. Spread icing over cold cake immediately.

Variations
Chocolate Add 2 or 3 tablespoons cocoa to icing sugar when sifting.
Coffee Add 3 teaspoons instant coffee granules to icing sugar when sifting.
Lemon Substitute lemon juice for milk, add 1 teaspoon grated rind.
Maple Syrup Substitute maple syrup for milk.
Orange Substitute orange juice for milk; 1 teaspoon grated rind can be added, if desired.
Passionfruit Add the pulp of 1 passionfruit and enough milk to give a spreadable consistency

Chocolate butter cream

preparation time **5 minutes** (plus standing time) cooking time **5 minutes**

125g **unsalted butter, chopped**
125g **dark eating chocolate, chopped**

Melt butter and chocolate in small heatproof bowl over hot water, cool to room temperature. Beat with wooden spoon until thick and spreadable.

Caramel icing

preparation time **5 minutes** cooking time **5 minutes**

60g butter
½ cup (110g) firmly packed brown sugar
2 tablespoons milk
¾ cup (120g) icing sugar, approximately

Melt butter in a small saucepan, add brown sugar and milk. Bring to boil, then reduce heat and simmer, stirring, for 2 minutes; cool. Stir in enough sifted icing sugar until of a spreadable consistency.

Rich chocolate glacé icing

preparation time **5 minutes** cooking time **5 minutes**

90g dark eating chocolate, chopped
1 teaspoon vegetable oil
¼ cup (60ml) water
2 cups (320g) icing sugar, approximately

Combine chocolate, oil and water in a medium saucepan, stir over low heat until chocolate is melted. Gradually beat in enough sifted icing sugar to until of a smooth, spreadable consistency.

Milk chocolate icing

preparation time **5 minutes** cooking time **5 minutes**

125g dark eating chocolate, chopped
60g butter
2 tablespoons sweetened condensed milk

Combine chocolate, butter and milk in a small heatproof bowl. Stir over hot water until smooth; cool. Beat icing with electric mixer until mixture thickens and changes slightly in colour.

Chocolate glaze

preparation time **5 minutes** cooking time **5 minutes**

150g dark eating chocolate, chopped
30g butter
2 teaspoons vegetable oil

Combine all ingredients in a small heatproof bowl. Stir over hot water until mixure is smooth. Use while still warm.

Vienna cream frosting

preparation time **5 minutes**

150g butter, chopped
2 cups (320g) icing sugar
2 tablespoons milk

Beat butter in a small bowl with electric mixer until as white as possible. Gradually beat in half the sifted icing sugar, all of the milk, then the remaining icing sugar.

Variations
Chocolate Sift 2 or 3 tablespoons cocoa with the icing sugar; add a little more milk if necessary.
Cinnamon Sift 2 teaspoons ground cinnamon with the icing sugar.
Coffee Dissolve 3 teaspoons instant coffee granules in 2 tablespoons hot water; cool. Substitute for milk.
Lemon Substitute lemon juice for milk; 1 teaspoon of grated rind can be added, if desired.
Orange Substitute orange juice for milk; 1 teaspoon of grated rind can be added, if desired.

Cream cheese frosting

preparation time **5 minutes**

90g cream cheese, chopped
90g butter, chopped
1 cup (160g) icing sugar

Beat cheese and butter in small bowl with electric mixer until as white as possible. Gradually beat in sifted icing sugar.

Variations

Choc-hazelnut Reduce cream cheese and butter to 60g each, and beat in 2 tablespoons chocolate hazelnut spread with cheese and butter.
Golden Beat in 2 tablespoons golden syrup with cheese and butter.
Honey Beat in 1 tablespoon honey with cheese and butter.
Passionfruit Reduce cream cheese and butter to 60g each, and stir in the pulp of 1 passionfruit after beating in icing sugar.
Treacle Beat in 1 tablespoon treacle with cheese and butter.

Chocolate cream topping

preparation time **5 minutes** cooking time **5 minutes**

½ cup (125ml) double cream
125g dark eating chocolate, chopped

Heat cream in small saucepan until boiling, remove from heat. Add chocolate, stir until smooth. Cool until thick and pourable.

Lemon icing

preparation time **5 minutes** cooking time **5 minutes**

1 ½ cups (240g) icing sugar
1 teaspoon soft butter
1 tablespoon lemon juice, approximately

Sift icing sugar into small heatproof bowl, stir in butter and enough juice to form a stiff paste. Stir over hot water until of a spreadable consistency.

Sour cream chocolate glaze

preparation time **5 minutes** cooking time **5 minutes**

100g dark eating chocolate, chopped
60g unsalted butter
½ cup (80g) icing sugar
¼ cup (60ml) sour cream

Combine all ingredients in a small saucepan. Stir over low heat until smooth. Bring to boil, then reduce heat and simmer, uncovered, for 2 minutes; cool for 5 minutes before using.

Citrus frosting

preparation time **5 minutes**

1½ cups (240g) icing sugar
1 teaspoon finely grated orange or lemon rind
30g soft butter
1½ tablespoons orange or lemon juice, approximately

Combine sifted icing sugar, rind and butter in a small bowl. Stir in enough juice to give a spreadable consistency.

Chocolate fudge frosting

preparation time **5 minutes** (plus refrigeration time) cooking time **5 minutes**

45g unsalted butter
2 tablespoons water
¼ cup (55g) caster sugar
¾ cup (120g) icing sugar
2 tablespoons cocoa

Combine butter, water and caster sugar in small saucepan. Stir over heat, without boiling, until sugar is dissolved. Sift icing sugar and cocoa into a small heatproof bowl. Gradually stir in hot butter mixture. Cover, and refrigerate until thick. Beat with wooden spoon until mixture is smooth and spreadable.

Chantilly cream

preparation time **5 minutes**

300ml whipping cream
1 tablespoon caster sugar
½ teaspoon vanilla extract

Beat ingredients in a small bowl with electric mixer until soft peaks form.

Passionfruit cream

preparation time **5 minutes**

300ml whipping cream
1 tablespoon caster sugar
2 passionfruit

Beat cream and sugar in small bowl with electric mixer until soft peaks form; fold in passionfruit pulp.

Liqueur cream

preparation time **5 minutes**

Any favourite liqueur can be used in this cream

300ml whipping cream
1 tablespoon liqueur
1 tablespoon icing sugar

Beat ingredients in a small bowl with electric mixer until soft peaks form.

Fluffy cocoa frosting

preparation time **5 minutes** (plus refrigeration time) cooking time **5 minutes**

50g butter
2 tablespoons water
¼ cup (55g) caster sugar
¾ cup (120g) icing sugar
2 tablespoons cocoa powder

1 Combine butter, water and caster sugar in a small pan. Stir over heat, without boiling, until sugar is dissolved.
2 Sift icing sugar and cocoa into a medium heatproof bowl. Gradually stir in hot butter mixture. Cover, and refrigerate until thick. Beat with a wooden spoon until of a spreadable consistency.

Butter cream

preparation time **5 minutes**

This is a basic butter cream recipe; the flavour can be varied by adding the finely grated rind of any citrus fruit or any essence to your taste.

125g butter, softened
1½ cups (240g) icing sugar
2 tablespoons milk

1 Beat butter in a small bowl with electric mixer until as white as possible. Gradually beat in half of the icing sugar, milk, then remaining icing sugar.
2 Flavour and colour butter cream as required.

Fluffy frosting

preparation time **10 minutes** cooking time **10 minutes**

1 cup (220g) caster sugar
⅓ cup (80ml) water
2 egg whites

1 Combine sugar and the water in a small saucepan. Stir with a wooden spoon over high heat, without boiling, until sugar dissolves. Boil, uncovered, without stirring, for about 3-5 minutes or until syrup is slightly thick.
2 If using a candy thermometer, the syrup is ready when it reaches 114°C (240°F). Otherwise, when syrup is thick, remove the pan from the heat, allow the bubbles to subside then test the syrup by dropping 1 teaspoon into a cup of cold water. It should form a ball of soft, sticky toffee when rolled gently between your fingertips.
3 The syrup should not change colour; if it does, it has been cooked for too long and you will have to discard it and start again.
4 While syrup is boiling, beat egg whites in a small bowl with electric mixer until stiff. Keep beating (or the whites will deflate) until the syrup reaches the correct temperature.
5 When syrup is ready, allow bubbles to subside then pour a very thin stream onto the egg whites with the mixer operating on medium speed. If syrup is added too quickly to the egg whites, the frosting will not thicken. Continue beating and adding syrup until all the syrup is used. Continue to beat until frosting stands in stiff peaks (frosting should be barely warm by this stage).
6 Tint frosting, if desired, by beating food colouring through while mixing, or by stirring through with a spatula at the end. Frosting can also be flavoured with a little essence of your choice.
7 For best results, frosting should be applied to a cake on the day it is served, while the frosting is still soft and has a marshmallow-like consistency. While you can frost the cake the day before, the frosting will become crisp and lose its glossiness – much like a meringue.
8 Be sure to cover the cake with frosting to the base near the board. This will form a seal and help to keep the cake fresh.

Almond icing

preparation time **10 minutes** makes **500g**

2⅓ cups (375g) icing sugar, sifted
1 cup (125g) almond meal
2 tablespoons brandy
1 egg yolk
1 teaspoon lemon juice
Icing sugar, extra

1 Combine icing sugar and almond meal in a bowl. Make a well in the centre, stir in brandy, egg yolk and lemon juice. When the mixture becomes too stiff to stir, use your hand to mix.
2 Knead on a surface dusted with sifted extra icing sugar.
3 Almond icing must be kept covered while not being handled as exposure to air will allow a crust to develop. It may be wrapped tightly in plastic and kept for up to 1 week in the refrigerator.

Fondant

preparation time **10 minutes** (plus standing time) makes **500g**

2 tablespoons water
3 teaspoons gelatine
2 tablespoons glucose syrup
2 teaspoons glycerine
3 cups (480g) icing sugar, sifted
Icing sugar, sifted, extra

1 Place the water in a small saucepan, add gelatine. Stir over low heat until gelatine is dissolved; do not boil. Remove from heat, stir in glucose syrup and glycerine; cool to warm.
2 Place icing sugar in large bowl, make well in centre, gradually stir in liquid. When mixture becomes too stiff to stir, use hand to mix.
3 Knead fondant on surface dusted with extra icing sugar until smooth, pliable and without stickiness.

Passionfruit icing

preparation time **5 minutes** cooking time **5 minutes**

1 ½ cups (240g) icing sugar
1 teaspoon soft butter
2 tablespoons passionfruit pulp, approximately

Place icing sugar in small heatproof bowl; stir in butter and enough passionfruit pulp to form a firm paste. Stir over hot water until icing is of a spreadable consistency, taking care not to overheat. Use immediately.

Mascarpone cream

Preparation time **5 minutes**

250g mascarpone
¼ cup (40g) icing sugar
2 tablespoons hazelnut liqueur
½ cup (120g) sour cream
½ cup (75g) roasted hazelnuts, chopped finely

Combine mascarpone, icing sugar, liqueur and sour cream in a medium bowl. Using a wooden spoon, stir until smooth. Stir in nuts.

Coconut ice frosting

preparation time **5 minutes**

2 cups (320g) icing sugar
1 ⅓ cups (110g) coconut
2 egg whites, lightly beaten
Pink food colouring

Combine sifted icing sugar in bowl with coconut and egg whites; mix well. Tint with a little pink food colouring, if desired.

Coffee icing

preparation time **5 minutes** cooking time **5 minutes**

2 cups (320g) icing sugar
15g butter
3 teaspoons instant coffee granules
2 tablespoons water

Sift icing sugar into small heatproof bowl. Stir in butter and combined coffee and water. Stir over hot water until icing is of a spreadable consistency.

Orange icing

preparation time **5 minutes** cooking time **5 minutes**

1 cup (160g) icing sugar
1 teaspoon soft butter
1 tablespoon orange juice, approximately
1 tablespoon coconut

Sift icing sugar into small heatproof bowl. Stir in butter and enough juice to form a stiff paste. Stir over hot water until icing is of a spreadable consistency.

Honey frosting

preparation time **5 minutes**

125g butter
125g cream cheese
¼ cup honey
30g dark eating chocolate, grated

Cream butter and cream cheese in a small bowl with electric mixer until light and fluffy. Stir in honey and chocolate.

Mocha frosting

preparation time **5 minutes** (plus standing time) cooking time **5 minutes**

60g dark eating chocolate, chopped
90g unsalted butter
1¼ cups (200g) icing sugar
1 teaspoon instant coffee granules
2 teaspoons hot water

Melt chocolate in a heatproof bowl over hot water; cool. Beat butter in a small bowl with electric mixer until creamy. Gradually beat in sifted icing sugar, chocolate, and combined coffee and water.

Orange cream cheese frosting

preparation time **5 minutes**

60g cream cheese
30g soft butter
1 teaspoon finely grated orange rind
1½ cups (240g) icing sugar

Beat cream cheese, butter and rind in a small bowl with electric mixer until light and fluffy. Gradually beat in sifted icing sugar; beat until smooth.

Pineapple frosting

preparation time **5 minutes**

30g butter
2 cups (320g) icing sugar
¼ cup (60ml) pineapple juice

Combine butter and sifted icing sugar in a bowl. Gradually stir in juice until mixture is smooth.

MUFFINS AND SCONES

Banana maple muffins

preparation time **15 minutes** cooking time **25 minutes** makes **12**

You will need about 2 small over-ripe bananas (260g) for this recipe.

2 cups (300g) self-raising flour
⅓ cup (50g) plain flour
½ teaspoon bicarbonate of soda
½ cup (110g) firmly packed brown sugar
¼ cup (60ml) maple-flavoured syrup
⅔ cup mashed banana
2 eggs, beaten lightly
1 cup (250ml) buttermilk
⅓ cup (80ml) vegetable oil

Coconut topping
15g butter
1 tablespoon maple-flavoured syrup
⅔ cup (30g) flaked coconut

1 Preheat oven to moderately hot (200°C/180°C fan-forced). Grease a 12-hole (⅓-cup/80ml) muffin pan.
2 Make coconut topping.
3 Sift dry ingredients into a large bowl; stir in maple syrup and banana, then egg, buttermilk and oil.
4 Divide mixture among holes of prepared pan; sprinkle with coconut topping. Bake for about 20 minutes. Stand muffins in pan for 5 minutes before turning onto a wire rack to cool.

Coconut topping Melt butter in small saucepan, add maple syrup and coconut; stir constantly over high heat until coconut is browned lightly. Remove from heat.

Citrus poppy seed muffins

preparation time **15 minutes** cooking time **20 minutes** makes **12**

125g softened butter, chopped
2 teaspoons finely grated lemon rind
2 teaspoons finely grated lime rind
2 teaspoons finely grated orange rind
²/₃ cup (150g) caster sugar
2 eggs, beaten lightly
2 cups (300g) self-raising flour
½ cup (250ml) milk
2 tablespoons poppy seeds
1 medium orange (240g)
Icing sugar, for dusting

1 Preheat oven to moderately hot (200°C/180°C fan-forced). Grease a
12-hole (¹/₃-cup/80ml) muffin pan.
2 Combine butter, rinds, caster sugar, egg, sifted flour and milk in medium
bowl; beat with electric mixer until just combined. Increase speed to medium;
beat until mixture is just changed in colour; stir in poppy seeds.
3 Divide mixture among holes of prepared pan; bake about 20 minutes.
Stand muffins in pan for 5 minutes before turning onto wire rack.
4 Peel rind thinly from orange, avoiding any white pith. Cut rind into thin
strips. To serve, dust muffins with icing sugar; top with orange strips.

Choc brownie muffins

preparation time **15 minutes** cooking time **20 minutes** makes **12**

2 cups (300g) self-raising flour
¹/₃ cup (35g) cocoa powder
¹/₃ cup (75g) caster sugar
60g butter, melted
½ cup (95g) choc chips
½ cup (75g) pistachios, chopped coarsely
½ cup (165g) chocolate hazelnut spread
1 egg, beaten lightly
¾ cup (180ml) milk
½ cup (120g) sour cream

1 Preheat oven to moderately hot (200°C/180°C fan-forced). Grease a 12-hole (⅓-cup/80ml) muffin pan.

2 Sift dry ingredients into large bowl; stir in remaining ingredients.

3 Divide mixture among holes of prepared pan; bake about 20 minutes. Stand muffins in pan 5 minutes before turning onto wire rack. Serve, dusted with sifted extra cocoa, if desired.

Lime syrup coconut muffins

preparation time **10 minutes** cooking time **25 minutes** makes **12**

2½ cups (375g) self-raising flour
1 cup (90g) desiccated coconut
1 cup (220g) caster sugar
1 tablespoon finely grated lime rind
1 cup (250ml) buttermilk
125g butter, melted
2 eggs

Lime syrup
½ cup (110g) caster sugar
¼ cup (60ml) water
2 teaspoons finely grated lime rind
⅓ cup (80ml) lime juice

1 Preheat oven to moderately hot (200°C/180°C fan-forced). Grease a 12-hole (⅓-cup/80ml) muffin pan.

2 Combine flour, coconut and sugar in large bowl; stir in combined remaining ingredients. Divide mixture among holes of prepared pan; bake 20 minutes.

3 Make lime syrup.

4 Transfer muffins to wire rack set over an oven tray; pour hot lime syrup over hot muffins. Drain syrup from tray and pour over muffins again.

Lime syrup Place ingredients in small saucepan; stir over heat, without boiling, until sugar dissolves. Simmer, uncovered, without stirring, 2 minutes.

White chocolate and macadamia muffins

preparation time **10 minutes** cooking time **20 minutes** makes **6**

2 cups (300g) self-raising flour
2/3 cup (150g) caster sugar
3/4 cup (140g) white choc chips
1/2 cup (75g) coarsely chopped macadamias, toasted
60g butter, melted
3/4 cup (180ml) milk
1 egg, beaten lightly

1 Preheat oven to moderately hot (200°C/180°C fan-forced). Grease a six-hole (3/4-cup/180ml) muffin pan.
2 Sift flour and sugar into large bowl; stir in remaining ingredients.
3 Divide muffin mixture among holes of prepared pan. Bake 20 minutes. Stand muffins in pan for 5 minutes before turning onto a wire rack to cool.

Raspberry and coconut muffins

preparation time **10 minutes** cooking time **20 minutes** makes **12**

2½ cups (375g) self-raising flour
90g butter, chopped
1 cup (220g) caster sugar
1 egg, beaten lightly
1¼ cups (310ml) buttermilk
1/3 cup (30g) desiccated coconut
150g fresh or frozen raspberries
2 tablespoons shredded coconut

1 Preheat oven to moderately hot (200°C/180°C fan-forced). Grease a 12-hole (1/3-cup/80ml) muffin pan.
2 Place flour in large bowl; using fingertips, rub in butter. Add sugar, egg, buttermilk, desiccated coconut and raspberries; mix until just combined.
3 Divide mixture among holes of prepared pan; sprinkle with shredded coconut. Bake about 20 minutes. Stand muffins in pan for 5 minutes before turning onto a wire rack to cool.

Blueberry muffins

preparation time **10 minutes** cooking time **20 minutes** makes **6**

2 cups (300g) self-raising flour
¾ cup (150g) firmly packed brown sugar
1 cup (150g) fresh or frozen blueberries
1 egg, lightly beaten
¾ cup (180ml) buttermilk
½ cup (125ml) vegetable oil

1 Preheat oven to moderately hot (200°C/180°C fan-forced). Grease a six-hole (¾-cup/180ml) muffin pan.
2 Sift dry ingredients into large bowl, stir in remaining ingredients.
3 Divide muffin mixture among holes of prepared pan. Bake for 20 minutes. Stand muffins in pan for 5 minutes before turning onto a wire rack to cool.

Mixed berry muffins

preparation time **10 minutes** cooking time **35 minutes** makes **6**

2¼ cups (335g) self-raising flour
1 cup (220g) caster sugar
1 teaspoon vanilla extract
2 eggs, beaten lightly
100g butter, melted
1 cup (250ml) milk
1 teaspoon finely grated lemon rind
200g fresh or frozen mixed berries

1 Preheat oven to moderately hot (200°C/180°C fan-forced). Grease a six-hole (¾-cup/180ml) muffin pan or coat six large paper muffin cases with cooking oil spray and place on an oven tray.
2 Sift flour into large bowl; add sugar then combined extract, egg, butter, milk and rind. Add berries; stir through gently.
3 Divide muffin mixture among holes of prepared pan. Bake for 35 minutes. Stand muffins in pan for 5 minutes before turning onto a wire rack.

Marmalade almond muffins

preparation time **15 minutes**   cooking time **20 minutes**   makes **12**

2 cups (300g) self-raising flour
125g butter, chopped
1 cup (80g) flaked almonds
²/₃ cup (150g) caster sugar
1 tablespoon finely grated orange rind
½ cup (170g) orange marmalade
2 eggs, beaten lightly
½ cup (125ml) milk
¼ cup (20g) flaked almonds, extra

Orange syrup
¼ cup (85g) orange marmalade
2 tablespoons water

1 Preheat oven to moderately hot (200°C/180°C fan-forced). Grease a
12-hole (¹/₃-cup/80ml) muffin pan.
2 Sift flour into large bowl; rub in butter. Stir in nuts, sugar and rind, then
marmalade, egg and milk. Divide mixture among holes of prepared pan;
sprinkle with extra nuts.
3 Bake muffins for about 20 minutes. Stand muffins in pan for a few minutes
before turning onto a wire rack.
4 Meanwhile, combine ingredients for orange syrup in small bowl. Drizzle
syrup over warm muffins.

Basic scones

preparation time **20 minutes** cooking time **15 minutes** makes **16**

2½ cups (375g) self-raising flour
1 tablespoon caster sugar
¼ teaspoon salt
30g butter
¾ cup (180ml) milk
½ cup (125ml) water, approximately

1 Preheat oven to very hot (240°C/220°C fan-forced). Grease a deep 19cm-square cake pan.

2 Sift flour, sugar and salt into large bowl; rub in butter with fingertips.

3 Make a well in the centre of flour mixture; add milk and almost all of the water. Using a knife, "cut" the milk and water through the flour mixture to form a soft, sticky dough. Add remaining water only if needed.

4 Turn dough onto a lightly floured surface; knead until smooth. Use your hand to press the dough out evenly to a thickness of 2cm.

5 Dip a 4.5cm cutter into flour; cut as many rounds as you can from the piece of dough. Place scones side-by-side, just touching, in prepared pan. Gently knead dough scraps, and repeat pressing and cutting dough. Place in pan; brush scone tops with a little extra milk. Bake for about 15 minutes.

Variations

Sultana and lemon At end of step 2, add ½ cup sultanas and 2 teaspoons finely grated lemon rind.

Cardamom marmalade At end of step 2, add 1 teaspoon ground cardamom and 2 teaspoons finely grated orange rind. Also, omit the water and increase milk to 1 cup. Stir in ⅓ cup orange marmalade with the milk.

Blueberry ginger At the end of step 2, add 3 teaspoons ground ginger and ½ cup fresh or frozen blueberries.

Buttermilk Replace the milk and the water in the basic scone mixture with approximately 1¼ cups buttermilk.

Honey and muesli At the end of step 2, add 1 teaspoon ground cinnamon and ½ cup toasted muesli. Also, omit the water and add ¼ cup honey just before adding the milk.

Apricot and almond At the end of step 2, add 1 teaspoon mixed spice, 1 cup chopped dried apricots and ⅓ cup chopped toasted slivered almonds.

Fruit and nut scrolls

preparation time **30 minutes** cooking time **25 minutes** makes **18**

You can use 1 ¼ cups (380g) bottled fruit mince instead of filling in this recipe.

3 cups (450g) self-raising flour
2 teaspoons caster sugar
50g butter
1 ⅓ cups (330ml) buttermilk, approximately

Filling
¼ cup (40g) sultanas
¼ cup (35g) dried currants
¼ cup (35g) chopped dried apricots
¼ cup (50g) chopped seeded prunes
1 medium (150g) apple, peeled, finely chopped
2 tablespoons flaked almonds
2 teaspoons grated orange rind
2 tablespoons orange juice
⅓ teaspoon ground cloves
2 teaspoons rum or brandy
¼ cup (50g) brown sugar

Apricot glaze
2 tablespoons apricot jam
2 teaspoons water

Icing
⅓ cup (55g) icing sugar
1 teaspoon hot water

1 Preheat oven to hot (220°C/200°C fan-forced). Grease oven trays.
2 Combine ingredients for filling in medium bowl; mix well.
3 Sift flour and sugar into large bowl, rub in butter. Stir in enough buttermilk to mix to a soft, sticky dough. Turn onto floured surface, knead until smooth.
4 Roll dough to 26cm x 36cm rectangle, spread with filling. Roll dough firmly from long side, like a swiss roll. Cut roll into 2cm slices. Place slices, cut-side up, about 3cm apart onto prepared trays. Bake about 15 minutes.
5 Meanwhile, make apricot glaze. Combine ingredients for icing in small bowl; stir until smooth. Brush scrolls with hot apricot glaze; pipe or drizzle with icing.

Apricot glaze Simmer jam and water in small pan until it thickens; strain.

Walnut coffee sticky buns

preparation time **20 minutes** cooking time **25 minutes** makes **24**

2 tablespoons instant coffee granules
2 tablespoons boiling water
1 ⅓ cups (330ml) milk
3 cups (450g) self-raising flour
¾ cup (165g) firmly packed brown sugar, extra
60g butter, chopped
50g butter, extra, melted
1 cup (100g) toasted walnuts, chopped

Walnut caramel
80g butter
¾ cup (165g) firmly packed brown sugar
1 tablespoon water
1 cup (100g) toasted walnuts, chopped

1 Preheat oven to moderately hot (200°C/180°C fan-forced). Lightly grease a 20cm x 30cm lamington pan.

2 Make walnut caramel.

3 Dissolve coffee in boiling water; stir in milk. Place flour and 1 tablespoon of sugar in medium bowl; rub in butter. Make a well in centre of dry ingredients; add coffee mixture to make a soft, sticky dough. Turn onto floured surface, knead until smooth.

4 Roll dough to 25cm x 50cm rectangle; brush with extra butter, sprinkle with remaining extra sugar and walnuts. Roll dough firmly from long side, like a swiss roll. Cut roll into 24 rounds. Place rounds tightly in prepared pan over walnut caramel.

5 Bake for about 20 minutes or until browned. Stand buns for 5 minutes before turning onto a wire rack to cool.

Walnut caramel Place butter, sugar and water in small saucepan; stir until sugar dissolves. Stir in walnuts. Pour into prepared pan.

tip This recipe is not suitable to freeze.

Spicy fruit scones

preparation time **20 minutes** (plus standing time) cooking time **15 minutes**
makes **16**

1¼ cups (310ml) hot strong strained black tea
¾ cup (135g) mixed dried fruit
3 cups (450g) self-raising flour
1 teaspoon ground cinnamon
1 teaspoon mixed spice
2 tablespoons caster sugar
20g butter
½ cup (125ml) sour cream, approximately

1 Preheat oven to hot (220°C/200°C fan-forced). Grease 23cm square slab
pan. Combine tea and fruit in small heatproof bowl, cover, stand 20 minutes.
2 Sift dry ingredients into large bowl, rub in butter. Stir in fruit mixture and
enough sour cream to mix to a soft, sticky dough.
3 Turn onto floured surface; knead until smooth. Press out to 2cm thickness,
cut into 5.5cm rounds; place into prepared pan. Bake about 15 minutes.

Carrot banana scones

preparation time **30 minutes** cooking time **20** makes **12**

You will need 1 large over-ripe banana (230g) and 1 medium carrot (120g).

2 cups (300g) white self-raising flour
½ cup (80g) wholemeal self-raising flour
½ teaspoon ground cardamom
40g butter
⅓ cup (65g) firmly packed brown sugar
½ cup mashed banana
⅓ cup finely grated carrot
¼ cup (30g) finely chopped walnuts
¼ cup (40g) finely chopped raisins
¾ cup (180ml) milk, approximately

Orange cream
50g cream cheese, chopped
50g butter, chopped
½ teaspoon finely grated orange rind
½ cup (80g) icing sugar

1 Preheat oven to very hot (240°C/220°C fan-forced). Grease 23cm round sandwich cake pan.

2 Sift flours and cardamom into large bowl, rub in butter. Add sugar, banana, carrot, nuts and raisins; stir in enough milk to mix to a soft, sticky dough. Turn onto floured surface, knead until smooth. Press out to 2cm thickness, cut into 5.5cm rounds, place into prepared pan. Bake about 20 minutes.

3 Meanwhile, make orange cream. Serve scones with orange cream

Orange cream Beat cheese, butter and rind in small bowl with electric mixer until as white as possible. Gradually beat in sifted icing sugar.

Pistachio lime syrup gems

preparation time **20 minutes** cooking time **15 minutes** makes **24**

Heat ungreased gem irons in hot oven for 5 minutes just before use; grease with cooking oil spray.

30g butter
1 teaspoon grated lime rind
⅓ cup (75g) caster sugar
1 egg
1¼ cups (185g) self-raising flour
⅔ cup (160ml) milk
¼ cup (35g) finely chopped pistachios

Lime syrup
2 tablespoons lime juice
2 tablespoons water
⅓ cup (75g) caster sugar

1 Preheat oven to moderately hot (200°C/180°C fan-forced).

2 Beat butter, rind, sugar and egg in small bowl with electric mixer until combined. Stir in sifted flour and milk in two batches.

3 Drop tablespoons of mixture into gem irons, then sprinkle with nuts. Bake for about 12 minutes.

4 Meanwhile, make lime syrup. Turn gems onto a wire rack, brush with hot lime syrup.

Lime syrup Combine ingredients in small saucepan; stir over heat, without boiling, until sugar dissolves. Simmer, uncovered, without stirring, 2 minutes.

Wholemeal date scones

preparation time **15 minutes** cooking time **15 minutes** makes about **15**

1 cup (150g) self-raising flour
1 cup (150g) wholemeal self-raising flour
1 cup (60g) unprocessed bran
¼ cup (25g) full cream milk powder
60g butter
1 cup (140g) dried seeded dates, chopped finely
1 cup (250ml) water, approximately

1 Preheat oven to moderately hot (200°C/180°C fan-forced). Lightly grease a 20 x 30cm lamington pan.
2 Sift flours into medium bowl, return husks from sifter to bowl, mix in bran and milk powder; rub in butter, then add dates. Make a well in centre of dry ingredients and stir in enough water to give a soft, sticky dough.
3 Turn dough onto a lightly floured surface and knead lightly until smooth. Press dough out to 1cm thickness and cut into rounds with 5cm cutter.
4 Place scones into prepared pan; bake 15 minutes. Serve hot with butter.

Apricot coconut muffins

preparation time **15 minutes** cooking time **20 minutes** makes **12**

2 cups (300g) self-raising flour
125g butter, chopped
¾ cup (165g) castor sugar
1 cup (150g) chopped dried apricots
1 cup (90g) coconut
¾ cup (180ml) milk
2 eggs

1 Preheat oven to moderately hot (200°C/180°C fan-forced). Grease a 12-hole (⅓-cup/80ml) muffin pan.
2 Place flour in large bowl, rub in butter. Add remaining ingredients, stir with large metal spoon until just combined. Divide mixture among holes of prepared pan.
3 Bake muffins for about 20 minutes. Turn onto a wire rack to cool.

Pumpkin scones

preparation time **20 minutes** cooking time **15 minutes** makes **about 16**

You will need to cook about 250g pumpkin for this recipe.

40g butter
¼ cup (55g) caster sugar
1 egg, beaten lightly
¾ cup cooked mashed pumpkin
2½ cups (375g) self-raising flour
½ teaspoon ground nutmeg
⅓ cup milk (125ml), approximately

1 Preheat oven to hot (220°C/200°C fan-forced). Lightly grease two 20cm round sandwich pans.
2 Beat butter and sugar in large bowl with electric mixer until light and fluffy; gradually beat in egg. Stir in pumpkin, then sifted dry ingredients and enough milk to make a soft sticky dough.
3 Turn dough onto floured surface, knead lightly until smooth. Press dough out to about 2cm thickness; cut 5cm rounds from dough. Place rounds, just touching, in prepared pans. Brush tops with a little milk.
4 Bake scones for about 15 minutes.

Banana date muffins

preparation time **20 minutes** cooking time **20 minutes** makes **12**

You will need about 2 large over-ripe bananas (460g) for this recipe.

2 cups (300g) self-raising flour
1 teaspoon mixed spice
½ cup (100g) firmly packed brown sugar
1 cup mashed bananas
1 cup (160g) seeded chopped dates
3 eggs, lightly beaten
⅓ cup (80ml) vegetable oil
⅓ cup (80ml) buttermilk

1 Preheat oven to moderately hot (200°C/180°C fan-forced). Grease a 12-hole (⅓-cup/80ml) muffin pan.
2 Sift dry ingredients into a large bowl, stir in remaining ingredients. Divide among holes of prepared pan. Bake about 20 minutes.

Chocolate orange dessert muffins

preparation time **35 minutes** cooking time **30 minutes** makes **12**

2 cups (300g) self-raising flour
½ cup (50g) cocoa powder
1¼ cups (275g) caster sugar
125g butter, melted
¾ cup (180ml) buttermilk
1 egg, beaten lightly
2 tablespoons orange-flavoured liqueur
2 teaspoons finely grated orange rind
12 (120g) chocolate orange thins

Crème anglaise
4 egg yolks
½ cup (110g) caster sugar
1⅔ cups (410ml) milk

1 Preheat oven to moderately hot (200°C/180°C fan-forced). Grease a 12-hole (⅓-cup/80ml) muffin pan.
2 Sift flour, cocoa and sugar into a large bowl; stir in butter, buttermilk, egg, liqueur and rind.
3 Divide muffin mixture among holes of prepared pan. Break each chocolate into three or four pieces; push pieces into each muffin, making sure that chocolate does not touch sides of muffin pan and that mixture almost covers the chocolate. Bake for about 20 minutes.
4 Meanwhile, make crème anglaise; serve with muffins.

Crème anglaise Beat egg yolks and sugar in a small bowl with electric mixer until thick and pale. Pour milk into small saucepan, bring to the boil. Whisk milk into yolk mixture. Return mixture to pan; stir over heat, without boiling, until mixture thickens and coats back of spoon.

Overnight date and muesli muffins

preparation time **10 minutes** (plus refrigeration time)
cooking time **20 minutes** makes **12**

1 ¼ cups (185g) plain flour
1 ¼ cups (160g) toasted muesli
1 teaspoon ground cinnamon
1 teaspoon bicarbonate of soda
½ cup (110g) firmly packed brown sugar
½ cup (30g) unprocessed bran
¾ cup (120g) coarsely chopped seedless dates
1 ½ cups (375ml) buttermilk
½ cup (125ml) vegetable oil
1 egg, beaten lightly

1 Combine ingredients in a large bowl; stir until just combined. Cover and refrigerate overnight.
2 Preheat oven to moderately hot (200°C/180°C fan-forced). Grease a 12-hole (⅓-cup/80ml) muffin pan.
3 Divide mixture among holes of prepared pan. Bake for about 20 minutes. Stand muffins in pan for 5 minutes before turning onto a wire rack to cool.

Apple and custard muffins

preparation time **20 minutes** cooking time **25 minutes** makes **12**

90g butter, melted
2 cups (300g) self-raising flour
1 cup (150g) plain flour
½ teaspoon ground cinnamon
¾ cup (165g) caster sugar
1 egg, beaten lightly
1 cup (250ml) milk
¼ cup (60ml) packaged thick custard
½ cup (110g) canned pie apples
2 tablespoons brown sugar
½ teaspoon ground cinnamon, extra

1 Preheat oven to moderately hot (200°C/180°C fan-forced). Grease a 12-hole (⅓-cup/80ml) muffin pan.

2 Combine butter, flours, cinnamon, caster sugar, egg and milk in a large bowl; stir until just combined.

3 Divide half the mixture among holes of prepared pan; make a well in centre of each muffin, drop 1 level teaspoon of custard and 2 level teaspoons of apple into each well. Top with remaining muffin mixture; sprinkle with combined brown sugar and extra cinnamon.

4 Bake muffins for about 25 minutes. Stand muffins in pan for a few minutes before turning onto a wire rack to cool.

Apple spice muffins

preparation time **15 minutes**   cooking time **25 minutes**   makes **6**

2 cups (300g) self-raising flour
½ teaspoon bicarbonate of soda
½ teaspoon ground cinnamon
1 teaspoon ground ginger
¼ teaspoon ground nutmeg
Pinch ground cloves
¼ cup (50g) brown sugar
½ x 410g can pie apples
1 egg, lightly beaten
¾ cup (180ml) milk
60g butter, melted
1 small (130g) apple
20g butter, melted, extra
2 tablespoons cinnamon sugar

1 Preheat oven to moderately hot (200°C/180°C fan-forced). Grease a six-hole (¾-cup/180ml) muffin pan.

2 Sift flour, soda, spices and brown sugar into a large bowl. Stir in pie apples, then egg, milk and butter.

3 Divide muffin mixture among holes of prepared pan. Peel, core and halve apple; slice each half thinly. Place an apple slice on top of each muffin, brush with extra butter and sprinkle with cinnamon sugar.

4 Bake muffins for about 25 minutes.

Hazelnut plum muffins

preparation time **15 minutes** cooking time **25 minutes** makes **12**

90g butter, melted
2½ cups (375g) self-raising flour
½ cup (55g) hazelnut meal
⅔ cup (150g) caster sugar
1 egg
1 cup (250ml) milk
½ cup (125ml) plum jam

1 Preheat oven to moderately hot (200°C/180°C fan-forced). Grease a 12-hole (⅓-cup/80ml) muffin pan.
2 Place butter, flour, hazelnut meal, sugar, egg and milk in large bowl, stir with a large metal spoon until just combined.
3 Divide half muffin among holes of prepared pan. Make a small well in the centre of each muffin, spoon 2 teaspoons jam into each well, then top with remaining muffin mixture.
4 Bake muffins for about 25 minutes. Turn carefully onto a wire rack to cool.

Fruit 'n' spice muffins

preparation time **15 minutes** cooking time **25 minutes** makes **12**

3 cups (450g) self-raising flour
2 teaspoons mixed spice
½ cup (110g) caster sugar
125g butter, chopped
1 cup (250ml) milk
2 eggs
1 cup (190g) mixed dried fruit

1 Preheat oven to moderately hot (200°C/180°C fan-forced). Grease a 12-hole (⅓-cup/80ml) muffin pan.
2 Combine flour, spice and sugar in large bowl; rub in butter. Add milk, eggs and fruit, stirring with large metal spoon until just combined.
3 Divide muffin mixture among holes of prepared pan. Bake for 25 minutes. Turn onto a wire rack to cool.

Blackberry streusel muffins

preparation time **20 minutes** (plus refrigeration time)
cooking time **20 minutes** makes **12**

2 cups (300g) self-raising flour
1 ¼ cups (170g) frozen blackberries
1 medium (150g) apple, peeled, coarsely grated
¾ cup (150g) firmly packed brown sugar
3 eggs, lightly beaten
⅓ cup (80ml) vegetable oil
⅓ cup (80ml) buttermilk

Streusel topping
⅓ cup (50g) plain flour
2 tablespoons brown sugar
1 teaspoon mixed spice
30g butter

1 Make streusel topping; refrigerate 30 minutes.
2 Preheat oven to moderately hot (200°C/180°C fan-forced). Grease
a 12-hole (⅓-cup/80ml capacity) muffin pan.
3 Sift flour into large bowl, then stir in remaining ingredients. Divide mixture
into holes of prepared pan. Coarsely grate streusel topping over muffins.
4 Bake muffins for about 20 minutes.

Streusel topping Sift flour, sugar and spice into a small bowl; rub in butter.
Roll mixture into a ball and wrap in plastic wrap.

Chocolate beetroot muffins

preparation time **20 minutes** cooking time **40 minutes** makes **12**

2 large (500g) beetroots
1 ¾ cups (260g) self-raising flour
⅓ cup (35g) cocoa powder
1 cup (220g) caster sugar
2 eggs, beaten lightly
⅓ cup (80ml) vegetable oil
⅓ cup (80ml) buttermilk

1 Preheat oven to moderately hot (200°C/180°C fan-forced). Grease a 12-hole (⅓-cup/80ml) muffin pan.

2 Wash and trim beetroot and cut off leaves, leaving about 3cm of stem attached. Boil, steam or microwave unpeeled beetroot until tender. Drain, rinse under cold water and drain again. Peel beetroot while still warm. Blend or process until smooth. You will need 1⅓ cups (330ml) beetroot puree.

3 Sift dry ingredients into a large bowl; stir in beetroot puree and remaining ingredients. Divide mixture among holes of prepared pan.

4 Bake muffins for about 25 minutes.

Strawberry and rhubarb muffins

preparation time **15 minutes** cooking time **20 minutes** makes **12**

You will need about 4 large trimmed rhubarb stems for this recipe.

125g strawberries, sliced thinly
3 cups (450g) wholemeal self-raising flour
½ cup (100g) firmly packed brown sugar
1 teaspoon ground cinnamon
1 teaspoon vanilla extract
60g margarine, melted
¾ cup (180ml) no-fat soy milk
2 eggs, beaten lightly
2 cups (250g) finely chopped rhubarb
¼ cup (60g) apple sauce

1 Preheat oven to moderately hot (200°C/180°C fan-forced). Grease a 12-hole (⅓-cup/80ml) muffin pan. Reserve 12 strawberry slices.

2 Combine flour, sugar and cinnamon in large bowl. Add extract, margarine, milk and eggs; mix to combine. Gently stir in remaining strawberries, rhubarb and apple sauce.

3 Divide muffin mixture among holes of prepared pan; top each with a reserved strawberry slice. Bake for about 20 minutes. Serve muffins warm or at room temperature.

Chocolate hazelnut muffins

preparation time **15 minutes** cooking time **20 minutes** makes **12**

2½ cups (375g) self-raising flour
½ teaspoon bicarbonate of soda
¼ cup (25g) cocoa powder
½ cup (100g) firmly packed brown sugar
125g butter, melted
2 eggs, beaten lightly
1 cup (250ml) buttermilk
1 cup (250ml) chocolate hazelnut spread

1 Preheat oven to moderately hot (200°C/180°C fan-forced). Grease
a 12-hole (⅓-cup/80ml) muffin pan.
2 Sift dry ingredients into a large bowl; stir in butter, eggs and buttermilk.
3 Spoon one-third of the mixture into holes of prepared pan; top with
1 level tablespoon of hazelnut spread. Top with remaining muffin mixture.
4 Bake muffins for about 20 minutes.

Wholemeal fig muffins

preparation time **10 minutes** cooking time **20 minutes** (plus cooling time)
makes **12**

2 cups (320g) wholemeal self-raising flour
1 cup (150g) self-raising flour
½ cup (110g) raw sugar
125g butter, chopped coarsely
1 cup (190g) coarsely chopped dried figs
2 eggs, beaten lightly
1 cup (250ml) milk

1 Preheat oven to moderately hot (200°C/180°C fan-forced). Grease a
12-hole (⅓ cup/80ml) muffin pan.
2 Combine flours and sugar in a large bowl; rub in butter. Add figs, then
combined eggs and milk. Using a fork, mix until just combined. Do not overmix – the mixture should be coarse and lumpy.
3 Divide mixture among holes of prepared pan; bake for about 20 minutes.
Turn onto wire racks to cool.

BISCUITS AND COOKIES

Coffee and hazelnut biscotti

preparation time **35 minutes** (plus setting time) cooking time **40 minutes** (plus cooling time) makes **20**

½ **cup (110g) caster sugar**
1 **egg, beaten lightly**
¾ **cup (110g) plain flour**
½ **teaspoon baking powder**
1 **tablespoon instant coffee granules**
1 **cup (150g) hazelnuts, toasted, chopped coarsely**
100g **dark eating chocolate, melted**

1 Preheat oven to moderate (180°C/160°C fan-forced). Grease an oven tray.

2 Whisk sugar and egg together in medium bowl; stir in flour, baking powder and coffee. Stir in nuts; mix to a sticky dough. Using floured hands, roll into a 20cm log. Place logs on prepared tray.

3 Bake for 25 minutes or until log is browned lightly and firm; cool on tray.

4 Using a serrated knife, cut log, diagonally, into 1cm slices. Place slices on an ungreased oven tray.

5 Bake for about 15 minutes or until dry and crisp, turning halfway through cooking. Transfer to wire racks to cool.

6 Spread chocolate over one cut side of each biscotti. Allow chocolate to set at room temperature.

tip Store biscotti in an airtight container for up to two weeks.

Lemon and pistachio biscotti

preparation time **20 minutes** (plus refrigeration time)
cooking time **40 minutes** (plus cooling time) makes **60**

60g butter, chopped coarsely
1 cup (220g) caster sugar
1 teaspoon vanilla extract
1 tablespoon finely grated lemon rind
4 eggs
2¼ cups (335g) plain flour
1 teaspoon baking powder
½ teaspoon bicarbonate of soda
1 cup (150g) shelled pistachios, chopped coarsely
2 tablespoons caster sugar, extra

1 Preheat oven to moderate (180°C/160°C fan-forced). Grease oven tray.
2 Beat butter, sugar, extract and rind in medium bowl with electric mixer until just combined. Add three of the eggs, one at a time, beating until combined after each addition. Stir in flour, baking powder, soda and nuts. Cover; refrigerate 1 hour.
3 Knead dough on a lightly floured surface until smooth but still sticky. Halve dough; shape each half into a 30cm log. Place logs on prepared tray. Combine remaining egg with 1 tablespoon water in small bowl. Brush egg mixture over logs; sprinkle thickly with extra sugar.
4 Bake for about 20 minutes or until firm; cool on trays. Using a serrated knife, cut logs, diagonally, into 1cm slices. Place on ungreased oven trays.
5 Bake for about 15 minutes or until dry and crisp, turning halfway through cooking; cool on wire racks.

tip Store biscotti in an airtight container for up to two weeks.

Aniseed biscotti

preparation time **20 minutes** (plus refrigeration time)
cooking time **45 minutes** makes **40**

125g butter, chopped
¾ cup (165g) caster sugar
3 eggs
2 tablespoons brandy
1 tablespoon grated lemon rind
1½ cups (225g) plain flour
¾ cup (110g) self-raising flour
¾ cup (120g) blanched almonds, toasted, chopped coarsely
1 tablespoon ground aniseed

1 Beat butter and sugar in large bowl with electric mixer until just combined. Add eggs one at a time, beating well after each addition. Add brandy and rind; mix well. Stir in flours, nuts and aniseed; cover, refrigerate 1 hour.
2 Preheat oven to moderate (180°C/160°C fan-forced). Lightly grease an oven tray.
3 Halve dough; shape each half into a 30cm log. Place on prepared tray.
4 Bake for 20 minutes or until lightly browned and firm; stand logs on oven tray for 10 minutes.
5 Using a serrated or electric knife, cut logs diagonally into 1cm slices. Place slices on ungreased oven trays.
6 Bake for about 25 minutes or until dry and crisp, turning halfway through cooking. Transfer to wire racks to cool.

tip Store biscotti in an airtight container for up to two weeks.

Apricot and pine nut biscotti

preparation time **20 minutes** cooking time **50 minutes** makes **50**

1 ¼ cups (275g) caster sugar
2 eggs
1 teaspoon vanilla extract
1 ½ cups (225g) plain flour
½ cup (75g) self-raising flour
½ cup (125g) coarsely chopped glacé apricots
¼ cup (40g) pine nuts, toasted
2 teaspoons water

1 Preheat oven to moderate (180°C/160°C fan-forced). Grease oven tray.
2 Whisk sugar, eggs and extract in medium bowl. Stir in sifted flours, apricots, pine nuts and the water; mix to a sticky dough.
3 Knead dough on lightly floured surface until smooth; divide into two portions. Using floured hands, roll each portion into a 30cm log. Place logs on prepared tray.
4 Bake for 25 minutes or until browned lightly. Cool on tray 10 minutes.
5 Reduce oven temperature to slow (150°C/130°C fan-forced).
6 Using a serrated knife, cut logs diagonally into 1cm slices. Place slices, in a single layer, on ungreased oven trays.
7 Bake in slow oven for about 25 minutes or until dry and crisp, turning over halfway through cooking. Transfer to wire racks to cool.

tips Store biscotti in an airtight container for up to two weeks. To toast nuts, place in a heavy-based frying pan, stir constantly over medium to high heat until nuts are evenly browned. Remove from pan.

Mini florentines

preparation time **10 minutes** cooking time **6 minutes** (plus cooling time) makes **45**

¾ **cup (120g) sultanas**
2 **cups (80g) corn flakes**
¾ **cup (60g) flaked almonds, toasted**
½ **cup (110g) red glacé cherries**
⅔ **cup (160ml) sweetened condensed milk**
60g **white eating chocolate, melted**
60g **dark eating chocolate, melted**

1 Preheat oven to moderate (180°C/160°C fan-forced). Line oven trays with baking paper.
2 Combine sultanas, corn flakes, nuts, cherries and condensed milk in a medium bowl. Drop heaped teaspoons of mixture onto prepared trays, allowing 5cm between each florentine.
3 Bake florentines for about 6 minutes or until browned lightly; cool on trays.
4 Spread half of the florentines with white chocolate and the remaining half with dark chocolate; run a fork through the chocolate to make a wave pattern. Allow chocolate to set at room temperature.

tips Florentines can be stored in an airtight container for up to two weeks.

Amaretti

preparation time **15 minutes** cooking time **15 minutes** makes **20**

1 **cup (125g) almond meal**
1 **cup (220g) caster sugar**
2 **large egg whites**
½ **teaspoon vanilla extract**
2 **drops almond essence**
20 **blanched almonds**

1 Preheat oven to moderate (180°C/160°C fan-forced).
2 Beat almond meal, sugar, egg whites, extract and essence in medium bowl with electric mixer on medium speed for 3 minutes; stand 5 minutes.
3 Spoon mixture into piping bag fitted with 1cm plain tube; pipe on oven

tray in circular motion from centre, to make biscuits about 4cm in diameter, leaving 2cm between each. Top with almonds.

4 Bake biscuits for about 12 minutes or until tops are browned lightly. Stand biscuits on trays for 5 minutes before transferring to wire rack to cool.

tip Amaretti can be made three days ahead and stored in an airtight container.

Gingernuts

preparation time **15 minutes** (plus standing time) cooking time **15 minutes** makes **about 35**

90g butter
⅓ cup (110g) brown sugar
⅓ cup (175g) golden syrup
1 ⅓ cups (225g) plain flour
¾ teaspoon bicarbonate of soda
1 teaspoon ground cinnamon
1 tablespoon ground ginger
¼ teaspoon ground cloves

1 Preheat oven to moderate (180°C/160°C fan-forced). Grease oven trays.
2 Combine butter, sugar and golden syrup in small saucepan; stir over heat until butter is melted. Remove from heat, stir in sifted dry ingredients. Stand until mixture feels warm to the touch.
3 Roll 2-level-teaspoon portions of mixture into balls and place about 3cm apart on prepared trays; flatten slightly.
4 Bake biscuits for about 12 minutes or until browned. Loosen biscuits; cool on trays.

Coconut macaroons

preparation time **15 minutes** cooking time **45 minutes** (plus cooling time)
makes **18**

1 egg, separated
1 egg yolk
¼ cup (55g) caster sugar
1²⁄₃ cups (120g) shredded coconut

1 Preheat oven to slow (150°C/130°C fan-forced). Grease oven trays.
2 Beat egg yolks and sugar in small bowl with electric mixer until creamy;
stir in coconut.
3 Beat egg white in small bowl with electric mixer until firm peaks form; stir
gently into coconut mixture.
4 Drop heaped teaspoons of mixture onto prepared trays. Bake 15 minutes.
5 Reduce oven temperature to very slow (120°C/100°C fan-forced). Bake a
further 30 minutes or until golden brown. Loosen biscuits; cool on trays.

Chocolate lace crisps

preparation time **25 minutes** (plus refrigeration time)
cooking time **20 minutes** makes **24**

100g dark cooking chocolate, chopped coarsely
80g butter, chopped
1 cup (220g) caster sugar
1 egg, beaten lightly
1 cup (150g) plain flour
2 tablespoons cocoa powder
¼ teaspoon bicarbonate of soda
¼ cup (40g) icing sugar

1 Melt chocolate and butter in a small saucepan over low heat. Transfer to
a medium bowl; stir in caster sugar, egg and sifted flour, cocoa and soda.
Cover; refrigerate about 15 minutes or until mixture is firm enough to handle.
2 Preheat oven to moderate (180°C/160°C fan-forced). Grease oven trays;
line with baking paper.
3 Roll level tablespoons of mixture into balls; roll each ball in icing sugar and
place on trays 8cm apart. Bake for about 15 minutes; cool on trays.

Almond jam cookies

preparation time **15 minutes** cooking time **25 minutes** makes about **30**

185g butter, chopped
¾ cup (165g) caster sugar
2 egg yolks
1 teaspoon vanilla extract
½ cup (60g) almond meal
1½ cups (225g) plain flour
½ teaspoon baking powder
2 tablespoons apricot jam, approximately
1 teaspoon finely grated lemon rind
2 tablespoons raspberry jam, approximately

1 Preheat oven to moderately slow (170°C/150°C fan-forced).
2 Beat butter, sugar, yolks and extract in a medium bowl with electric mixer until just combined. Stir in almond meal, flour and baking powder; mix well.
3 Roll level teaspoons of the mixture into balls and place about 5cm apart on ungreased oven trays. Press a hollow in each ball about 1cm deep and 1.5cm wide using the handle end of a lightly floured wooden spoon.
4 Combine apricot jam with half the rind. Combine raspberry jam with remaining rind. Carefully spoon a little apricot jam into half the cookies; spoon raspberry jam into remaining cookies.
5 Bake cookies for 25 minutes or until cookies are browned; cool on trays.

Pistachio bread

preparation time **25 minutes** (plus standing time) cooking time **45 minutes**
makes **40**

3 **egg whites**
⅓ **cup (75g) sugar**
¼ **teaspoon ground cardamom**
1 **teaspoon finely grated orange rind**
¾ **cup (110g) plain flour**
¾ **cup (110g) shelled pistachios**

1 Preheat oven to moderate (180°C/160°C fan-forced). Grease an 8cm
x 26cm bar cake pan; line base and two long sides with baking paper,
extending paper 2cm above edge.
2 Beat egg whites in bowl with electric mixer until soft peaks form. With
motor operating, gradually add sugar, beating until dissolved between additions.
Fold in cardamom, rind, flour and nuts; spread into prepared pan.
3 Bake bread 30 minutes. Cool in pan. Wrap in foil; stand overnight.
4 Preheat oven to slow (150°C/130°C fan-forced). Using a serrated or
electric knife, cut bread into 3mm diagonal slices; place on ungreased oven
trays. Bake 15 minutes or until dry and crisp; transfer to wire racks to cool.

Bran and apricot cookies

preparation time **15 minutes** cooking time **10 minutes** makes **about 25**

1 **cup (70g) all-bran**
1 **cup (150g) self-raising flour**
1 **cup (90g) desiccated coconut**
½ **cup (110g) firmly packed brown sugar**
½ **cup (125g) chopped glacé apricots**
125g **butter, melted**
1 **egg, lightly beaten**

1 Preheat oven to moderately hot (200°C/180°C fan-forced). Grease oven trays.
2 Combine all-bran, sifted flour, coconut, sugar and apricots in a bowl; stir
in butter and egg. Place level tablespoons of mixture about 5cm apart on
prepared trays.
3 Bake cookies for about 10 minutes, or until lightly browned; cool on trays.

Maple cinnamon swirls

preparation time **20 minutes** (plus refrigeration time)
cooking time **15 minutes** makes **about 50**

2 cups (300g) plain flour
185g butter, chopped
½ cup (110g) firmly packed brown sugar
1 egg yolk
2 tablespoons maple-flavoured syrup

Filling
¼ cup (60ml) maple-flavoured syrup
½ cup (40g) finely chopped walnuts, toasted
3 teaspoons cinnamon sugar

1 Process flour, butter and sugar until mixture resembles breadcrumbs. Add yolk and maple syrup; process until mixture forms a ball. Knead dough on lightly floured surface until smooth; cover and refrigerate 1 hour.
2 Combine ingredients for filling in medium bowl; mix well.
3 Roll dough between sheets of baking paper to a 28cm x 48cm rectangle; spread filling evenly over dough, leaving a 1cm border. Using paper as a guide, roll dough tightly from long side to enclose filling. Wrap roll in plastic wrap; refrigerate for 30 minutes.
4 Preheat oven to moderate (180°C/160°C fan-forced). Grease oven trays.
5 Remove plastic from roll, cut into 1cm slices. Place slices about 2cm apart on prepared trays.
6 Bake swirls for 15 minutes or until browned. Stand swirls for 5 minutes before transferring to wire racks to cool.

Glazed lemon shortbreads

preparation time **20 minutes** cooking time **40 minutes** makes **60**

2 tablespoons rice flour
⅓ cup (80g) icing sugar
2 cups (300g) plain flour
250g butter
1 teaspoon finely grated lemon rind
2 teaspoons lemon juice, approximately

Lemon glaze
1 cup (160g) icing sugar
½ teaspoon finely grated lemon rind
¼ cup (60ml) lemon juice

1 Preheat oven to moderately slow (170°C/150°C fan-forced). Grease a 20cm x 30cm lamington pan.
2 Sift dry ingredients into bowl, rub in butter; stir in rind and enough juice to make ingredients cling together. Turn dough onto a lightly floured surface, knead lightly until smooth.
3 Press dough evenly into prepared pan; mark into finger lengths. Bake for about 40 minutes or until firm.
4 Cut shortbread into finger lengths in pan; let stand for 10 minutes. Transfer shortbread fingers to wire rack to cool.
5 Beat ingredients for lemon glaze in bowl until well combined. Dip one end of each shortbread finger in glaze; place on a foil-covered tray to set.

Honey snap biscuits

preparation time **15 minutes** cooking time **10 minutes** makes **about 45**

80g butter
⅓ cup (115g) honey
½ cup (110g) firmly packed brown sugar
½ teaspoon vanilla extract
¾ cup (110g) plain flour
½ teaspoon ground ginger

1 Preheat oven to moderate (180°C/160°C fan-forced). Grease oven trays.
2 Combine butter, honey and sugar in a small saucepan; stir over a medium

heat until the butter is melted. Remove from the heat, stir in vanilla.

3 Sift flour and ginger into a medium bowl; stir in butter mixture, beat with a wooden spoon until smooth.

4 Drop heaped teaspoons of mixture about 8cm apart onto prepared trays, about six at a time. The biscuits will spread during cooking.

5 Bake biscuits for about 8 minutes, or until golden brown. Stand biscuits on trays for 5 minutes before transferring to wire rack to cool.

tip These biscuits are delicious served with ice-cream or fruit desserts.

Fudgy-wudgy chocolate cookies

preparation time **10 minutes** cooking time **10 minutes** makes **24**

125g butter, chopped
1¼ cups (250g) firmly packed brown sugar
1 egg
1 teaspoon vanilla extract
1 cup (150g) plain flour
¼ cup (35g) self-raising flour
1 teaspoon bicarbonate of soda
⅓ cup (35g) cocoa powder
½ cup (85g) raisins
¾ cup (100g) macadamia nuts, toasted, chopped coarsely
½ cup (95g) dark choc chips
75g dark eating chocolate, chopped coarsely

1 Preheat oven to moderate (180°C/160°C fan-forced). Line three oven trays with baking paper.

2 Beat butter, sugar, egg and extract in medium bowl with electric mixer until smooth. Stir in combined sifted flours, soda and cocoa; stir in raisins, nuts, choc chips and eating chocolate.

3 Drop rounded tablespoons of mixture onto prepared trays about 4cm apart; press each with a fork to flatten slightly.

4 Bake biscuits for 10 minutes. Stand biscuits on trays for 5 minutes, before transferring to wire rack to cool.

tip These cookies can be made up to four days ahead; stored in an airtight container.

Coffee snaps

preparation time **15 minutes** cooking time **10 minutes** makes about **70**

125g butter, softened
1 ¼ cups (250g) firmly packed brown sugar
3 teaspoons instant coffee granules
½ teaspoon vanilla extract
1 egg
¾ cup (110g) plain flour
¾ cup (110g) self-raising flour
2 tablespoons (70g) coffee beans (70 beans)

1 Preheat oven to moderate (180°C/160°C fan-forced). Grease oven trays.
2 Beat butter, sugar, coffee and extract in small bowl with electric mixer until pale and fluffy. Add egg, beating until just combined. Stir in sifted flours.
3 Roll rounded teaspoons of the mixture into balls, place 3cm apart on prepared trays; top each with a coffee bean.
4 Bake biscuits for about 10 minutes. Stand biscuits on trays for 5 minutes before transferring to wire rack to cool.

Chocolate chip cookies

preparation time **40 minutes** (plus refrigeration time)
cooking time **15 minutes** makes **40**

250g butter, softened
¾ cup (165g) sugar
¾ cup (165g) firmly packed brown sugar
1 egg
1 teaspoon vanilla extract
2 ¼ cups (335g) plain flour
1 teaspoon bicarbonate of soda
300g dark eating chocolate, chopped coarsely

1 Beat butter, sugars, egg and extract in large bowl with electric mixer until light and fluffy. Stir in combined sifted flour and soda, in two batches; stir in chocolate. Cover; refrigerate for 1 hour.
2 Preheat oven to moderate (180°C/160°C fan-forced). Grease oven trays.
3 Roll level tablespoons of the dough into balls; place on prepared trays 3cm apart. Bake, uncovered, for about 12 minutes. Cool on trays.

Passionfruit butter yoyo bites

preparation time **20 minutes** cooking time **15 minutes** makes **36**

250g unsalted butter, chopped
½ cup (80g) icing sugar
1 teaspoon vanilla extract
1½ cups (225g) plain flour
½ cup (75g) cornflour

Passionfruit butter
80g unsalted butter
⅔ cup (150g) icing sugar
1 tablespoon passionfruit pulp

1 Preheat oven to moderately slow (170°C/150°C fan-forced). Line two oven trays with baking paper.
2 Beat butter, sugar and extract in medium bowl with electric mixer until light and fluffy; stir in sifted dry ingredients, in two batches.
3 Roll rounded teaspoons of mixture into balls; place on prepared trays, about 3cm apart. Press a fork dusted with flour gently onto each biscuit to flatten slightly.
4 Bake biscuits for about 12 minutes or until firm. Stand biscuits 5 minutes on trays before transferring to wire rack to cool.
5 Make passionfruit butter; sandwich biscuits together with passionfruit butter.

Passionfruit butter Beat butter and sugar in small bowl with electric mixer until light and fluffy; stir in passionfruit pulp.

tip One rounded teaspoon is equivalent to 2 level teaspoons.

Pistachio shortbread mounds

preparation time **25 minutes** cooking time **25 minutes** makes **40**

½ cup (75g) shelled pistachios
250g butter, chopped
1 cup (160g) icing sugar
1½ cups (225g) plain flour
2 tablespoons rice flour
2 tablespoons cornflour
¾ cup (90g) almond meal
⅓ cup (55g) icing sugar, extra

1 Preheat oven to slow (150°C/130°C fan-forced). Lightly grease oven trays.
2 Toast nuts in a small heavy-based frying pan until lightly browned; remove from pan. Coarsely chop ⅓ cup (50g) of the nuts; leave remaining nuts whole.
3 Beat butter and sifted icing sugar in small bowl with electric mixer until light and fluffy; transfer mixture to large bowl. Stir in sifted flours, almond meal and chopped nuts.
4 Shape level tablespoons of mixture into mounds; place mounds on prepared trays about 3cm apart. Press one reserved whole nut on top.
5 Bake mounds for about 25 minutes. Stand mounds on tray for 5 minutes, before transferring to wire rack to cool. Serve dusted with extra icing sugar.

tips Store biscuits in an airtight container for up to two weeks. Suitable to freeze for up to three months.

Macadamia shortbread

preparation time **20 minutes** cooking time **20 minutes** makes **24**

250g butter, chopped
½ cup (110g) caster sugar
2 teaspoons vanilla extract
2 cups (300g) plain flour
½ cup (75g) rice flour
½ cup (75g) finely chopped macadamias
2 tablespoons caster sugar, extra

1 Preheat oven to moderately slow (170°C/150°C fan-forced). Lightly grease oven trays.
2 Beat butter, sugar and extract in small bowl with electric mixer until pale and fluffy; transfer mixture to large bowl. Stir in sifted flours and nuts, in two batches. Press ingredients together. Turn onto lightly floured surface; knead until smooth (do not over-knead).
3 Divide mixture into two portions. Roll each portion, between two sheets of baking paper, into a 23cm circle. Press an upturned 22cm loose-based fluted flan tin into shortbread to cut rounds. Cut each round into 12 wedges. Place on prepared trays; mark with a fork, sprinkle with extra sugar.
4 Bake shortbread about 20 minutes. Stand shortbread on tray 10 minutes before transferring to wire rack to cool.

tips Store biscuits in an airtight container for up to three weeks. Suitable to freeze for up to three months.

Lemon shortbreads

preparation time **20 minutes** cooking time **15 minutes** makes **40**

250g butter, chopped
1 teaspoon finely grated lemon rind
⅓ cup (55g) icing sugar
1½ cups (225g) plain flour
½ cup (75g) cornflour
½ cup (85g) mixed peel, chopped finely

1 Preheat oven to moderate (180°C/160°C fan-forced). Lightly grease oven trays.
2 Beat butter, rind and sifted icing sugar in small bowl with electric mixer until just changed in colour. Stir in sifted flours in two batches.
3 Place mixture into large piping bag fitted with fluted tube; pipe mixture into rosettes, about 2cm apart, onto prepared trays. Sprinkle with mixed peel.
4 Bake shortbreads about 15 minutes. Stand on tray 10 minutes before transferring to wire rack to cool.

Chocolate melting moments

preparation time **15 minutes** cooking time **10 minutes** makes **28**

125g butter, chopped
2 tablespoons icing sugar
¾ cup (110g) plain flour
2 tablespoons cornflour
2 tablespoons cocoa powder
¼ cup (85g) chocolate hazelnut spread

1 Preheat oven to moderate (180°C/160°C fan-forced). Lightly grease two oven trays.
2 Beat butter and sugar in small bowl with electric mixer until light and fluffy. Stir in sifted dry ingredients, in two batches.
3 Spoon mixture into piping bag fitted with 5mm fluted tube. Pipe directly onto prepared trays about 3cm part.
4 Bake biscuits for about 10 minutes or until firm. Stand 5 minutes; transfer to wire rack to cool. Sandwich biscuits with hazelnut spread to serve.

tip Strawberry or raspberry jam can be used instead of hazelnut spread.

Triple-choc cookies

preparation time **10 minutes** cooking time **10 minutes** makes **36**

125g butter, chopped
1¼ cups (275g) firmly packed brown sugar
1 egg
1 teaspoon vanilla extract
1 cup (150g) plain flour
¼ cup (35g) self-raising flour
1 teaspoon bicarbonate of soda
⅓ cup (35g) cocoa powder
½ cup (85g) chopped raisins
½ cup (95g) milk choc chips
75g white eating chocolate, chopped coarsely
75g dark eating chocolate, chopped coarsely

1 Preheat oven to moderate (180°C/160°C fan-forced). Lightly grease oven trays.
2 Beat butter, sugar, egg and extract in small bowl with electric mixer until smooth; do not overbeat. Stir in sifted dry ingredients, then raisins and all the chocolate.
3 Drop level tablespoons of mixture onto prepared trays about 5cm apart. Bake for about 10 minutes. Stand cookies on trays 5 minutes before transferring to wire rack to cool.

tips Cookies can be stored in an airtight container for up to three weeks. Suitable to freeze for up to three months.

Choc-hazelnut cookie sandwiches

preparation time **25 minutes** (plus refrigeration time)
cooking time **10 minutes** makes **30**

80g butter, chopped
¼ cup (55g) caster sugar
1 egg
1 teaspoon vanilla extract
½ cup (50g) hazelnut meal
¾ cup (110g) plain flour
¼ cup (25g) cocoa powder
1 tablespoon cocoa powder, extra

Choc-hazelnut cream
100g dark eating chocolate, melted
50g butter
⅓ cup (110g) chocolate hazelnut spread

1 Beat butter, sugar, egg and extract in small bowl with electric mixer until light and fluffy; stir in hazelnut meal, sifted flour and cocoa. Wrap dough with plastic wrap; refrigerate 1 hour or until firm.
2 Preheat oven to moderate (180°C/160°C fan-forced). Lightly grease two oven trays.
3 Roll dough between two sheets of baking paper until 3mm thick. Using 4cm fluted cutter, cut rounds from dough; place on prepared trays.
4 Bake biscuits for about 8 minutes. Stand biscuits for 5 minutes on trays before transferring to wire rack to cool.
5 Make choc-hazelnut cream; spoon into piping bag fitted with large fluted tube. Pipe cream onto one biscuit; sandwich with another biscuit. Place on wire rack set over tray; repeat with remaining biscuits and cream. When all sandwiches are on rack, dust with extra sifted cocoa.

Choc-hazelnut cream Beat cooled chocolate, butter and hazelnut spread in small bowl with electric mixer until thick and glossy.

Caramello chocolate cookies

preparation time **15 minutes** cooking time **20 minutes** makes **24**

1 egg
⅔ cup (150g) firmly packed brown sugar
¼ cup (60ml) vegetable oil
½ cup (75g) plain flour
⅓ cup (50g) self-raising flour
¼ teaspoon bicarbonate of soda
100g dark eating chocolate, melted
250g caramello chocolate squares

1 Preheat oven to moderate (180°C/160°C fan-forced). Grease two oven trays.
2 Beat egg, sugar and oil in small bowl with electric mixer until mixture changes in colour. Stir in sifted dry ingredients and dark chocolate; stir until mixture becomes firm.
3 Centre one caramello square on 1 heaped teaspoon chocolate mixture; roll into a ball, enclosing caramello. Place balls on prepared trays, allowing 6cm between each cookie. Bake about 10 minutes. Stand cookies for 5 minutes; transfer to wire rack to cool.

tips Chocolate squares with strawberry or peppermint centres can be used instead of caramello squares.

Polenta and orange biscuits

preparation time **15 minutes** cooking time **15 minutes** makes **30**

125g butter, softened
2 teaspoons finely grated orange rind
2/3 cup (110g) icing sugar
1/3 cup (55g) polenta
1 cup (150g) plain flour

1 Preheat oven to moderate (180°C/160°C fan-forced). Grease oven trays; line with baking paper.
2 Beat butter, rind and icing sugar in small bowl with electric mixer until light and fluffy; stir in polenta and flour.
3 Shape mixture into a 30cm-rectangular log; cut log into 1cm-wide slices.
4 Place slices on trays 2cm apart. Bake for about 15 minutes. Stand biscuits on trays for 5 minutes before transferring to wire rack to cool.

Snickerdoodles

preparation time **25 minutes** (plus refrigeration time)
cooking time **15 minutes** makes **50**

250g butter, softened
1 teaspoon vanilla extract
½ cup (110g) firmly packed brown sugar
1 cup (220g) caster sugar
2 eggs
2¾ cups (410g) plain flour
1 teaspoon bicarbonate of soda
½ teaspoon ground nutmeg
1 tablespoon caster sugar, extra
2 teaspoons ground cinnamon

1 Beat butter, extract and sugars in small bowl with electric mixer until light and fluffy. Add eggs one at a time, beating until just combined. Transfer mixture to large bowl.

2 Stir combined sifted flour, soda and nutmeg, in two batches, into egg mixture. Cover; refrigerate for 30 minutes.

3 Preheat oven to moderate (180°C/160°C fan-forced).

4 Combine extra caster sugar and cinnamon in small shallow bowl. Roll level tablespoons of dough into balls, then roll in cinnamon sugar.

5 Place balls on ungreased oven trays, about 7cm apart. Bake for about 12 minutes. Cool on trays.

Refrigerator cookies

preparation time **20 minutes** (plus refrigeration time)
cooking time **10 minutes** makes **50**

250g butter, softened
1 cup (160g) icing sugar
2½ cups (375g) plain flour

1 Beat butter and sifted sugar in small bowl with electric mixer until light and fluffy. Transfer to large bowl.
2 Stir flour, in two batches, into butter mixture. Knead dough on lightly floured surface until smooth. Divide dough in half; roll each half into a 25cm log. Enclose in plastic wrap; refrigerate about 1 hour or until firm.
3 Preheat oven to moderate (180°C/160°C fan-forced). Grease oven trays.
4 Cut rolls into 1cm slices; place on prepared trays 2cm apart. Bake, uncovered, for about 10 minutes or until browned lightly. Turn cookies onto wire rack to cool.

tips Keep this dough, rolled into a log shape and tightly sealed in plastic wrap, in the refrigerator for up to three days or in the freezer for up to three months. The frozen dough should be defrosted in the refrigerator before slicing and baking. Flavour dough with chopped toasted nuts or finely grated citrus rind, if desired.

Greek almond biscuits

preparation time **30 minutes** cooking time **15 minutes** makes **25**

3 cups (375g) almond meal
1 cup (220g) caster sugar
3 drops almond essence
3 egg whites, beaten lightly
1 cup (80g) flaked almonds

1 Preheat oven to moderate (180°C/160°C fan-forced). Line oven trays with baking paper.
2 Combine almond meal, sugar and essence in large bowl. Add egg white; stir until mixture forms a firm paste.
3 Roll level tablespoons of the mixture into flaked almonds; roll into 8cm logs, press on any remaining almonds. Curve each log into a crescent shape.
4 Place biscuits on prepared trays; bake 15 minutes. Cool on trays.

tip Store in an airtight container for up to one week; freeze up to three months.

Choc-orange hazelnut crescents

preparation time **20 minutes** (plus refrigeration time)
cooking time **15 minutes** makes **25**

125g butter
2 teaspoons finely grated orange rind
2 tablespoons caster sugar
¾ cup (110g) plain flour
½ cup (50g) hazelnut meal
60g dark eating chocolate, melted

1 Beat butter, rind and sugar in small bowl with electric mixer until light and fluffy. Stir in sifted flour and hazelnut meal. Turn dough onto lightly floured surface; knead until smooth. Cover; refrigerate 30 minutes.
2 Preheat oven to moderate (180°C/160°C fan-forced). Grease oven trays.
3 Roll rounded teaspoons of mixture into logs 7cm long; curve each into a crescent shape. Place on prepared trays about 3cm apart.
4 Bake crescents for about 15 minutes. Cool crescents on trays before transferring to wire racks; pipe or drizzle with melted chocolate.

Chocolate peppermint cookies

preparation time **15 minutes** (plus standing and refrigeration time)
cooking time **6 minutes** makes **50**

125g butter
180g dark eating chocolate, chopped
¼ cup (55g) firmly packed brown sugar
¼ cup (60ml) light corn syrup
1 egg, lightly beaten
1¼ cups(185g) plain flour
¼ cup (35g) self-raising flour
100g hard peppermint boiled sweets, roughly crushed

1 Combine butter, chocolate, sugar and corn syrup in pan and stir over heat until smooth; let stand for 5 minutes. Stir in egg and sifted flours. Cover; refrigerate for 1 hour.

2 Preheat oven to moderate (180°C/160°C fan-forced). Grease oven trays.

3 Roll rounded teaspoons of mixture into balls; place onto prepared trays about 5cm apart. Press sweets gently onto each cookie.

4 Bake cookies for about 6 minutes or until firm. Stand cookies on trays for 5 minutes before transferring to wire rack to cool.

Chocolate fudge cookies

preparation time **25 minutes** (plus refrigeration time)
cooking time **10 minutes** makes **20**

2 eggs
¼ cup (55g) firmly packed brown sugar
180g dark eating chocolate, melted
½ cup (125ml) vegetable oil
1¼ cups (185g) plain flour
¼ cup (35g) self-raising flour
100g white eating chocolate, chopped coarsely
1 cup (190g) choc chips

1 Beat eggs and sugar in small bowl with electric mixer until frothy. Stir in combined cooled dark chocolate and oil, then sifted flours, white chocolate and choc chips. Cover; refrigerate 1 hour.
2 Preheat oven to moderate (180°C/160°C fan-forced). Grease oven tray.
3 Roll 1½ level teaspoons of mixture into balls, place on prepared tray about 4cm apart.
4 Bake cookies for about 10 minutes or until just firm; cool on trays.

Spicy date and pecan cookies

preparation time **20 minutes** (plus refrigeration time)
cooking time **12 minutes** makes **50**

180g butter
½ cup (110g) caster sugar
1 egg yolk
2 teaspoons vanilla extract
1½ cups (225g) self-raising flour
1 teaspoon ground cinnamon
½ teaspoon ground nutmeg
⅔ cup (90g) seeded dried chopped dates
½ cup (60g) pecans, chopped
⅔ cup (80g) pecan halves

1 Beat butter, sugar, egg yolk and extract in small bowl with electric mixer until light and fluffy. Stir in sifted flour and spices, then dates and chopped pecans. Cover; refrigerate for 30 minutes.

2 Preheat oven to moderately hot (200°C/180°C fan-forced). Grease oven trays.

3 Roll rounded teaspoons of mixture into balls, place on prepared trays about 4cm apart. Top with pecan halves.

4 Bake cookies for about 12 minutes; cool on trays.

Macadamia and white chocolate cookies

preparation time **25 minutes** cooking time **12 minutes** makes **40**

125g butter
1 cup (220g) firmly packed brown sugar
1 egg
2 teaspoons vanilla extract
1 cup (150g) plain flour
½ cup (75g) self-raising flour
1 cup (150g) chopped unsalted roasted macadamia nuts
1 cup (70g) shredded coconut
¾ cup (60g) rolled oats
200g white eating chocolate, chopped

1 Preheat oven to moderately hot (200°C/180°C fan-forced). Grease oven trays.

2 Beat butter, sugar, egg and extract in small bowl with electric mixer until light and fluffy. Transfer mixture to a large bowl; stir in sifted flours, nuts, coconut, oats and chocolate.

3 Shape level tablespoons of mixture into balls, place on prepared trays about 3cm apart, flatten slightly.

4 Bake cookies for about 12 minutes; cool on trays.

Scorched peanut cookies

preparation time **15 minutes** cooking time **12 minutes** makes **50**

125g butter
¼ cup (70g) crunchy peanut butter
¾ cup (165g) firmly packed brown sugar
1 egg
1½ cups (225g) plain flour
½ teaspoon bicarbonate of soda
¾ cup (110g) scorched peanuts

1 Preheat oven to moderately hot (200°C/180°C fan-forced). Grease
oven tray.
2 Beat butter, peanut butter, sugar and egg in small bowl with electric
mixer until well combined. Transfer mixture to large bowl; stir in sifted dry
ingredients and nuts.
3 Roll rounded teaspoons of mixture into balls with lightly floured hands.
Place onto a prepared tray, about 3cm apart; flatten each slightly with a fork.
4 Bake cookies for about 12 minutes; cool on trays.

Almond raspberry fingers

preparation time **15 minutes** cooking time **20 minutes** makes **12**

125g butter
1 teaspoon finely grated lemon rind
½ cup (80g) icing sugar
1 cup (150g) plain flour
⅓ cup (80ml) raspberry jam

Topping
2 cups (250g) almond meal
2 tablespoons caster sugar
2 eggs, beaten lightly
1½ tablespoons dark rum

1 Preheat oven to moderately hot (200°C/180°C fan-forced). Grease oven tray.
2 Beat butter, rind and icing sugar in small bowl with electric mixer until smooth; stir in sifted flour. Knead gently on a lightly floured surface until dough is smooth.
3 Roll dough between sheets of baking paper to a 23cm square. Place on prepared tray; prick lightly with a fork. Bake for about 10 minutes.
4 Meanwhile, combine ingredients for topping in bowl; mix well.
5 Remove dough from oven; spread gently with jam while still hot.
6 Spoon topping into a piping bag fitted with a large fluted tube. Pipe topping in lines over jam, about 1cm apart.
7 Bake for another 10 minutes. Cut into fingers while still warm; cool on tray.

Bran butter biscuits

preparation time **20 minutes**   cooking time **12 minutes**   makes **25**

½ cup (80g) wholemeal plain flour
2 teaspoons baking powder
1 teaspoon raw sugar
½ cup (30g) unprocessed wheat bran
60g butter, chopped
2 tablespoons water, approximately
1½ tablespoons unprocessed wheat bran, extra

1 Preheat oven to moderate (180°C/160°C fan-forced). Grease oven trays.
2 Sift flour and baking powder into medium bowl, stir in sugar and bran; rub in butter. Add enough water to mix to a soft dough. Knead dough gently on lightly floured surface until smooth.
3 Roll dough between sheets of baking paper until 2mm thick. Cut into 5cm rounds. Place about 3cm apart on prepared trays; sprinkle with extra bran.
4 Bake biscuits for about 12 minutes. Cool on trays.

Muesli cookies

preparation time **15 minutes**   cooking time **15 minutes**   makes **30**

185g butter, melted
1 cup (130g) toasted muesli
1 cup (90g) coconut
1 cup (90g) rolled oats
½ cup (75g) self-raising flour
½ cup (110g) raw sugar
¼ cup (35g) sesame seeds
1 tablespoon honey
1 egg, lightly beaten

1 Preheat oven to moderate (180°C/160°C fan-forced). Grease oven trays.
2 Combine ingredients in a medium bowl; mix well.
3 Mould level tablespoons of mixture into balls, place on prepared trays about 3cm apart; flatten slightly.
4 Bake cookies for about 15 minutes. Cool on trays.

Cherry almond bars

preparation time **20 minutes** (plus refrigeration time)
cooking time **15 minutes** makes **35**

90g butter
1 teaspoon finely grated lemon rind
⅓ cup (75g) caster sugar
1 egg yolk
1 cup (150g) plain flour
⅓ cup (55g) blanched almonds
⅓ cup (70g) glacé cherries
250g dark eating chocolate, melted
2 teaspoons vegetable oil

1 Beat butter, rind, sugar and yolk in small bowl with electric mixer until smooth. Stir in sifted flour, almonds and cherries.
2 Use floured hands to shape mixture into a 4cm x 20cm bar shape; wrap in foil. Refrigerate for 1 hour or until firm.
3 Preheat oven to moderate (180°C/160°C fan-forced). Line oven trays with baking paper.
4 Cut bar into 5mm slices, using a serrated knife. Place slices on prepared trays about 3cm apart.
5 Bake biscuits for about 15 minutes; cool on trays. Dip half of each biscuit in combined chocolate and oil; leave to set on wire racks.

Chocolate wheaties

preparation time **20 minutes** cooking time **12 minutes** makes **35**

90g butter
½ cup (110g) firmly packed brown sugar
1 egg, beaten lightly
¼ cup (20g) desiccated coconut
¼ cup (25g) wheatgerm
¾ cup (120g) wholemeal plain flour
½ cup (75g) self-raising flour
150g dark eating chocolate, melted

1 Preheat oven to moderate (180°C/160°C fan-forced). Grease oven trays.
2 Beat butter and sugar in small bowl with electric mixer until smooth; add egg and beat until combined. Stir in coconut, wheatgerm and flours.
3 Roll rounded teaspoons of mixture into balls, place on plepared trays about 3cm apart; flatten each ball with a fork.
4 Bake biscuits for about 12 minutes. Cool on trays.
5 Dip half of each biscuit in chocolate; leave to set on wire racks.

Orange coconut biscuits

preparation time **20 minutes** cooking time **15 minutes** makes **70**

125g butter
2 teaspoons finely grated orange rind
1 cup (220g) caster sugar
1 egg
1 cup (90g) coconut
2 cups (300g) self-raising flour
2 tablespoons orange juice
½ cup (85g) mixed peel, finely chopped

1 Preheat oven to moderate (180°C/160°C fan-forced). Grease oven trays.
2 Beat butter, rind, sugar and egg in a medium bowl with electric mixer until smooth. Stir in coconut, sifted flour and juice.
3 Roll rounded teaspoons of mixture into balls; press one side lightly onto mixed peel. Place balls, peel-side up, on prepared trays about 4cm apart.
4 Bake biscuits for about 15 minutes. Cool on trays.

Hazelnut almond sticks

preparation time **15 minutes** cooking time **15 minutes** makes **35**

3 egg whites
¾ cup (165g) caster sugar
1½ cups (165g) hazelnut meal
1½ cups (185g) almond meal
¼ cup (35g) plain flour
150g dark eating chocolate, chopped
10g butter, melted

1 Preheat oven to moderate (180°C/160°C fan-forced). Line oven trays with baking paper.

2 Beat egg whites in a small bowl with electric mixer until soft peaks form. Gradually add sugar, beat until dissolved between additions. Transfer mixture to large bowl; stir in nuts and sifted flour.

3 Spoon mixture into a piping bag fitted with a 1.5cm plain tube; pipe 8cm lengths on prepared trays, about 4cm apart.

4 Bake sticks for about 15 minutes or until sticks are dry to touch. Transfer to wrie racks to cool.

5 Place chocolate and butter in small heatproof bowl, stir over hot water until melted. Dip one end of sticks into chocolate mixture; place on wire racks. Drizzle or pipe more chocolate mixture over plain end of sticks; leave to set.

Crunchy peanut cookies

preparation time **25 minutes** (plus refrigeration time)
cooking time **10 minutes** makes **25**

¾ cup (110g) self-raising flour
¼ teaspoon bicarbonate of soda
½ teaspoon ground cinnamon
¾ cup (165g) caster sugar
½ cup (45g) rolled oats
⅓ cup (30g) coconut
1 teaspoon finely grated lemon rind
½ cup (125ml) crunchy peanut butter
1 tablespoon golden syrup
2 tablespoons water, approximately

1 Sift flour, soda and cinnamon into medium bowl; stir in sugar, oats, coconut and rind, then peanut butter, golden syrup and enough water to mix to a soft dough. Knead gently on lightly floured surface until smooth; cover and refrigerate for 30 minutes.
2 Preheat oven to moderate (180°C/160°C fan-forced). Grease oven trays.
3 Divide dough in half. Roll each half between sheets of baking paper until 5mm thick; cut into 6cm rounds, place on prepared trays, about 3cm apart.
4 Bake for about 10 minutes. Cool on wire racks.

Viennese orange kisses

preparation time **25 minutes** cooking time **12 minutes** makes **25**

220g butter
2 tablespoons finely grated orange rind
½ cup (80g) icing sugar
1 tablespoon cornflour
1 cup (150g) plain flour
½ cup (75g) self-raising flour

Orange cream
60g butter
1 cup (160g) icing sugar
2 tablespoons orange juice

1 Preheat oven to moderate (180°C/160°C fan-forced). Grease oven trays.
2 Beat butter, rind and sifted icing sugar in small bowl with electric mixer until smooth. Stir in sifted flours.
3 Spoon mixture into a piping bag fitted with a medium fluted tube. Pipe 3cm stars on prepared trays, about 3cm apart.
4 Bake biscuits for about 12 minutes. Cool on wire racks.
5 Make orange cream. Sandwich kisses with orange cream. Dust with extra sifted icing sugar, if desired.

Orange cream Beat butter and sifted sugar in small bowl with electric mixer until smooth; beat in juice.

Apricot muesli bars

preparation time **15 minutes** cooking time **30 minutes** makes **8**

125g butter, chopped
½ cup (110g) firmly packed brown sugar
1 tablespoon honey
2¼ cups (200g) rolled oats
¼ cup (40g) sunflower kernels
¼ cup (20g) desiccated coconut
½ teaspoon ground cinnamon
½ cup (75g) chopped dried apricots
2 tablespoons dark choc bits

1 Preheat oven to moderately slow (170°C/150°C fan-forced). Grease 20cm x 30cm lamington pan.
2 Combine butter, sugar and honey in medium saucepan; stir over low heat until sugar is dissolved.
3 Transfer honey mixture to medium bowl; stir in oats, sunflower kernels, coconut, cinnamon and apricots. Press mixture into prepared pan; sprinkle with choc bits.
4 Bake for about 30 minutes. Cut into pieces while still warm; cool in pan.

Mocha shortbread sticks

preparation time **25 minutes** cooking time **12 minutes** makes **40**

250g butter
⅓ cup (55g) icing sugar
1 cup (150g) plain flour
1 cup (150g) cornflour
2 teaspoons instant coffee granules
2 teaspoons hot water
1 tablespoon cocoa
2 teaspoons hot water, extra

Coffee filling
1½ teaspoons instant coffee granules
3 teaspoons hot milk
40g butter
¾ cup (120g) icing sugar

1 Preheat oven to moderate (180°C/160°C fan-forced). Grease oven trays.
2 Beat butter and sifted icing sugar in medium bowl with electric mixer until smooth; stir in sifted flours.
3 Divide mixture in half. Stir combined coffee and water into one half of mixture and blended sifted cocoa and extra water in remaining half.
4 Spoon coffee mixture carefully into one side of a piping bag fitted with a medium fluted tube. Spoon cocoa mixture into other side of piping bag. Pipe 5cm lengths of mixture on prepared trays, about 3cm apart.
5 Bake sticks for about 12 minutes or until firm. Cool on wire racks.
6 Make coffee filling.
7 Sandwich biscuits with filling; serve dusted with extra sifted icing sugar, if desired.

Coffee filling Dissolve coffee in milk; cool. Beat butter, coffee mixture and sifted sugar in small bowl with electric mixer until pale in colour.

Sour cream cookies

preparation time **25 minutes** cooking time **8 minutes** makes **24**

60g butter
¼ cup (55g) caster sugar
1 egg yolk
½ teaspoon vanilla extract
1 cup (150g) self-raising flour
¼ teaspoon bicarbonate of soda
¼ teaspoon ground nutmeg
2 teaspoons sour cream

Citrus icing
1 cup (160g) icing sugar
½ teaspoons finely grated orange rind
1 tablespoon lemon juice
2 teaspoons orange juice, approximately

1 Preheat oven to hot (220°C/200°C fan-forced). Grease oven trays.
2 Beat butter, sugar, yolk and extract in small bowl with electric mixer until smooth. Stir in sifted dry ingredients and cream.
3 Roll rounded teaspoons of mixture into balls, place on prepared trays, about 3cm apart; flatten with a fork.
4 Bake cookies for about 8 minutes. Cool on wire racks.
5 Meanwhile, make citrus icing. Dip tops of cooled biscuits into icing; leave to set on wire racks.

Citrus icing Sift icing sugar into a small heatproof bowl. Stir in rind, lemon juice and enough orange juice to make a stiff paste. Stir over hot water until icing is spreadable.

Viennese shortbread biscuits

preparation time **20 minutes** cooking time **15 minutes** makes **35**

250g butter
¼ cup (55g) caster sugar
½ teaspoon vanilla extract
1 ¾ cups (260g) plain flour
¼ cup (35g) rice flour
300g dark eating chocolate, melted
3 teaspoons vegetable oil

1 Preheat oven to moderate (180°C/160°C fan-forced). Grease oven trays.
2 Beat butter, sugar and extract in small bowl with electric mixer until smooth. Add sifted flours; beat until just combined.
3 Spoon mixture into piping bag fitted with a medium fluted tube. Pipe 2cm x 6cm shapes on prepared trays, about 3cm apart.
4 Bake biscuits for about 15 minutes. Cool on trays.
5 Combine melted chocolate with oil. Dip one end of each biscuit in chocolate mixture; leave to set on wire racks.

Sugar and spice cookies

preparation time **25 minutes** cooking time **12 minutes** makes **30**

125g butter
⅓ cup (75g) raw sugar
1 egg
½ teaspoon vanilla extract
2 tablespoons wheatgerm
1 cup (160g) wholemeal plain flour
2 tablespoons wholemeal self-raising flour
⅓ cup (75g) raw sugar, extra
1 teaspoon ground cinnamon

1 Preheat oven to moderate (180°C/160°C fan-forced). Grease oven trays.
2 Beat butter, sugar, egg and extract in small bowl with electric mixer until smooth. Stir in wheatgerm and sifted flours.
3 Roll rounded teaspoons of mixture into balls; toss in combined extra sugar and cinnamon. Place on prepared trays, about 3cm apart; flatten with fork.
4 Bake for about 12 minutes or until lightly browned; cool on wire racks.

Walnut coffee biscuits

preparation time **35 minutes** cooking time **15 minutes** makes **15**

1²⁄₃ cups (250g) plain flour
125g butter, chopped
¼ cup (55g) caster sugar
1 egg, lightly beaten
1 teaspoon vanilla extract
⅓ cup (35g) walnuts, approximately

Filling
60g butter
¼ cup (40g) icing sugar
1 cup (120g) ground walnuts
1 tablespoon milk

Coffee icing
1½ cups (240g) icing sugar
1 teaspoon soft butter
3 teaspoons instant coffee granules
1 tablespoon hot water

1 Preheat oven to moderate (180°C/160°C fan-forced). Grease oven trays.
2 Sift flour into medium bowl, rub in butter. Stir in sugar, egg and extract; mix to a soft dough.Knead gently on lightly floured surface until smooth.
3 Roll dough between sheets of baking paper until 3mm thick. Cut into 6cm rounds; place on prepared trays, about 3cm apart.
4 Bake biscuits for about 15 minutes. Cool on wire racks.
5 Make filling; make coffee icing.
6 Sandwich biscuits together with filling; spread with coffee icing and top with walnuts.

Filling Beat butter and icing sugar in small bowl with electric mixer until combined. Stir in remaining ingredients.

Coffee icing Sift icing sugar into small heatproof bowl. Stir in butter, and enough combined coffee and water to make a stiff paste. Stir over hot water until icing is of a spreadable consistency.

Pecan shortbreads

preparation time **35 minutes** (plus refrigeration time)
cooking time **20 minutes** makes **50**

250g butter
⅓ cup (75g) caster sugar
1 teaspoon vanilla extract
2¼ cups (335g) plain flour
¼ cup (50g) rice flour
⅓ cup (40g) finely chopped pecans
1 cup (100g) pecans, approximately, extra
100g dark eating chocolate, melted

1 Beat butter, sugar and extract in small bowl with electric mixer until light and fluffy. Transfer to a large bowl. Stir in sifted flours and chopped nuts, mix to a soft dough.
2 Turn dough onto lightly floured surface, knead until smooth; cover and refrigerate for 30 minutes.
3 Preheat oven to moderately slow (170°C/150°C fan-forced). Grease oven trays.
4 Roll dough between sheets of baking paper until 6mm thick. Cut 8cm diamonds from dough; place on prepared trays about 3cm apart.
5 Bake biscuits for about 20 minutes or until lightly browned. Stand biscuits on trays for 5 minutes before tranferring to wire racks to cool.
6 Place extra pecans on top of each biscuit, securing with a little melted chocolate; pipe remaining melted chocolate over biscuits.

Italian walnut biscuits

preparation time **20 minutes** cooking time **10 minutes** makes **35**

1½ cups (240g) blanched almonds
1 egg white
½ cup (110g) caster sugar
2 tablespoons dark rum
¾ cup (110g) plain flour
1 egg white, lightly beaten, extra
⅔ cup (70g) walnuts, finely chopped

1 Preheat oven to hot (220°C/200°C fan-forced). Grease oven trays.
2 Blend or process almonds until finely chopped. Add egg white, sugar and rum; process until combined. Transfer mixture to medium bowl, add sifted flour, mix to a soft dough.
3 Knead dough gently on a lightly floured surface until smooth. Roll between sheets of baking paper until 5mm thick. Cut dough into 4cm rounds, place on prepared trays about 3cm apart; brush rounds with extra egg white and sprinkle with walnuts.
4 Bake biscuits for 10 minutes or until lightly browned. Cool on wire racks.

Butterscotch buttons

preparation time **20 minutes** cooking time **30 minutes** makes **40**

125g butter
½ cup (110g) brown sugar, firmly packed
1 tablespoon golden syrup
1 teaspoons vanilla extract
1¼ cups (185g) self-raising flour

1 Preheat oven to slow (150°C/130°C fan-forced). Grease oven trays.
2 Beat butter, sugar, golden syrup and extract in small bowl with electric mixer until light and fluffy; stir in sifted flour.
3 Roll 2 level teaspoons of mixture into balls, place on prepared trays about 5cm apart; flatten slightly with a fork.
4 Bake biscuits for 30 minutes or until firm. Transfer to wire rack to cool.

tips This recipe can be made a week ahead; store in an airtight container. These biscuits are suitable to freeze.

Honey jumbles

preparation time **35 minutes** (plus refrigeration time)
cooking time **15 minutes** makes **40**

60g butter
½ cup (110g) brown sugar, firmly packed
¾ cup (185g) golden syrup
1 egg, beaten lightly
2½ cups (375g) plain flour
½ cup (75g) self-raising flour
½ teaspoon bicarbonate of soda
1 teaspoons ground cinnamon
½ teaspoon ground cloves
2 teaspoons ground ginger
1 teaspoon mixed spice

Icing
1 egg white
1½ cups (240g) icing sugar
2 teaspoons plain flour
1 tablespoon lemon juice, approximately
Pink food colouring

1 Combine butter, sugar and golden syrup in medium saucepan, stir over low heat until sugar is dissolved and butter is melted; cool for 10 minutes.
2 Transfer mixture to large bowl; stir in egg and sifted dry ingredients in two batches. Turn dough onto a floured surface and knead gently until mixture loses its stickiness. Cover; refrigerate 30 minutes.
3 Preheat oven to moderately slow (170°C/150°C fan-forced). Grease oven trays.
4 Divide dough into eight portions; roll each portion into 2cm thick sausages. Cut each portion into 5 x 6cm lengths. Place onto prepared trays, about 3cm apart. Round the ends with lightly floured fingers, flatten gently with the heel of your hand.
5 Bake jumbles for about 12 minutes; cool on trays.
6 Make icing. Spread honey jumbles with pink and white icing.

Icing Lightly beat egg white in small bowl; gradually stir in sifted icing sugar and flour. Stir in enough juice to make a spreadable consistency. Tint half the icing with pink colouring. Keep icing covered with a damp cloth while in use.

tips Honey jumbles are best made a day before eating. Overnight the flavour from the spices will develop and the texture will soften so the biscuits have a more cake-like consistency. Store them uncovered, at room temperature. Un-iced biscuits are suitable to freeze.

Monte carlos

preparation time **30 minutes** cooking time **10 minutes** makes **28**

180g butter
½ cup (110g) brown sugar, firmly packed
1 teaspoon vanilla extract
1 egg
1¼ cups (185g) self-raising flour
¾ cup (105g) plain flour
¼ teaspoon bicarbonate of soda
⅔ cup (60g) coconut
½ cup (150g) raspberry jam, approximately

Vienna cream
60g butter
½ teaspoon vanilla extract
¾ cup (120g) icing sugar
2 teaspoons milk

1 Preheat oven to moderately hot (200°C/180°C fan-forced). Grease oven trays.
2 Beat butter, sugar and extract in small bowl with electric mixer until just combined. Add egg and beat only until combined. Stir in sifted flours, soda and coconut in two batches.
3 Roll two level teaspoons of mixture into ovals; place onto prepared trays about 5cm apart. Flatten ovals slightly and use the back of a fork to roughen the surface. Bake for about 7 minutes. Transfer to a wire rack to cool.
4 Make vienna cream; sandwich biscuits with vienna cream and jam.

Vienna cream Beat butter, sifted icing sugar and extract in a small bowl with electric mixer until fluffy; beat in milk.

tips These biscuits can be made a week ahead; store in an airtight container. Unfilled biscuits are suitable to freeze.

Chewy peanut butter bars

preparation time **15 minutes** cooking time **10 minutes**
(plus refrigeration time) makes **24**

60g butter, chopped
¼ cup (90g) honey
½ cup (110g) firmly packed brown sugar
⅓ cup (95g) smooth peanut butter
2 tablespoons marmalade
1 cup (90g) rolled oats
1½ cups (50g) rice bubbles
½ cup (35g) shredded coconut
½ cup (75g) mixed dried fruit
¼ cup (55g) finely chopped glacé pineapple

1 Grease a 23cm-square slab pan.
2 Combine butter, honey, sugar, peanut butter and marmalade in a large saucepan; stir over low heat, without boiling, until sugar is dissolved. Bring to a boil; remove from heat. Stir in remaining ingredients; mix well.
3 Press mixture firmly into prepared pan; refrigerate until firm.

Rock cakes

preparation time **20 minutes** cooking time **15 minutes** makes **18**

2 cups (300g) self-raising flour
¼ teaspoon ground cinnamon
90g butter
⅓ cup (75g) caster sugar
1 cup (160g) sultanas
2 tablespoons mixed peel
1 egg, beaten lightly
½ cup (125ml) milk, approximately
1 tablespoon caster sugar, extra

1 Preheat oven to moderately hot (200°C/180°C fan-forced). Grease oven trays.
2 Sift flour and cinnamon into large bowl; rub in butter, then stir in sugar and fruit. Stir in egg, then enough milk to give a moist but firm consistency.
3 Place 2-level-tablespoon portions of mixture onto prepared trays about 5cm apart. Sprinkle cakes with a little extra sugar.
4 Bake cakes for about 15 minutes. Loosen cakes; cool on trays.

Caramel corn flake chews

preparation time **15 minutes** cooking time **20 minutes** makes **25**

These biscuits do not contain any flour.

125g butter
½ cup (55g) brown sugar, firmly packed
¼ cup (35g) caster sugar
½ cup (45g) coconut
3 cups (120g) corn flakes, lightly crushed
1 egg, beaten lightly
½ cup (60g) finely chopped mixed nuts

1 Preheat oven to moderate (180°C/160°C fan-forced). Lightly grease oven trays.
2 Melt butter in large saucepan; add sugars and cook, stirring, until combined. Remove pan from heat, stir in coconut, corn flakes, egg and nuts; stir gently until combined.
3 Place level tablespoons of mixture about 3cm apart on prepared trays.
4 Bake for about 15 minutes. Stand on trays for 5 minutes before transferring to wire rack to cool.

tips This recipe can be made a week ahead; store in airtight container. These biscuits are suitable to freeze.

Orange poppy seed shortbread bars

preparation time **15 minutes** cooking time **35 minutes** makes **24**

200g softened butter, chopped
2 teaspoons grated orange rind
½ cup (80g) icing sugar
2 cups (300g) plain flour
1 tablespoon poppy seeds
1 tablespoon orange juice

1 Preheat oven to moderately slow (170°C/150°C fan-forced). Grease a 20cm x 30cm lamington pan.
2 Beat butter, rind and sugar in medium bowl using electric mixer until light and fluffy. Stir in flour, poppy seeds and juice. Press mixture together firmly.
3 Press shortbread mixture into prepared pan; mark into finger lengths.
4 Bake shortbread for about 35 minutes. Cut into finger lengths while still in pan; cool in pan.

tip This recipe can be made a week ahead; store in an airtight container.

Hazelnut and chocolate biscuits

preparation time **40 minutes** (plus refrigeration time)
cooking time **20 minutes** (plus cooling time) makes **18**

60g butter
2 tablespoons caster sugar
2 tablespoons brown sugar
½ cup (75g) plain flour
1½ tablespoons rice flour
1 tablespoon cornflour
1 tablespoon milk
1½ tablespoons finely chopped toasted hazelnuts

Hazelnut spread
¼ cup (75g) chocolate hazelnut spread
30g dark cooking chocolate, melted

1 Beat butter and sugars in small bowl with electric mixer until pale and fluffy. Stir in sifted flours in two batches; stir in milk and nuts.

2 Divide mixture in half. Knead each half until smooth; roll each half into 30cm log. Wrap logs in plastic wrap; refrigerate 1 hour or until firm.

3 Preheat oven to slow (150°C/130°C fan-forced). Grease oven trays.

4 Cut logs into 8mm slices; place on prepared trays about 3cm apart.

5 Bake for about 20 minutes. Cool on wire rack.

6 Meanwhile, make hazelnut spread; sandwich biscuits a teaspoon of hazelnut spread. Serve dusted with icing sugar, if desired.

Hazelnut spread Combine spread and chocolate in a bowl; refrigerate, stirring often, until spreadable.

tip Biscuits can be made several days ahead. Join biscuits on day of serving.

Passionfruit butter biscuits

preparation time **25 minutes** (plus refrigeration time)
cooking time **20 minutes** makes **40**

250g butter, softened
1 ⅓ cups (220g) icing sugar
2 cups (300g) plain flour
½ cup (75g) cornflour
⅓ cup (50g) rice flour
2 tablespoons passionfruit pulp

1 Process butter, sugar and flours in food processor for 2 minutes or until mixture is combined. Add passionfruit; process until mixture clings together.

2 Transfer mixture to lightly floured surface; knead gently until smooth.

3 Divide mixture in half. Roll each half into 26cm log; wrap in plastic wrap and refrigerate for 1 hour.

4 Preheat oven to moderately slow (170°C/150°C fan-forced). Lightly grease oven trays.

5 Cut logs into 1cm slices; place on prepared trays about 3cm apart.

6 Bake biscuits for about 20 minutes. Transfer to wire rack to cool.

Vanilla bean thins

preparation time **20 minutes** cooking time **5 minutes** makes **18**

1 vanilla bean
30g butter, softened
¼ cup (55g) caster sugar
1 egg white, beaten lightly
2 tablespoons plain flour

1 Preheat oven to moderately hot (200°C/180°C fan-forced). Grease oven trays; line with baking paper.
2 Halve vanilla bean lengthways and scrape seeds into medium bowl with butter and sugar; discard vanilla pod. Whisk until combined. Stir in egg white and flour. Spoon mixture into piping bag fitted with 5mm plain tube.
3 Pipe 6cm-long strips (making them slightly wider at both ends), 5cm apart on prepared trays. Bake for about 5 minutes or until the edges are lightly browned; cool biscuits on trays.

Maple-syrup butter cookies

preparation time **20 minutes** cooking time **15 minutes** makes **24**

125g butter, softened
1 teaspoon vanilla extract
⅓ cup (80ml) maple syrup
¾ cup (110g) plain flour
¼ cup (35g) cornflour

1 Preheat oven to moderate (180°C/160°C fan-forced). Grease oven trays; line with baking paper.
2 Beat butter, extract and maple syrup in small bowl with electric mixer until light and fluffy; stir in combined sifted flours. Spoon mixture into piping bag fitted with 1cm fluted tube.
3 Pipe 4cm stars about 3cm apart onto trays. Bake about 15 minutes; cool cookies on trays.

Sicilian creams

preparation time **35 minutes** cooking time **20 minutes** (plus cooling time)
makes **12**

1¾ cups (260g) self-raising flour
60g butter
½ cup (110g) caster sugar
1 teaspoon grated lemon rind
1 teaspoon vanilla extract
1 egg
¼ cup (60ml) milk
¼ cup (60ml) cream
2 tablespoons icing sugar
1 tablespoon water
1 tablespoon liqueur
1 tablespoon icing sugar, extra

1 Preheat oven to moderate (180°C/160°C fan-forced). Lightly grease
oven trays.
2 Place flour in large bowl; rub in butter. Add sugar; mix well. Make well in
centre of mixture; add combined rind, extract, egg and milk. Using a wooden
spoon, mix to a soft, pliable dough.
3 Turn dough onto a lightly floured surface; knead gently until smooth.
Dough should be soft and pliable.
4 Roll dough out gently until 1cm thick. Cut into rounds using 5cm cutter;
place on prepared trays, about 2.5cm apart.
5 Bake biscuits for about 15 minutes.
6 Beat cream and icing sugar in small bowl with electric mixer until firm
peaks form.
7 Using fine serrated knife, split each biscuit in half, horizontally; brush cut
side of each top half of biscuit with combined water and liqueur. Sandwich
biscuits with cream; serve, dusted with extra icing sugar.

tips Use liqueurs such as galliano, grand marnier and amaretto. Sicilian
creams are best assembled close to serving.

Hazelnut pinwheels

preparation time **20 minutes** (plus refrigeration time)
cooking time **20 minutes** makes **30**

1¼ cups (185g) plain flour
100g butter, chopped
½ cup (110g) caster sugar
1 egg yolk
1 tablespoon milk, approximately
⅓ cup (110g) chocolate hazelnut spread
2 tablespoons hazelnut meal

1 Process flour, butter and sugar until mixture resembles breadcrumbs. Add egg yolk; process with enough milk until mixture forms a ball.
2 Knead dough on a lightly floured surface until smooth. Cover; refrigerate for 1 hour.
3 Roll dough between two sheets of baking paper to form a 20cm x 30cm rectangle; remove top sheet of paper. Cover dough evenly with hazelnut spread, then sprinkle with hazelnut meal. Using paper as a guide, roll dough tightly from long side to enclose the filling. Wrap roll in plastic wrap and refrigerate for 30 minutes.
4 Preheat oven to moderate (180°C/160°C fan-forced). Grease oven trays; line with baking paper.
5 Remove plastic wrap from dough; cut roll into 1cm-wide slices. Place slices on prepared trays about 2cm apart.
6 Bake for about 20 minutes. Stand pinwheels on trays for 5 minutes before transferring to a wire rack to cool.

Golden pecan twists

preparation time **25 minutes** cooking time **10 minutes** makes **30**

2 tablespoons golden syrup
⅓ cup (40g) finely chopped pecans
125g butter, softened
¼ teaspoon vanilla extract
⅓ cup (75g) caster sugar
1 egg yolk
1 cup (150g) plain flour

1 Preheat oven to moderate (180°C/160°C fan-forced). Grease oven trays; line with baking paper.

2 Combine half the golden syrup with the nuts in small bowl.

3 Beat butter, extract, sugar, remaining golden syrup and egg yolk in small bowl with electric mixer until light and fluffy; fold in flour.

4 Shape rounded teaspoons of mixture into balls; roll each ball into a 12cm log. Twist each log into a loop, overlapping one end over another.

5 Place twists on prepared trays 3cm apart; top each twist with ½ teaspoon of nut mixture. Bake for about 10 minutes; cool twists on trays.

Cashew ginger squares

preparation time **20 minutes** cooking time **25 minutes** makes about **12**

125g butter
¼ cup (55g) caster sugar
1 cup (150g) self-raising flour
1 teaspoon ground ginger

Topping
½ cup (80g) icing sugar
60g butter
2 tablespoons golden syrup
1 cup (150g) unsalted roasted cashews, chopped coarsely
¼ cup (50g) finely chopped glacé ginger

1 Preheat oven to moderate (180°C/160°C fan-forced). Grease a 20cm x 30cm lamington pan; line base and two long sides with baking paper, extending paper 2cm above edge.

2 Beat butter and sugar in small bowl with electric mixer until light and fluffy; stir in sifted flour and ginger. Spread mixture evenly over base of prepared pan.

3 Bake for about 20 minutes or until lightly browned; cool in pan.

4 Make topping; spread hot topping evenly over cold base. Cool, then cut into squares.

Topping Combine sifted icing sugar, butter and syrup in small saucepan; stir over heat until butter is melted. Stir in nuts and ginger.

GLOSSARY

AFTER-DINNER MINTS Thin chocolates filled with mint-flavoured fomdant cream.

ALLSPICE Also known as pimento or Jamaican pepper, allspice tastes like a combination of nutmeg, cumin, clove and cinnamon. Available from most supermarkets and specialty spice stores.

ALMONDS

Blanched Brown skins removed.

Candied Toffee-coated almonds. Also known as vienna almonds.

Flaked Paper-thin slices.

Meal Also known as ground almonds; nuts are powdered to a coarse flour-like texture. Used in baking or as a thickener.

Paste A combination of ground almonds or almond meal, sugar and egg or glucose which is used as a cake icing, sometimes later covered with fondant. Generally has a stronger flavour than marzipan but is not as pliable.

Slivered Small pieces cut lengthways.

AMARETTI BISCUITS Small Italian-style macaroons (biscuit or cookie) made with ground almonds.

AMARETTO An almond-flavoured liqueur.

ANISE Also known as aniseed or sweet cumin; the seeds are the fruit of an annual plant native to Greece and Egypt. Dried, they have a strong licorice flavour which is used in alcoholic drinks such as Pernod and Ouzo, cough mixtures and baking. Whole and ground seeds are available.

ANISEED Also called anise or sweet cumin. Dried, they have a strong licorice flavour. Available whole and as ground seeds.

APPLES, GREEN The granny smith apple is crisp and and juicy with a rich green skin; good to eat and ideal for cooking.

APRICOTS Used in sweet and savoury dishes; have a velvety, golden-orange skin and aromatic sweet flesh. Also dried.

ARROWROOT A starch made from the rhizome of a Central American plant, used mostly for thickening. Cornflour can be used but will not give as clear a glaze.

BABA PAN A tall, cylindrical, ring-shaped fluted cake pan.

BAKING PAPER Also called parchment, silicon paper or non-stick baking paper; not to be confused with greaseproof or waxed paper. Used to line pans before cooking, baking and to make piping bags.

BAKING POWDER A raising agent consisting mainly of two parts cream of tartar to one part bicarbonate of soda (baking soda). The acid and alkaline combination, when moistened and heated, gives off carbon dioxide which aerates and lightens the mixture during baking.

BEER Beverage brewed from malted barley and other cereals, yeast, and water, and flavoured with hops. Usually 5% alcohol or lower.

BEETROOT Also known as red beets; firm, round root vegetable. Can be eaten raw, grated, in salads; boiled and sliced; or roasted then mashed like potatoes.

BICARBONATE OF SODA Also known as baking soda.

BISCOTTI In Italian, 'bis' means twice and 'cotto' means cooked, hence the name. Their purpose-built dry texture means that biscotti will last well if kept airtight. These delicious biscuits go well with after-dinner coffee and are also available ready-made from most supermarkets and delicatessens.

BISCUITS Also known as cookies.

BLIND BAKING A cooking term describing a pie shell or pastry case baked before filling is added. To bake blind, ease pastry into pan or dish, place on oven tray; cover pastry with baking paper, fill with dried beans, rice or proper baking 'beans' (also called pie weights). Bake in moderately hot (200°C/180°C fan-forced) oven 10 minutes, remove paper and beans; bake for another 10 minutes or until browned lightly. cool before adding filling. Dried beans and rice used to weigh down the pastry are not suitable for eating; cool after use, then store in an airtight jar and reuse each time you bake blind.

BLOOD ORANGE Are thought to have occurred in nature by accident in 17th-century Sicily. In season for all too short a time in winter, blood oranges, with their red-streaked, salmony-coloured flesh, have a sweet, non-acidic pulp and juice with a slight strawberry or raspberry taste; even the skin is not as bitter as other citrus. Available in autumn and winter from greengrocers.

BRAN UNPROCESSED Made from the outer layer of a cereal, most often the husks of wheat, rice or oats.

BRANDY Spirit distilled from wine.

BRAZIL NUT A triangular nut with a hard shell; has white flesh encased with a brown skin.

BRIOCHE Rich French yeast-risen bread made with butter and eggs. Available from pâtisseries or specialty bread shops.

BUTTER Use salted or unsalted (sweet) butter; 125g is equal to 1 stick butter

BUTTERMILK Sold in the refrigerated dairy compartments in supermarkets. Originally just the liquid left after cream was separated from milk, today it is commercially made similarly to yogurt.

CACHOUS Small, round, cake-decorating sweets available in silver, gold or various colours.

CARAWAY SEEDS A member of the parsley family, it is available in seed or ground form and can be used in sweet and savoury dishes.

CARDAMOM Native to India and used in its cuisine; belonging to the ginger family, it attains a sweet yet spicy flavour. Available in pod, seed or ground form from most supermarkets and spice stores.

CASHEWS We prefer to use unsalted roasted cashews. They are available from health food stores and most supermarkets.

CHEESE

Mascarpone A cultured cream product made in much the same way as yogurt. It's whitish to creamy yellow in colour, with a soft, creamy texture.

Ricotta Soft white cow-milk cheese, roughly translated as 'cooked again'; made from whey, a by-product of other cheese making, to which fresh milk and acid are added. Ricotta is a sweet, moist cheese with a fat content of around 8.5% and a slightly grainy texture.

Cottage cheese Fresh, white, unripened curd cheese with a grainy consistency nd a fat content of 15% to 55%.

CHENILLE STICKS Also known as pipe cleaners.

CHERRIES Soft stone fruit varying in colour from yellow to dark red. Sweet cherries are eaten whole and in desserts while sour cherries such as the bitter Morello variety are used in jams, preserves, pies and savoury dishes, particularly as an accompaniment to game birds and meats.

Maraschino Are preserved in sugar syrup with flavourings and colour; sometimes have stems.

CHILLI

Dried flakes Deep-red, dehydrated chilli slices and whole seeds.

Powder The Asian variety is the hottest, made from dried ground thai chillies.

Thai red Small, hot and red in colour.

CHOCOLATE

Choc bits Also known as chocolate chips and chocolate morsels; available in milk, white and dark chocolate. Made of cocoa liquor, cocoa butter, sugar and an emulsifier, these hold their shape in baking and are ideal for decorating.

Compound For dipping and coating.

Dark eating Made of cocoa liquor, cocoa butter and sugar.

Dark cooking We used premium quality dark cooking chocolate, not compound.

White Eating chocolate.

White melts Discs of compounded white chocolate ideal for melting or moulding.

CHOCOLATE HAZELNUT SPREAD
Also known as Nutella.

CHOCOLATE-COATED COFFEE BEANS
Chocolate-coated roasted coffee beans.

CHOCOLATE-COATED SULTANAS
sultanas dipped in chocolate.

CINNAMON STICK Dried inner bark of the shoots of the cinnamon tree.

CITRUS PEEL Dried tangerine peel, available in Asian food stores.

CLOVES Dried flower buds of a tropical tree; can be used whole or in ground form. Have a strong scent and taste so should be used minimally.

COCOA POWDER Dried, unsweetened, roasted then ground cocoa beans.

COCONUT

Cream Is obtained commercially from the first pressing of the coconut flesh, without the addition of water; the second pressing (less rich) is sold as milk. Available in cans and cartons at supermarkets.

Desiccated Unsweetened, concentrated, dried finely shredded coconut flesh.

Flaked Dried flaked coconut flesh.

Shredded Thin strips of dried coconut.

COCONUT MACAROONS Made from coconut, egg white and cornflour.

COINTREAU Citrus-flavoured liqueur.

CONFECTIONERY

Allsorts Layered sweets consisting of licorice and fondant.

Freckles Chocolate discs covered with hundreds and thousands.

Jelly rings Soft sugar-coated jubes in ring shapes.

Jersey caramels Made from sugar, glucose, condensed milk, flour, oil and gelatine.

Licorice An aniseed-flavoured confection which is available in straps, tubes and twisted ropes.

Marshmallows Available pink and white; made from sugar, glucose, gelatine and cornflour.

M&Ms Made from chocolate, sugar and flour.

Snickers bars Made from chocolate, peanuts, glucose, sugar, milk powder, butter and egg white.

Violet crumble bars Chocolate-dipped honeycomb; made from chocolate, sugar, glucose and gelatine.

COPHA A solid white shortening based on coconut oil. Kremelta and Palmin can be substituted.

CORELLA PEARS Miniature dessert pear up to 10cm long

CORN FLAKES Crisp flakes of corn.

CORNFLOUR Also known as cornstarch; used as a thickening agent in cooking.

CORN SYRUP An imported product available in some supermarkets, delicatessens and health food stores. Made from cornstarch, it is a popular ingredient in American cooking for frostings, jams and jellies.

CREAM We used fresh pouring cream (or pure cream). It has no additives, and contains a minimum fat content of 35%.

Thickened A whipping cream that contains a thickener. Has a minimum fat content of 35%.

CRAISINS Dried cranberries; are sold in most supermarkets.

CREAM OF TARTAR The acid ingredient in baking powder; added to confectionery mixtures to prevent sugar crystallising. Keeps frostings creamy and improves volume when beating egg whites.

CREME FRAICHE A French variation of sour cream; is a mildly acidic, high fat, slightly nutty tasting thick cream. Crème fraîche can be used interchangeably with sour cream in some recipes; the former can also be whipped like cream and does not split or curdle when boiled. Available from most supermarkets and delicatessens.

CUMIN Also known as zeera or comino; is the dried seed of a plant having a spicy, nutty flavour. Available in seed form or dried and ground, from supermarkets.

CUMQUAT Orange-coloured citrus fruit about the size of walnuts. Usually preserved or used for making jam, the skin is always retained.

CURRANTS Dried, tiny, almost black raisins so-named after a grape variety that orignated in Corinth, Greece.

CUSTARD

Packaged Ready-made pouring custard, available in cartons from supermarket dairy sections.

Powder Instant mixture used to make pouring custard; similar to North American instant pudding mixes.

DARK RUM We use an underproof rum (not overproof) for a more subtle flavour.

DECORATING GEL Also called piping gel. Available from shops which specialise in cake decorators' supplies; it can be coloured as desired and piped or brushed where needed.

DOLLY VARDEN PAN Spherical, bombe-shaped cake pan.

DRAMBUIE Honey- and herb-flavoured Scotch whisky.

EGGS Some recipes in this book call for raw or barely cooked eggs; exercise caution if there is a salmonella problem in your area.

ESSENCES Also known as extracts; generally the by-product of distillation of plants. Can be set in alcohol or in a more pure form in glycerine.

FIG Small, soft, pear-shaped fruit with a sweet pulpy flesh full of tiny edible seeds. Also available dried.

FLOUR

Gluten-free Available from health food stores.

Plain An all-purpose wheat flour.

Rice A very fine flour, made from ground white rice, flour milled from rye.

Self-raising Plain flour sifted with baking powder in the proportion of 1 cup flour to 2 teaspoons baking powder.

Soy Flour made from ground soya beans.

Wholemeal plain Also known as all-purpose wholewheat flour, has no baking powder added.

Wholemeal self-raising Wholewheat flour that has baking powder added.

FRANGELICO Hazelnut-flavoured liqueur.

FRUIT MEDLEY Combination of dried sultanas, apricots, apples, nectarines, peaches and pears.

FRUIT MINCE Also called mincemeat. A mixture of dried fruits such as raisins, sultanas and candied peel, nuts, spices, apple, brandy or rum. Is used as a filling for cakes, puddings and fruit mince pies.

GALLIANO Clear yellow-coloured Italian liqueur made from and infusion of varies herbs and flowers.

GELATINE We used powdered gelatine; also available in sheets called leaf gelatine.

GINGER

Fresh Also known as green or root ginger; the thick gnarled root of a tropical plant. Can be kept, peeled, covered with dry sherry in a jar and refrigerated, or frozen in an airtight container.

Glace Fresh ginger root preserved in sugar syrup. Crystallised ginger can be substituted if rinsed with warm water and dried before using.

Ground Also known as powdered ginger; used as a flavouring in cakes, pies and puddings but cannot be substituted for fresh ginger.

GLACE FRUIT Fruit cooked in heavy sugar syrup then dried.

GLUCOSE SYRUP Also called liquid glucose, is made from wheat starch; used in jam and confectionery. Available from health food stores and supermarkets.

GOLDEN SYRUP A by-product of refined sugarcane; pure maple syrup or honey can be substituted.

GRAND MARNIER Orange-flavoured liqueur based on Cognac-brandy.

GRAPEFRUIT So named because they grow in clusters, it is the largest citrus fruit available. A pink-fleshed version is also available.

GRENADINE A non-alcoholic syrup made from pomegranate juice; bright red in colour, it's used to colour and flavour drinks and desserts. Imitation cordial is also available.

HAZELNUT Also known as filberts; plump, grape-size, rich, sweet nut with a brown inedible skin. Remove skin by rubbing heated nuts together in a tea towel.

Meal Also known as ground hazelnuts.

HONEYCOMB Is the structure made of beeswax that houses the honey; this edible chewy comb, saturated with honey, is available in health food stores and some supermarkets.

HUNDREDS AND THOUSANDS
Nonpareils; tiny sugar-syrup-coated sugar crystals that come in a variety of bright colours and are used to decorate cakes and party foods.

ICE-CREAM We used a good quality ice-cream having 5g of fat per 100ml.

INSTANT PUDDING MIX A blancmange-style dessert mix.

IRISH CREAM A smooth and creamy natural blend of fresh Irish cream, the finest Irish spirits, Irish whiskey, cocoa and vanilla.

IRISH WHISKEY The Irish were the first to make whiskey; theirs is a smooth, light, dry type made from distilled fermented barley and other grains.

JAM Also known as preserve or conserve; most often made from fruit.

KAFFIR LIME Also known as magrood, leech lime or jeruk purut; wrinkled, bumpy-skinned green fruit of a small citrus tree originally grown in South Africa and Southeast Asia. Give Thai food a unique aromatic flavour; usually only the zest is used.

Kaffir lime leaves Also known as bai magrood; look like two glossy dark green leaves joined end to end, forming a rounded hourglass shape. Sold fresh, dried or frozen, the dried leaves are less potent so double the number called for in a recipe if you substitute them for fresh leaves. A strip of fresh lime peel may be substituted for each kaffir lime leaf.

KAHLUA Coffee-flavoured liqueur.

KIRSCH Cherry-flavoured liqueur.

LARD Fat obtained from melting down and clarifying pork fat; available packaged.

LEMON BUTTER Also known as lemon curd, lemon cheese or lemon spread.

LIMONCELLO Italian lemon-flavoured liqueur, was originally made from the juice and peel of lemons grown along the coast of Amalfi. Served chilled after meals, on ice-cream, fruit salad and, of course, in cocktails, this refreshing apéritif is perfect on a hot summer night.

MACADAMIA NUTS Native to Australia, rich and buttery nut; store in refrigerator because of high oil content.

MADEIRA A fortified wine originally from the Portuguese island of the same name. Types range from golden and dry to rich, sweet and dark; can be served as an aperitif but is also an excellent cooking wine.

MADEIRA CAKE Buttery plain cake similar to pound cake but flavoured with lemon.

MALIBU Coconut-flavoured rum.

MANDARIN Small, loose-skinned citrus fruit also known as tangarine. Segments are also available canned in a light syrup.

MANGO Tropical fruit originally from India or South-east Asia, with skin colour ranging from green through yellow to deep red. Fragrant deep yellow flesh surrounds a large flat seed. Mango cheeks in a light syrup are available canned.

MAPLE-FLAVOURED SYRUP is made from sugar cane and is also known as golden or pancake syrup. It is not a substitute for pure maple syrup.

MAPLE SYRUP A thin syrup distilled from the sap of the maple tree. Maple-flavoured syrup is not an adequate substitute for the real thing.

MARSALA A sweet fortified wine.

MASCARPONE A cultured cream product made in much the same way as yogurt; whitish to creamy yellow in colour, with a soft, creamy texture. It's a fresh, unripened, smooth, triple-cream cheese with a rich, sweet taste, slightly acidic. Available from most supermarkets and delicatessens.

MARMALADE A preserve, usually based on citrus fruit.

MARZIPAN Made from ground almonds, sugar and glucose. Similar to almond paste but is not as strong in flavour but is finer in consistency and more pliable. Cheaper brands often use ground apricot kernels and sugar.

MAYONNAISE We use whole egg mayonnaise in our recipes.

MILK We used full-cream homogenised milk unless otherwise specified.

Buttermilk Sold alongside fresh milk products in supermarkets and is commercially made, by a method similar to yoghurt. Despite the implication of its name, it is low in fat and is a good substitute for dairy products such as cream or sour cream, good in baking and in salad dressings.

Sweetened condensed From which 60% of the water has been removed; the remaining milk is sweetened with sugar.

MIXED DRIED FRUIT A combination of sultanas, raisins, currants, mixed peel and cherries.

MIXED PEEL Candied citrus peel.

MIXED SPICE A blend of ground spices usually cinnamon, allspice, cloves and nutmeg. Available from supermarkets and specialty spice stores.

MOLASSES A thick, dark brown syrup, the residue of sugar refinement. Available in light, dark and blackstrap varieties it has a slightly bitter taste. An essential ingredient in American cooking, molasses is used in gingerbread and shoofly pie.

MUESLI Also known as granola, a combination of grains (mainly oats), nuts and dried fruits. Some manufacturers toast their product in oil and honey, adding crispness and kilojoules.

MUFFIN PAN Sold in a plethora of shapes and sizes, there are three standard sizes readily available – mini, regular and texas.

NON-REACTIVE PAN Saucepan made of a material that does not react adversely to foods cooked in it, includes stainless steel, cast iron, glass and enamel (chip-free). Do not use copper, aluminium or iron.

NUTMEG Its aromatic, full-bodied flavour goes well with pumpkin, kumara, cheese sauces, and sweet spicy cakes. Available ground or whole, from most supermarkets and specialty spice stores.

OIL

Olive Made from ripened olives. Extra virgin and virgin are the best; extra light or light refers to the taste not fat levels.

Peanut Pressed from ground peanuts; most commonly used oil in Asian cooking because of its high smoke point (capacity to handle high heat without burning).

Spray We used a cholesterol-free cooking-oil spray made from canola oil.

Vegetable Any number of oils sourced from plants rather than animal fats.

ORANGE FLOWER WATER Concentrated flavouring made from orange blossoms.

PANETTONE A sweet Italian yeast bread with raisins and candied orange, is usually tall and cylindrical and translates as 'big bread'. Can also be sliced and used as the 'bread' in bread and butter pudding.

Available from some supermarkets and delicatessens.

PAPAYA A large, pear-shaped red-orange tropical fruit. Sometimes used unripe (green) in cooking.

PEANUT BUTTER Peanuts ground to a paste; available in crunchy and smooth varieties from supermarkets.

PEANUTS Not in fact a nut but the pod of a legume.

PECANS Native to the USA and now grown locally; golden-brown, buttery and rich. Good in savoury as well as sweet dishes; especially good in salads.

PEPITAS Dried pumpkin seeds.

PINE NUTS Also known as pignoli; not in fact a nut but a small, cream-coloured kernel from pine cones.

PISTACHIO Pale green, delicately flavoured nut inside hard off-white shells. To peel, soak shelled nuts in boiling water for about 5 minutes; drain, then pat dry with absorbent paper. Rub skins with cloth to peel.

PLAIN CAKE CRUMBS Made from plain uniced cake.

POLENTA Also known as cornmeal; a flour-like cereal made of dried corn (maize) sold ground in several different textures; also the name of the dish made from it.

POMEGRANATE Leathery, dark-red-skinned fruit the size of oranges, are filled with hundreds of seeds, each of whish is wrapped in the edible lucent-crimson pulp that gives it a unique tangy sweet-sour flavour. Available during autumn and winter from greengrocers.

Molasses Not to be confused with pomegranate syrup or grenadine (a sweet red liquid used in cocktails); is made from the juice of pomegranate seeds boiled down to a thick syrup.

Available from Middle Eastern food stores, specialty food stores and delicatessens.

POPPY SEEDS Small, dried, bluish-grey seeds of the poppy plant. Poppy seeds have a crunchy texture and a nutty flavour. Can be purchased whole or ground in most supermarkets.

PRUNES Commercially or sun-dried plums.

PUFFED RICE Gluten-free cereal made from whole brown rice grains. Available from health food stores

PUMPKIN Sometimes used interchangeably with the word squash, the pumpkin is a member of the gourd family and is used in cooking both as one of many ingredients in a dish or eaten on its own. Various types can be substituted for one another.

QUINCE Yellow-skinned fruit with hard texture and astringent, tart taste; eaten cooked or as a preserve.

RAISINS Dried sweet grapes

READY-ROLLED PASTRY Packaged sheets of frozen puff and shortcrust pastry. Available from supermarkets.

RHUBARB Classified as a vegetable, is eaten as a fruit and so considered as one. Leaves must be removed before cooking as they contain traces of poison; the edible pink-red stalks are chopped and cooked.

RICE BUBBLES Puffed rice product made with malt extract; contains gluten

ROLLED OATS Oats that have been husked, steamed-softened, flatted with rolers, dried and packaged for consumption as a cereal product.

ROSEWATER Extract made from crushed rose petals, called gulab in India; used for its aromatic quality in many sweetmeats and desserts.

SAFFRON One of the most expensive spices in the world. Available from supermarkets and specialty spice stores.

SAVARIN PAN A heatproof ring mould named after the baba-like rum-soaked, rich yeast cake for which it was designed; its used has been extended to include uncooked recipes requiring ring moulds, such as a jelly mould.

SEGMENTING Cutting citrus fruits in such a way that the pieces contain no pith, seed or membrane. The thickly peeled fruit is cut towards the centre inside each membrane, forming wedges.

SEMOLINA Made from crushed durum wheat hearts, ground to a very fine flour; is used for making pasta and breads. Available from supermarkets.

SESAME SEEDS Black and white are the most common; a good source of calcium. To toast, spread seeds evenly on oven tray, toast briefly in moderate (180°C/160°C fan-forced) oven.

SEVILLE ORANGES Very tart in flavour; suitable only for jam-making.

SHERRY Fortified wine consumed as an aperitif or used in cooking. Sold as fino (light, dry), amontillado (medium sweet, dark) and oloroso (full-bodied, very dark).

SILVER CACHOUS Small, round, cake-decorating sweets, available in gold and other colours.

SOUR CREAM Thick, smooth and slightly acidic cream; adds richness to soups and stews, also dolloped on potatoes and soups.

SPATULA A flat, narrow, fairly long kitchen utensil used, depending on the material, to scrape the sides of mixing bowls, turn foods in fry pans, spread frostings, and so forth.

SOFT ICING Ready-to-use cake fondant available in 500g packets and 375g tubs; the tubs are labelled 'prepared icing'.

SPONGE FINGERS Also called savoiardi sponge finger biscuits; Italian-style crisp fingers made from sponge-cake mixture.

SPONGE ROLL We prefer to us a 250g swiss roll filled with jam or a 225g French roll filled with jam or cream.

SPONGE ROLLETTES We prefer to use 9cm long sponge rolls filled with jam or jam and cream; these are generally purchased in 250g packets of six.

SPRINKLES Also known as cake tops; tiny pellet-shaped bits of chocolate used for decorating

SUGAR We used coarse, granulated table sugar, also known as crystal sugar, unless otherwise specified.

Black Less refined than brown sugar and containing moremolasses; mostly used in Christmas cakes, black sugar is available from health food stores.

Brown An extremely soft, fine granulated sugar retaining molasses for its characteristic colour and flavour.

Caster Also known as superfine or finely granulated table sugar.

Coffee crystals Large golden-coloured crystal sugar made to enhance the flavour of coffee.

Demarara Small-grained golden-coloured crystal sugar.

Icing Also known as confectioners' sugar or powdered sugar; pulverised granulated sugar crushed together with a small amount (about 3%) cornflour added.

Pure icing Also known as confectioners' sugar or powdered sugar.

Raw Natural brown granulated sugar.

SUNFLOWER KERNELS From driedhusked sunflower seeds.

SWEET BISCUITS Any plain sweet biscuit (or cookie) can be used; chocolate biscuits used were uniced.

SWISS ROLL PAN Also known as a jelly-roll pan, measuring 26cm x 32cm in area; its slightly raised sides (averaging 2cm in height) help contain the mixture (usually cake batters, egg mixtures or various light doughs) being baked in it, preventing the swiss roll, sponge, roulade, jam roll, slice, pizza base, etc from rising. Often the baked item is removed from the pan and rolled while still hot and malleable, then later unrolled, spread with various sweet or savoury fillings, and rolled again before slicing. Can also be a rectangular baking pan having 2cm-deep sides used to make a swiss roll, genoise, jam roll, roulade, jelly roll or even pizza base; usually 26cm x 32cm in area.

TIA MARIA Coffee-flavoured liqueur.

TOASTING Almonds and shredded coconut can be toasted in the oven; spread evenly onto oven tray, toast in moderate oven (180°C/160°C fan-forced) for about 5 minutes. Desiccated coconut and sesame seeds toast more evenly by stirring over heat in a heavy pan; the natural oils will brown both ingredients.

TREACLE Thick, dark syrup not unlike molasses; a by-product of sugar refining.

TURKISH DELIGHT A gel-like Middle Eastern sweet coated in icing sugar. Commonly flavoured with rosewater or orange flower water, can also contain pistachios or almonds.

UNPROCESSED BRAN Made from the outer layer of a cereal, most often the husks of wheat, rice or oats.

VANILLA

Bean Dried, long, thin pod from a tropical golden orchid grown in Central and South America and Tahiti; the minuscule black seeds inside the bean are used to impart a luscious vanilla flavour in baking and desserts. A whole bean can be placed in the sugar container to make the vanilla sugar often called for in recipes.

Essence Obtained from vanilla beans infused in alcohol and water.

Extract Obtained from vanilla beans infused in water. A non-alcoholic version of essence.

WAFER Thin crisp biscuit generally served with ice-cream and creamy desserts; can also be layered with sweet cream filling

WALNUTS A rich, buttery and flavourful nut. Should be stored in the refrigerator because of its high oil content.

WHEAT GERM Small creamy flakes milled from the embryo of the wheat.

WHITE VINEGAR Made from spirit of cane sugar.

WHISKY We used a good quality Scotch whisky.

YEAST Allow 2 teaspoons (7g) dried granulated yeast to each 15g fresh yeast.

YOGURT We used plain, unflavoured yogurt, unless stated otherwise.

INDEX

A

allergy-free cakes
 allergy-free fruit cake, 183
 dairy-free fruit cake, 179
 egg-free chocolate cake, 181
 egg-free date and nut cake, 177
 egg-free fruit cake, 180
 egg-free ginger jumble cake, 184
 fat-free angel food cake, 179
 flourless chocolate dessert cake, 174
 flourless hazelnut chocolate cake, 185
 gluten-free berry cupcakes, 184
 gluten-free carrot cake with orange frosting, 178
 gluten-free chocolate cake, 175
 gluten-free, dairy-free raspberry muffins, 182
 gluten-free orange syrup cake, 176
 wheat-free sponge, 182
almond
 almond butter cake, 20
 almond honey spice cake, 172
 almond icing, 296
 almond jam cookies, 327
 almond orange halva cake, 165
 almond raspberry fingers, 347
 almond rum dessert cake, 253
 amaretti, 324
 apricot and almond scones, 306
 cherry almond bars, 349
 cherry almond cake, 202
 chocolate, nut and coffee ice-cream cake, 226
 coffee almond cakes, 59
 dark chocolate and almond torte, 93
 egg-free date and nut cake, 177

(*almond* continued)
 fruity white chocolate bars, 209
 glacé peach and almond cake, 110
 gluten-free fruit and almond loaves, 268
 greek almond biscuits, 342
 hazelnut almond sticks, 351
 little lime almond cakes, 57
 marmalade almond muffins, 305
 mini choc chip almond cakes, 49
 peach and almond cake, 225
 pear and hazelnut almond cakes, 58
 rum and citrus fruit cake, 132
 siena cake, 151
 strawberry and almond cakes, 56
 vanilla bean cherry financier, 139
 vanilla pear almond cake, 138
amaretti, 324
angel food cake, fat-free, 179
aniseed biscotti, 322
apple
 apple and custard muffins, 314
 apple buttermilk cake, 129
 apple chocolate cake, 194
 apple pecan cake with maple frosting, 16
 apple spice muffins, 315
 apple sponge, 70
 apple walnut cake, 202
 buttery apple cinnamon cakes, 44
 date squares, 150
 norwegian apple cake, 133
apricot
 apricot and almond scones, 306
 apricot and pine nut biscotti, 323
 apricot coconut muffins, 311
 apricot coconut rolls, 216
 apricot loaf, 110
 apricot muesli bars, 353
 apricot upside-down cakes, 45

O

oat loaves, little blueberry, 144
olive oil cake, citrus, 125
olive oil cake with blueberries, 34
one-bowl cakes
apple chocolate cake, 194
apple walnut cake, 202
buttery butterscotch cake, 200
carrot and prune cake, 193
cherry almond cake, 202
choc-carrot cake, 189
chocolate butterscotch cake, 188
chocolate fudge cake, 197
chocolate mayonnaise cake, 205
cinnamon teacake, 186
cream cheese and chocolate
brownies, 187
cream cheese lemon cake, 206
double lemon loaf, 208
fruity white chocolate bars,
209
fudgy choc nut brownies, 191
golden caramel cake, 200
hazelnut butter cake, 203
honey-iced coffee cake, 196
lemon delicious cake, 207
maple syrup cake, 207
marmalade cake, 206
melt 'n' mix coconut cake, 186
mixed spice cake, 210
mocha yogurt cake, 208
moist orange cake, 195
one-bowl sultana loaf, 198
orange date cake, 201
pineapple and macadamia loaf,
191
prune loaf, 210
quick honey gingerbread cake,
192
quick-mix chocolate cake, 189
rich chocolate cake, 199
rum and raisin coffee cake, 204
sherried sultana cake, 190
vanilla butter cake, 197
wholemeal banana coconut cake,
204
wholemeal honey beer fruit cake,
211

orange
almond orange halva cake, 165
blackberry and orange mascarpone
cake, 224
blueberry cake with orange syrup,
159
boiled passionfruit and orange fruit
cake, 134
buttery orange cake, 15
choc-chip orange sour cream cake, 104
chocolate orange dessert muffins,
313
chocolate orange liqueur cake, 221
choc-orange hazelnut crescents, 342
citrus olive oil cake, 125
currant cakes with orange glaze, 55,
164
gluten-free orange syrup cake, 176
moist orange cake, 195
moist whole orange cake, 108
orange and brandy syrup, 165
orange and passionfruit swirl cake,
114
orange coconut biscuits, 350
orange cream, 309, 352
orange cream cheese frosting, 299
orange date cake, 201
orange frosting, 178
orange glacé icing, 288
orange icing, 195, 298
orange macaroon cake, 143
orange marmalade cake, 145
orange poppy seed shortbread bars,
364
orange poppy seed syrup cake, 154
orange syrup, 104, 154, 159, 176
orange syrup cake, 158
orange vienna cream frosting, 290
orange yogurt cake, 26
petite orange coconut loaves, 137
pistachio and polenta cake with
blood orange syrup, 222
pistachio butter cake with orange
honey syrup, 170
polenta and orange biscuits, 338
pumpkin citrus syrup cake, 161
viennese orange kisses, 352
see also mandarin
overnight date and muesli muffins, 314

P

packet mix cakes
    apricot coconut rolls, 216
    banana cinnamon cake, 217
    berry jelly cake, 216
    black forest torte, 212
    chocolate cream cake, 220
    chocolate orange liqueur cake, 221
    chocolate pudding cake, 217
    coffee hazelnut supreme, 218
    colin caterpillar, 283
    construction site, 285
    daisy bunch, 284
    funny face cupcakes, 280
    girlie ghost, 279
    honey roll, 219
    howdy sheriff, 276
    irresistible choc-on-choc cake, 213
    lucy ladybird, 287
    minted tropical cake, 214
    picture perfect, 281
    rich fudge cake, 215
    sleeping moon, 277
papaya and banana cake, tropical, 128
passionfruit
    banana cake with passionfruit icing, 109
    boiled passionfruit and orange fruitcake, 134
    orange and passionfruit swirl cake, 114
    passionfruit and lemon syrup cake, 169
    passionfruit and mango charlotte, 252
    passionfruit butter, 214, 333
    passionfruit butter biscuits, 365
    passionfruit butter yoyo bites, 333
    passionfruit cream, 293
    passionfruit cream cheese frosting, 291
    passionfruit curd, 73, 74
    passionfruit glacé icing, 288
    passionfruit icing, 109, 297
    passionfruit sponge roll, 72
peach and almond cake, 225
peach and almond cake, glacé, 110
peach jam puddings with vanilla custard, little, 227
peanut butter bars, chewy, 362
peanut cookies, crunchy, 352
peanut cookies, scorched, 346
pear
    pear and hazelnut almond cakes, 58
    pear crumble cake, 136
    vanilla pear almond cake, 138
    walnut cake with roasted caramel pears, 254
pecan
    apple pecan cake with maple frosting, 16
    golden pecan twists, 368
    pecan and chocolate brownies, 232
    pecan shortbreads, 358
    pecan sour cream cake, 33
    spicy date and pecan cookies, 344
peppermint
    chocolate peppermint cake, 96
    chocolate peppermint cookies, 343
    peppermint cream, 96, 97
petite orange coconut loaves, 137
picture perfect, 281
pine nut biscotti, apricot and, 323
pineapple
    hummingbird cake, 115
    pineapple and macadamia loaf, 191
    pineapple frosting, 299
    pineapple teacake, 142
pistachio
    chocolate, nut and coffee ice-cream cake, 226
    lemon and pistachio biscotti, 321
    pistachio and polenta cake with blood orange syrup, 222
    pistachio bread, 328
    pistachio butter cake with orange honey syrup, 170
    pistachio lime syrup gems, 310
    pistachio shortbread mounds, 334
plum
    coffee mudcake with chilli plum syrup, 173
    hazelnut plum muffins, 316
    plum and cinnamon cake, 124